ANTHONY SMITH

MATO GROSSO

LAST VIRGIN LAND

An account of the Mato Grosso based on the Royal Society and
Royal Geographical Society expedition to central Brazil 1967–9

MICHAEL JOSEPH

This book was designed and produced by
George Rainbird Ltd, Marble Arch House,
44 Edgware Road, London W2.
for Michael Joseph Ltd,
52 Bedford Square, London WC1.

House Editor: Tony Birks
Designer: Gwyn Lewis
Maps: Tom Stalker-Miller

Filmset in Monophoto Baskerville 11 on 14 pt
by Westerham Press Ltd, Westerham, Kent.
Printed and bound by Dai Nippon, Tokyo, Japan.

SBN 7181 07349

PRINTED IN JAPAN

FOREWORD

By Lord Blackett, President, The Royal Society, 1965–70
and Sir Gilbert Laithwaite, President, The Royal Geographical Society, 1966–9

In 1965 the Brazilian authorities began building a highway through the Mato Grosso, a vast, remote and almost unexplored region of Brazil, as part of a great South American highway system. They invited several countries, Great Britain among them, to send teams of scientists to study the area in the vicinity of this road at a turning-point in its history.

The Royal Geographical Society and the Royal Society were quick to respond to this generous invitation. It is not often that scientists – botanists, zoologists, geographers – have the chance to study a habitat in a fast developing country in its pristine condition. A reconnaissance party was sent out in 1966. Between July 1967 and July 1969 a total of 44 British and 20 Brazilian scientists were at work, some 500 miles road journey from Brasília, on an expedition which, with the co-operation of Brazilian scientists and research organizations, became an Anglo-Brazilian enterprise.

The situation demanded something different from the traditional expedition. In order to carry out scientific investigations in some depth, the Base Camp became a small temporary field research station in the midst of a large area that was very poorly known from the scientific point of view and hardly at all disturbed by man and his animals. Some of the work, however, was done much farther afield, notably along the Suiá Missú and Xingú rivers, a refuge of the dwindling Indian tribes who once overran the Mato Grosso.

The careful study of the undeveloped natural environment, by scientists of many disciplines, can provide much information which is essential when the time comes to develop. Indeed, if the kind of scientific information which the expedition obtained is not available to the developers, or is not heeded by them, disaster may befall not only the natural environment, but also the people concerned, be they peasants or labourers, capitalists or politicians.

An enterprise of this magnitude and complexity required the co-operation of a great number of people, and the Royal Society and the Royal Geographical Society wish to record their thanks to these people. The contribution of Mr Iain Bishop, as leader of the expedition, and his wife, Angela, was of the greatest importance. Many Brazilian organizations assisted the expedition, particularly the University of Brasília. Special mention should be made of Professor Lobato Paraense who was appointed by the National Research Council as co-ordinator of the Brazilian interests in the expedition.

5

The British Council in Rio de Janeiro and in Brasília, especially Dr Vere Atkinson, Mr Peter Hewitt and their colleagues, assisted greatly by solving the numerous day-to-day problems of the 44 British scientists coming into Brazil with their equipment and leaving with their specimens. The Joint Committee of the two Societies which planned the expedition had as its Chairman Sir Ashley Miles, Biological Secretary of the Royal Society from 1963 to 1968. The Societies are particularly grateful to him and other members of the Committee, especially Sir David Martin of the Royal Society and Mr L. P. Kirwan, Director of the Royal Geographical Society, and to Mr George Hemmen and Miss Christine Johnson at the expedition's London headquarters. The author would like to add his special thanks to his assistant Jill Southam and to the many scientists who helped in preparing and checking the book.

Funds for the expedition came mainly from the Royal Society, which gratefully acknowledges the financial support also given by the Royal Geographical Society, the Astor Foundation of New York, the Ministry of Overseas Development, Times Newspapers Limited and other sources.

Blackett

Gilbert Laithwaite

'Such an offer of assistance through the last really large portion of unexplored territory on earth was of paramount ▷
importance' and the invitation to work in it was eagerly accepted. RIGHT *Little nightjar* Caprimulgus
parvulus.

OVERLEAF *The Bromeliaceae, often rivalling orchids in their beauty, have their distribution centre in Brazil.
It is also the home of large centipedes, of vast fish like the Sorubim that can be 5 ft. long, of birds like the
fork-tailed woodnymph, whose nest shows it to be a relative giant among humming birds.*

6

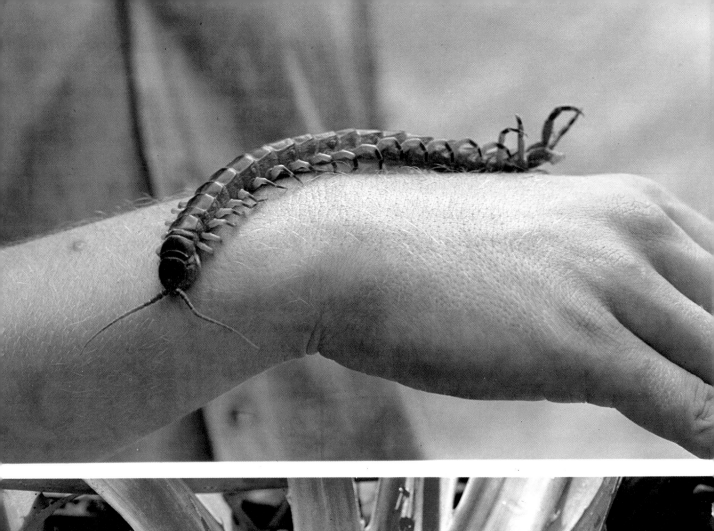

CONTENTS

FOREWORD 5

LIST OF COLOUR PLATES 12

PHOTOGRAPHIC ACKNOWLEDGMENTS 13

INTRODUCTION 17

1 THE LOST WORLD 21
A river through Eden · the largest anthills in the world · expeditions and immigrants · corruption in the Indian Protection Service · planning a road through the forest · the reconnaissance party reports

2 JOURNEY TO EDEN 54
Hazards of Brazilian Customs · alternative ways to the camp · hotel on the edge of nowhere · the ferry at Xavantina · coffee at Geraldão's · contending with biting insects · creating a common language

3 THE INDIANS 91
Human dehydration · the murder of Richard Mason · collecting urine from the Xavante · by boat down the Suiá Missú · the Villas Boas brothers · lip disc Indians · prompt aid for an injured Suiá · the São Marcos mission · a relay race with a tree trunk · Indians at work and prayer · Arabs v. Indians

4 A SQUARE FOR RESEARCH 131
Soil pits and laterite · a method of dealing with wasps · termites, ants and spiders · Taituba and Brazilians in camp · two contrasting wasp men · the leader and his wife · the silence of sub-camps

5 DOCTORS IN THE XINGÚ 165
A device for keeping blood · searching for the Kran-Acorore · the mirrors are smashed · the disfiguring Leishmaniasis · rats as hosts, flies as vectors · a craze for self-medication · Indian drugs of unknown value · 'You-dirty-Txikao-you' · doctors' diaries and diets

6 MAMMALS, BIRDS, FISH AND PLANTS 193
Calling up a jaguar · keeping trapped animals alive · coral snakes and false corals · an enthusiasm for killing · 263 species of birds · tape recording electric fish · the offensive candiru · fire-resistant plants

7 RICH MAN, POOR MAN 215
Squatters by the roadside · 'Are all the children yours?' · a steam engine fed on sawdust · Dr Paulo's investment · axemen's hazards · a fazenda cut off from the road · the importance of football · isolation

8 THE END OF THE FOREST 251
Grape juice on the verandah · cut and burn · droop-eared cattle · the cowboys of Brazil · the economics of the fazenda · financing farms from income tax · traffic on the forest road

9 ATÉ LOGO 273
The inheritors of the scientists' camp · scavengers for odds and ends · an upside-down view of conservation · fertilization and apathy · the disappearing Eden

LIST OF PARTICIPANTS 284

INDEX 286

◁ *The Harpy Eagle is the world's largest but is short-winged and can fly through the forest after monkeys. Indians capture these birds, cage them, and use the feathers for decoration.*

LIST OF COLOUR PLATES

Two macaws in flight   Half title

Humming-bird at the nectar   Frontispiece

Little nightjar incubating   7

Large centipede (above) and a Bromeliad   8

Sorubim, the catfish (above), and nest with eggs of the fork-tailed woodnymph   9

Caged Harpy eagle   10

Frieze of butterflies on bark   15

Decorated Txikão Indians   16

Ox-bow lake by the Suiá Missú (above) and Tucunaré roasting   25

Suiá Missú river from the air   26–7

Palms within the forest   28

The Txikão Matampó, heir to the chieftancy   37

Claudio (above) and Orlando Villas Boas   38

Xavante Indian in Xavantina   43

Old shapes for new: unfurled leaf (left) and Brasília cathedral   44–5

Rivers of the Xingú   46

The road straight through the forest   51

The swampy borderland of pantanal   52

Horsemen where the Garças meets the Araguaia   61

Mato Grosso arthropods: spiders and the tabanid fly   62–3

Lookout-point over the new road   64

Geraldão: opulence and coffee   73

Leaf-cutting ants at work   74

A tick in a scientific arm   79

Hidden creatures: coati, snake, deer and insect   80–1

Base-camp seen from the air   82

Beauty of a Brazilian exotic flower   87

Legendary teeth of a piranha   88

The Xingú Kuarup ceremony, watched by the older women and young children   97–100

Diauarum from the air (above) and from the river   109

Txukuhamae Indian with a lip disc   110

The Xingú Indians invite others to wrestling bouts, and watch the form   115–8

São Marcos Indians operating a tractor   123

Physical activity with Buriti log, spiritual welfare before the cross   124

Suiá Missú turtle   133

The Mato Grosso insect world   134–5

Venom from the fangs of a Bothrops   136

Apoica wasps, with much stung Christine and Bill Hamilton   145

Wasp nest hanging from a tree   146

Taituba   151

Coral snake   152–3

Seven Brazilians who worked at camp   154

Angela Bishop with capybara (above); Rhino beetles with each other   159

Yellow butterflies feeding (above) and camp at supper-time   160

Indian life in the Xingú: the building of a fish-trap   169–72

Txukuhamae woman with pipe and child   181

Mata collado, most lethal plant   182

Snowy egret, and a wing-spread of other birds   187–9

Caught: a tanager (above) and a maned wolf   190

The three-toed sloth climbed out of reach   195

Monkey in the bushes (above) and a bat in the hand   196

A catch of fish (above), a box of insects, and an assortment of plants for classification   205–8

Japanese mother, Brazilian father, and family   217

Qualea ingens   218

Burning forest makes the land black, but fit for the cow   223–5

Steam-engine, creator of fazendas   226

Hoatzin, misfit of a bird   231

Sunset on the Xingú (above) and Jacana on the water   232

The monkey who aimed (above) and the
pium who never missed 241

Txukuhamae village of Pororí 242–3

A caboclo from the north-east 244

Gerente and wife on their verandah (above);
the gang in their forest 253

Camp in the rainy season 254

The inheritors: from Rio Grande do Sul (above),
from the Xavante mission, from the corrals 259–61

Forest liana 262

Bulldozer making the new road 267

Settlers: every right or none 268

Young girl by the Araguaia 277

The world about her: orchids, butterflies,
petals, and sedge 278–9

The axe-man who had been rich 280

PHOTOGRAPHIC ACKNOWLEDGMENTS

Sources of black-and-white and colour illustrations are given below; where the picture credited is in colour, this is indicated by italic type.

George Argent, *25 above*, 41 right, *80 below*, *151*, *160 above*, *208 top left*; Iain Bishop, *45*, *154 top right*, *154 centre left*, 162 right, 199 right, 201, 213; Douglas Botting, *26–7*, *38 below*, 43, 44, 46, 52, 61, *62 below*, 74, *81 above*, *81 below*, 82, 88, 102 left, 102 right, *109 above*, *109 below*, 121, *123*, *124 above*, *124 below*, 128, *133*, *134 centre left*, *135 centre*, *135 bottom left*, 146, *154 bottom right*, 162 left, *190 below*, *195*, *196 above*, *205 below*, *206 top left*, *206 top centre*, *208 centre right*, *208 bottom right*, 217, 220, *223*, 226, 231, *232 above*, *232 below*, 234, 239, *241 above*, *241 below*, *242–3*, 244, 247, *253 above*, *257*, *259 above*, *259 below*, *260–1*, 267, 268, 275, 277, *278 below*, *279 below*, 280, 283; Kenneth Brecher, *17*; Geoffrey Bridgett, *2*, 22, 48, 77, *79*, 89, 90, *94*, *98–9*, 106 left, 106 right, 107 left, 107 right, 112, *115*, *116–7*, *118*, 130, *134 bottom left*, *134 bottom right*, *135 top left*, *135 bottom right*, 136, 138, 143 right, *154 top centre*, *159 below*, *160 below*, 164, 167, 202, *206 centre right*, 236; Stuart Daultrey, 23; Hilary Fry, *7*, *9 below*, *62 above*, *135 top right*, *159 above*, 187, *188–9 (all)*; David Gifford, *154 bottom left*, *206 bottom right*, *207 centre right*; Barry Goldsmith, *207 top left*, *208 top right*; Jim Green, *15*, *134 top right*, *135 centre right*, *196 below*; John Guillebaud, 95; Bill Hamilton, 28, 64, 143 left, *145 bottom left*; Christine Hamilton, *145 bottom right*; Ray Harley, *8 above*, *134 top left*, *145 above*, *152–3*, *154 top left*, 182, *206 top right*, *206 bottom left*, *207 top right*, *207 bottom right*, *208 centre left*, *278 above*; John Hemming, 93 left, 93 right; Philip Hugh-Jones, *10*, *25 below*, *37*, *100*, *110*, *180*; Ruth Jackson, *9 above*, 35, 67, 198; Hugh I. Jones, *135 centre left*, *169*, *170–1*, *172 above*, *172 below*; Margaret Knight, 134 centre; Tony Mathews, *154 centre right*, *207 top centre*, 210, 262; Rosemary McConnell, *63*, *205 above*; David Philcox, *8 below*, *207 centre left*, *208 bottom left*; Prospec SA and the Departamento Naçional da Producao Mineral, Brazil, 84; Jim Ratter, *206 centre left*, *207 bottom right*, *279 above*; Maud Richards, *134 centre right*; Paul Richards, *218*; David Thomas, *1*, *80 above*; The Wellcome Parasitology Unit, Belém (Ralph Lainson), 175; Jack Woodall, *38 above*.

The day has passed delightfully. Delight itself, however, is a weak term to express the feelings of a naturalist, who, for the first time, has wandered by himself in a Brazilian forest. . . . To a person fond of natural history, such a day brings with it a deeper pleasure than he can hope to experience again.

Charles Darwin

Let me parenthetically insert just one word to those who undertake to develop it. Let these men remember the disasters encountered by so many of the enthusiasts who, in the middle and early part of the last century, started to develop the western part of the United States, without any earthly understanding of what development of a raw frontier meant. Let all would-be emigrants remember that the frontier opens equally great chances for both success and failure.

Theodore Roosevelt

'Here is delight', say the naturalists. 'Here there is nothing, nada*', say the settlers.* ▷

INTRODUCTION

In the beginning was the land, with its plants and animals. It was a tropical land, moist and humid. Ever since the Andes had risen up to block off the west, the abundant rain had come predominantly from the Atlantic. It was also returned to the Atlantic, almost entirely in one colossal waterway. The Amazon basin, the largest drainage system on Earth, possessed at any one time a fifth of the world's fresh water in its soil, in its streams, rivers and tributaries, with the whole vast network making the most enormous river of any continent.

In the beginning there were no men, but the Bering Straits were presumably the means to the end of this anomaly. What other way could men have come, say 20,000 years ago? What else could they do but fan out, adapting themselves to the cold tundra, to the open plains, to the swamps, and then to the eternal forests of equatorial South America? No one will ever know how many people were living in the New World when Columbus found a part of it in 1492. No one will ever know how many Indians were living in the country to be named Brazil when it was discovered on 22 April, 1500 by Pedro Alvares Cabral. Even this one part of South America is thought to have had three million, perhaps six million. Portugal had a smaller population living in a far smaller country, but it was to take over the colossal Amazon basin—and all its Indians.

The inevitable confusion of discovery in South America, of conquests and claims, led the Pope to anticipate trouble and settle differences by dividing the spoil. In his eyes, and according to the Treaty of Tordesillas, there were only two contenders and the English, for example, were incensed by such partiality; but it was decreed by treaty in 1494, and then by papal sanction in 1506, that all land more than 370 leagues west (and south) from the Cape Verde Islands should belong to Spain, and all land within this demarcation should belong to Portugal.

There was a difference between these two Iberian conquerors. The Spanish were

◁ *'The forest has all our needs', say the Indians. 'It gives us our food and the material for our homes. It gives us medicine, and wood for our bows.' It also gave them their security, until their land was invaded by the aeroplane.*

17

more militant. Fired by their religion they fell upon their knees, it has been said, and then fell upon the Indians. The Portuguese were more casual, and for years they had no real notion of their inheritance. To this day there are still Indian tribes living in the forest who have not yet experienced the Old World's confrontation of the New. Not until 1958 did anyone reach the geographical centre of Brazil, admittedly a spot of no great significance, but the recent date of this journey is important. By comparison the very centre of the United States must have been encountered, and trampled on, and passed by, long before anyone knew how to compute the spot.

The Brazilian Portuguese achieved their ends, and the subjugation of this huge territory together with its inhabitants, by more casual deliberation. The Indians were shot or maimed, either for religious or cruder reasons, with the colonizer's disregard for aborigines that was to become traditional in new lands. Sometimes they were befriended but given, in the warm handshake, a charge of Old World disease. To begin with they were put to work, although Negroes imported from the Portuguese African possessions were subsequently preferred. And always the Indian blood was absorbed, as marriages and matings and the resulting interrelationships extinguished the Indians quite as effectively as bullets from a musket, or the smallpox virus from a diseased invader. 'There is no racial problem here,' Jorge Amado has written, 'for the simple reason that we are all mulattos.' The Indians have played their part and have disappeared, save for the 60,000, perhaps 100,000, still reckoned to exist in the country. Strangely the more martial Spaniards, rarely averse to putting whole areas to the sword and with those rich empires beckoning them on, are now left in several places with large groups of pure and expanding Indian stock. These surviving communities, so much a problem of Ecuador, Bolivia and Peru, do not have a comparable counterpart around the Amazon.

The hinterland of Brazil was traditionally regarded not so much as a region for future development, nor as an eternity of soil for homesteaders to settle, but as a wealth to be exploited. As armies, as groups, or even as individuals, the Portuguese have gone into Brazil to find and to take. They have not always come out, and those that have emerged have not always been richer, but the custom of plundering rather than developing has had a venerable history. The *bandeirantes*, respected soldier-citizens and undoubtedly courageous, travelled with official backing to extend Portuguese influence, and never had to account for their methods. The *seringueiros*, more recent invaders from the same mould, collected rubber from the wild trees, but were usually desperately in debt and particularly prepared to defend themselves by shooting first. No seringueiro, and no bandeirante before him, can be likened to the North American pioneers who received 640 acres from the government, and considered that both their due and their lot.

Nevertheless there was settlement. Of course this occurred along the Amazon river, the natural ingress to the heart of Brazil, and also along the country's coastal belt; access to the sea was always vital. The open country in the south, relatively free of trees and yet with a good rainfall, was another easy access point, but every incursion to the interior was inevitably accompanied by backward glances. In North America there were similar problems and an early development of the Atlantic seaboard states, but the huge central artery of the Mississippi travelling to the southward helped men to forget about the east coast. Also the lure of California and the Pacific coast then helped men still further on their way to the west. The barrier of the Rockies has never been so formidable as the wall of the Andes, quite apart from the Spaniards on the other side. So Brazilians have looked either to the Amazon, or eastwards to the Atlantic coast, to Rio, to Santos and São Paulo. Their country cannot look to the west, however beneficial this might be to the development of that formidable interior, the largest tropical forest in the world.

With this proviso development has proceeded, insofar as the lie of the land has permitted it and the Indians have been unable to keep it permanently at bay. There have been Portuguese as far south as Rio de Janeiro ever since a ship was blown into Guanabara Bay in 1502, and western civilization has flourished there for centuries, spreading its tentacles into the land; but any tentacles which reached out towards certain areas have been abruptly lopped off. Various tribes acquired respected reputations for their resistance, and among them were the Xavante. They fought in Goiás, and then retreated to the Araguaia river. Soon their frontier was even further west, but at the Rio das Mortes they stopped. That river, only some 800 miles from Rio de Janeiro, provided an effective defensive line, and behind it the Xavante and other tribes of the Xingú held firm. Even for the first four decades of this current twentieth century anyone crossing that river was likely to be clubbed to death, or shot with an arrow, by the first Indians who saw him. There was development to the south of this area, and even to the west, but the actual enclave of the headwaters of the Xingú river became an Indian fortress.

It was a huge area, virtually impenetrable, and therefore those headwaters became the source of legend. In the early years of this century, the place was the only unexplored area on Earth large enough to be concealing a whole civilization, and by this token alone it was presumed to be hiding such a civilization. Its very impenetrability, and the effectiveness of its retribution on any invader, further suggested some living Machu Picchu. Colonel Percy Harrison Fawcett was the most famous believer in a Xingú capital, and he died in 1925 trying to find it. Various other explorers traversed the area by keeping to the rivers, but such restricted exploration settled nothing. The world's largest uninvestigated region would remain the source of legend until examined to its core.

No early invader could have been expected to predict that this particular part of South America would have been the last large major region to withstand the onslaught of the Old World's invasion. This north-eastern section of Brazil's Mato Grosso state is neither outstandingly remote nor inaccessible. It has few of the normal trappings of a traditional fortress. It is a plateau of forest and river, a rich tangle of natural defences. It is abundant, for those who know how to live there, and a bewilderment for those who do not. The Xavante and others knew the forest, and knew how to keep it for themselves. Anyone on foot was at their mercy.

Not so anyone in the air. Not so those who parachuted themselves and their supplies into clearings, who built airstrips, who were replenished, and who knew there was no city in the heart of all that forest but merely groups of dissident Indian bands. In the 1940s the Xavante collapsed, and began to die. It all happened very quickly. A brand new town, Aragarças, was built where the Araguaia met the Garças. Another—Xavantina—named in their honour, but a testament to their defeat, was built on the Rio das Mortes, and a ferry was instituted to chug people across to the other side.

Later, with the country's capital suddenly 600 miles nearer, as it leapt overnight from Rio to Brasília, the process of dismembering the fortress continued. One task of the new Central Brazil Foundation was to drive a road from south to north, with Aragarças as its starting point and Manaus on the Amazon as its triumphant conclusion. This 1,200-mile leap would open up the Brazilian backwoods, the hinterland that had been closed for so long. In doing so it would finally topple the Xingú enclave and other lesser fortresses along the way. The great north road would mean that the last great unexplored territory was to be prepared for pacification, for settlement, for the extinction of all that used to be. 'Nobody goes to Central Brazil' wrote David Maybury-Lewis of Harvard in 1965, 'they make expeditions to it.' The purpose of the road was to open it all up, to make him wrong, to let people go there, just as they now go to Nebraska or even Arizona. No one makes expeditions to those places any more.

The Central Brazil Foundation realized it was carving a way through the past. It realized how much might be lost in the turmoil of bulldozers and the subsequent upheaval. Consequently, it issued invitations to scientists to come and see, to take note, to record, and to preserve at least some facts from the past. In Britain the Royal Society and the Royal Geographical Society received and accepted the invitation. They offered to mount a large expedition to be encamped on and around the new road in its virgin setting. They would arrange scientists and money and equipment. They would organize a flow of personnel to map, collect, photograph, observe and record all they could before the people came.

It is the area they were investigating, the work of those scientists, the Xingú enclave, and the development that has already come and will continue to come, which form the subject of this book. It is about the northern Mato Grosso, why it was, and why it could not remain as it used to be. It is about the end of an era.

1 THE LOST WORLD

From horizon to horizon, it is an unending carpet of trees. For hour after hour it is like this, broken only by the occasional streaks of water. From high up the rivers seem to be its only outstanding characteristic, as they meander about and glint with bright reflection from the sun. From lower down, and in a humbler aeroplane, they are even more important, providing a firm guide for the navigator, some sort of solace for thoughts of engine failure, and just as an entity in such a featureless sea of green. For the Indian invading this part of the continent they must have provided access routes, and for the settled Indian they must have been all-important. As a respite from the perpetuity of vegetation they are as refreshing as any oasis in any desert.

Take the Suiá Missú, for example, the waters of the Suiá Indians. This river is just one tributary of the mighty Xingú, itself only one of the many tributaries of the colossal Amazon further to the north. The unheard-of Suiá Missú is about 800 miles long, but may be substantially more or less because it has never been mapped. It starts by the ridge of the Serra do Roncador and within a hundred miles, or more, or less, it is wide enough to have torn apart the everlasting forest canopy. By then it has acquired the slow-moving dignity of a river and, at a mile or two an hour, its waters set off peacefully for the Xingú, for the Amazon, for the open sea. From source to ocean the journey must take a couple of months to be completed, more in the sluggish drought of winter and probably less when the rains are on, but the river is never uncomfortably fast.

It meanders prodigiously. It travels some four times further than any plane flying straight along its path. It makes its way within the broad valley of its own creation, like the zig-zag pattern on the back of a snake, and beyond the width of that restraining valley is the forest on either side. Within the valley are the river's own convolutions and the remains of all its former wanderings. Each curve tends to become so distorted and so circular that the river is eventually forced to take the short cut and nip off the unnecessary detour. The resulting ox-bow then survives to exist as a lake alongside the river that has abandoned it. On each side of the Suiá Missú are hundreds of these former fragments, all of a different age and all of a different depth and form in

The river was a sinuous fragment from the past, a lost world in danger of being found.

consequence. Some, freshly made, are like the river itself, but without a flow. Some are half empty, and muddy or sandy on their banks. Others are no more than a swamp, a remnant of a lake, and still others are full of growth as the forest has re-invaded this gentle affront to its universality.

The river had an unforgettably primitive quality about it. The water, particularly at the drier times of the year, was deliciously clear and the fish swam by in their droves. It was always possible to see the sting-rays undulating over the sandy bottom, and to watch others suddenly shiver themselves into a yet faster speed. Such fish never appeared to slow down but to proceed in a series of accelerations. At the shallowness of every bank there were small fish always desperate for food but desperately vulnerable themselves. Birds never seemed to fail with any dive, but predatory fish would often miss and be seen to miss in that exquisite clarity before sheering off after their unsuccessful attack.

Whereas the river was so clearly a beautiful thing, quite untouched, quite unharmed, those lakes it had budded off appeared yet more deeply embedded in the past. Perhaps the lack of any form of current helped the notion that time itself had stood still with them. If they had cayman swimming there, the six-foot form of alligator common in the area, this effect was heightened. Either there were eyes and nostrils above the surface or nothing more visible than a wake steaming along on its own through the water.

To paddle into one of these lakes was always exhilarating. They were of every shape and form—kidney, lozenge, moon, square, heart, round, arrow—and of every consistency. Once, after a group of us had pushed a boat over the muddy bank enclosing a small, circular lake, two large fish bounded away with a tremendous splash. Both these *tucunaré* were caught with ridiculous simplicity—only two casts being necessary—and that denuded the pool. No other large fish were there, only small minnows nibbling

To travel along it was to feel a sense of privilege for its was pristine and most beautiful.

repeatedly at an undulating black shape of minute tucunaré. Their cloud spread out when danger receded but coalesced at once into a firm, black toffee apple when the predators attacked and again proceeded to bite hungrily at the writhing thing.

That little lake with its fish summed up so well the story to be told in this book. It had a sense of antiquity to it, and was indeed an undisturbed place with natural selection promoting all kinds of survivors—until mankind arrived. Then, with two quick casts of the line, the lake was instantly exploited and abruptly left to itself. We pushed ourselves over the bank back to the river to satisfy our inquisitive appetites elsewhere.

Those of us who were fortunate in seeing this place at that time realized we were trespassing upon the past. We knew the old ways would soon be gone for good, and felt privileged to take note and witness so much of that ancient world. We were totally delighted with the Suiá Missú, that long sinuous fragment of natural peace whose gentleness eroded the soft earth on one side and built up white banks of sand on the other. The sandbanks were always a pleasure. They were steepest where the river was narrowest, and larger when the river itself was larger. Up them the turtles would trudge to lay their eggs (August being the favoured month) and a cayman would often be seen basking on their warm sand. Should the river be clear, or brown and green from the rains, its sandbanks were always white and ideal stopping places for the traveller. Whether soft, squeaky and dry, or firm and wet, they were the only portions of land without vegetation in that area, and were entirely welcome.

For the main part the act of travelling along that river, to see no more than the next bend or the next sandbank, was to experience total movement. Whereas the fish all dart backwards the birds all seem to fly forward, as if willing to be driven forever to the sea. Herons struggle upwards and then glide slowly down to the water's edge once again but further on. The kingfishers—and there were five different kinds—all scurried across the

river at no height at all, and then zoomed up on to a convenient branch in the traditional kingfisher manner. The Muscovy ducks splashed and flapped off lengthily downstream before becoming firmly airborne. The sun-bitterns, of anachronistic appearance
with high wings and odd colours, flew noisily from one bank and then hurried up the
same bank some fifty yards further on. With the fish swimming back, the birds flying
forward, and the water being both static in appearance and yet forever moving, the
river had a great sense of permanent impermanence to it. It was eternally travelling and
forever the same, but in the early morning there was a heavy mist over the water and
time then stood even stiller. At night the water changed from its daytime clarity into
inky blackness, but at all times the current moved on and on in its perpetual subjugation
to the Amazon so many hundreds of miles away.

To climb up the banks of the Suiá Missú, to attempt to scuttle up them much as the
sun-bitterns had done, was to enter a tangle of earthy branches. Every year the water
level climbed high up these banks either to strip the earth away or to deposit more of it,
and either to leave dead branches or merely to coat the living ones with mud. It took
time to batter one's way through the quick and the dead, past the springy living things
and the brittle, rotten stumps whose sudden disintegrations could be equally disarming.
Beyond this immediate confrontation lay a forest of short trees with a thick canopy that
kept the ground free from other vegetation. All these trees had to stand in water for
several months of each year and their bare poles covered the ground monotonously.
This uniformity could be broken by the sight of more water, perhaps a lake, perhaps a
new ox-bow, or perhaps just another bend of the river.

To the novice all is confusion. To the man who knows the place it is a superb defensive
system, and a boat wearily travelling round each major loop could be ambushed time
and time again, a point not without relevance to the invasion of this Indian country.
From the air the novice's confusion is easy to understand, and the river system makes a
riveting spectacle. The sight of a small boat determinedly hurrying along that maze has
a pathetic quality to it, an air of desperate endeavour much like some tiny insect's
random efforts to escape from the concrete danger of a major highway.

On either side of this particular river's main valley system lies the forest, the *mata
seca*, the dry forest. It is of lesser stature than the rain forest, both in height and density,
but it has an all-embracing regularity to it that is staggering. From horizon to horizon
the green mat of trees makes one crave (and particularly when in an aircraft whose
instruments have been largely replaced by pictures of the saints) for some relief, for an
open patch, a clearing or a landing place other than the carpet of branches at least
sixty feet above the ground. In such uniformity any change in the scene is immediately

In its meanderings the river had nipped off small portions of its length and these remained as lakes on either side ▷
*of the main flow. They were often full of fish, such as tucunaré, that tasted all the better for being roasted
traditionally. The Suiá Missú* OVERLEAF, *wandering peacefully past its sandbanks, was a maze that only
made sense from the air.*

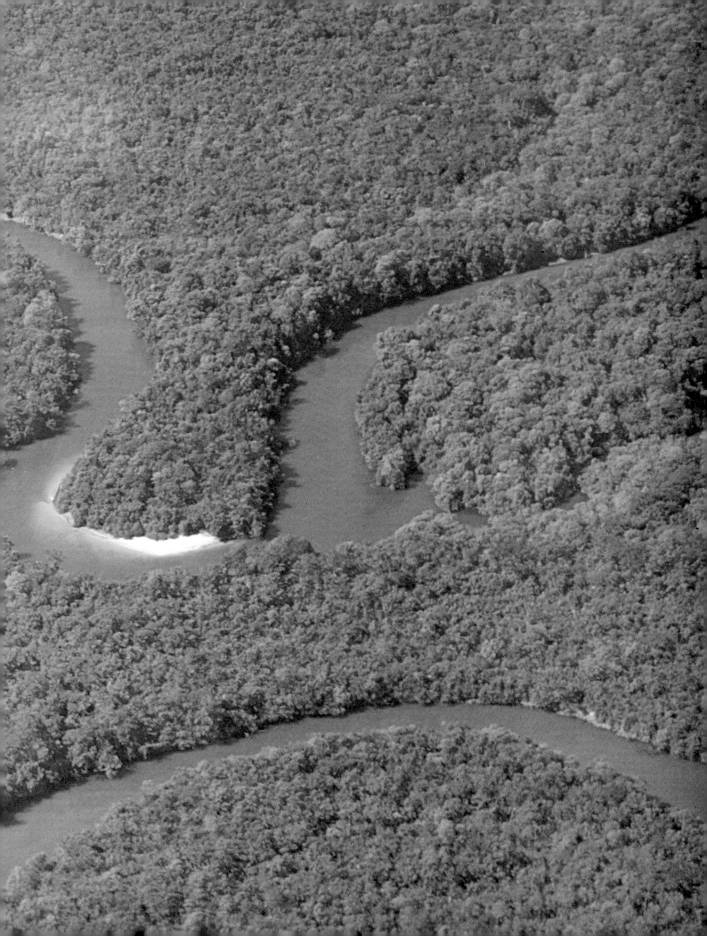

detectable. It may be a bunch of *Mauritia* palms showing the presence of a moister area. Or sudden flashes of light between the branches meaning that some hundreds or thousands of the dry forest trees are actually standing in water.

Just as it is hard to believe that the Suiá Missú will not yield some change around the next corner, so is it difficult to realize the vastness of the forest when walking in it and your eyes can see no further than fifty yards. In many ways it is a forest of death more than the exuberant life one might have expected from above. There are great dead trunks, either lying flat, or leaning on the living, or even standing vertically and surprisingly on their own. There are all the brittle lower branches, and there are the husks of former forest giants. Some tall trees, obviously flourishing at the top, are supported by half-rotten trunks, either soft and dusty on the outside or having a tough shell around a cavernous interior. One longs to find a whole tree, a tree whose bark is as pristine as a Norway spruce, whose leaves are uneaten, whose interior is entire. Even to find a whole leaf is a problem; the insects see to that.

Any possible notion that the forest resembles some mixed coppice of Western Europe is immediately dispelled by the ants, the termites and the ticks. They are forever present. The balls of earth hanging in the trees are termite homes, and they all have slender covered pathways leading to the ground. There are termite mounds on the ground, perhaps six feet high, and there are similar excavations within the ground, within the older trees. The fluffier kinds of nests are made by the ants, and they too hang from the trees, or within the trees. Sit anywhere and there will instantly be an energetic ant upon your trousers. Dig virtually anywhere, and there will be termites. Do not even pause, or dig, or sit, and you will have acquired ticks. (This triumvirate of tick, ant and termite makes it impossible to believe that the dry forest zone, the mata seca, could ever be part of the temperate world.)

The largest ant nests in the mata are made by *Atta sextus*. The mounds are so large, perhaps 20 feet by 30 feet, that they seem at first to be part of the lie of the land. Leading up to them from every side, and thereby drawing these huge ant-made hillocks to one's attention, are the busy roadways along which supplies are being brought in. It has been estimated that a quarter of a million ants live within each large encampment, the biggest such communities in the world. It seems only right that they should exist, every hundred yards or so, in the mata seca of central Brazil. Walking in that enormous forest means going beneath and around a lot of trees, but it is easy to return from each outing more impressed with the arthropods who really rule the area. Everything has to escape their depredations to survive. No animal, for example, that cannot jump away from the ants or is without a protective shell or an effective repellent of an odour could survive in that formic forest. There would be no hope for it.

Quite suddenly the dry forest changes into the drier *cerrado*, a scattered assortment of small trees and shrubs much resembling a poorly kept orchard. The trees rarely grow

◁　*On every side there was forest making it hard to comprehend the scale of the landscape.*

straight from the ground but lean this way and that in a haphazard manner. The ground between them may be bare and hotly exposed to the sun. It may be covered with fallen leaves, and these are either surprisingly soft for the aridity of that environment or else huge and crackly. They can snap like poppadoms, and they are often the size of cabbage leaves, but there is no springiness to them as in the forest. The cerrado is a strange mixture of delicacy and roughness, of some fresh plant with its solitary bright flower and the gnarled trees on every side, of a soft fern and the savage razor sedge nearby. It is bereft of growth, compared to the forest, but it is still impossible to see through it for more than those fifty or so of visible forest yards.

Suddenly there is *campo*. It is quite remarkable in such an arboreal world to be abruptly standing in a place bereft of trees. On one side of it there may be the wilderness of the sun-baked cerrado. On the other there may be the hot-house profusion of a piece of forest alongside a stream. In between there exists the strange phenomenon of a thin sliver of tussocky grass, not very wide and not very long, and nothing in the campo grows taller than those tufts of grass. It is seemingly as out of place as a well-mown path running through the wilder parts of a stately garden for it appears to belong elsewhere, but these strips of campo are just as positive and natural a feature of the landscape as the tall trees of the forest or the scorched, stubby growth of the cerrado.

Nevertheless, as might almost be expected, the area is not disregarded by the arthropods. There are anthills and termite mounds in the cerrado and there are innumerable forms of both in the campo. The absence of almost anything else, save for the tufts of grass and the very occasional shrub and fern, makes the campo mounds all the more striking. Looking like lumps of granite, and also impressively hard, they are dotted here and there, perpetual reminders of the permanent presence of the termite and the ant. Central Brazil, whether forested and dark, or poorly covered and bright to the sun, is a place where people tend to rest standing up. To sit down is to invite the ant. There are enough invaders without the issuing of such open-ended invitations.

At least the expanses of campo enable a man to get his bearings. In the forest and in the cerrado it was possible to feel lost, and even to be lost in the precise sense, when within a very short distance either of a path or even of a road. A sense of direction was easily disrupted, particularly should something trip up the visitor and make him more immediately interested in a spiny palm than in his general location. To stand upright again, to squint at a vertical sun, to look for signs and to see none could be rapidly disarming. On the other hand to travel with the Indians was to realize that the place is as stacked with features as a modern city. A bird is shot; it is hidden in a tree; it is left there for the greater part of the day; and it is then picked up having been approached from quite a different direction. A *non sequitur* of a conversation is almost inevitable. 'How did you know where the tree was?' 'It was in the same place.'

Aqui não tem nada was a constant Brazilian refrain, frequently heard and frequently said in any wilderness—'Here there is nothing'. Conversely 'The forest has everything,' said the Indians. 'It supplies all our needs, the food to eat, timber and thatch, wood for bows and arrows, fruit and medicine.' The forest is either *nada* or everything. It depends on who you are.

One reason for the discrepancy is that the immigrants and the residents have not been looking for the same things. The history of this region, whether forest, cerrado or river, shows up the differing purposes, however single-minded. The bandeirantes, those free-booters who explored Brazil in its early days, were more like land-based pirates than selfless explorers. Of all the plunder that was most desirable and easily transportable nothing could match the value of precious stones. Although these men brought back tales of hardships, and did not always return with belts of Indian ears around their waists, they frequently did bring back diamonds, gold, emeralds and other desirable minerals. To a great extent the people of North America moved west in order to settle and develop the land. To a large degree those who moved into the centre of Brazil were intent upon exploitation rather than development, and nothing was quite so eminently exploitable as the precious stones and minerals.

Suddenly rubber became almost as good, for the tall *Hevea* trees grew well and natur-ally in the wetter parts of the forests. The seringueiros were no less forthright in their invasion, tapping the trees for their latex, shooting anyone who got in their way and usually desperately in debt to their masters. To the prospectors there was nothing if the right minerals were lacking. To the seringueiros there was also nothing if the desirable Hevea trees were inadequately dotted throughout the forest. To the ordinary man, per-haps fleeing from injustice or retribution, there was also nothing—until he had learnt how to make use of the forest's peculiar bounty.

To the Indian it was richly generous. Unlike those plains Indians to the north who cropped a single species, the buffalo, for all their needs, the forest Indians lived within a more varied larder. Each annual cycle brought its succession of fruits and nuts, for flowering in the tropics is more evenly scattered throughout the year than in the uneven temperate world. The forests, although without the thundering hoofed abundance of most of the world's grasslands, contained a wide variety of mammals, such as deer and tapir, pig and monkey, and cats of many sizes up to the jaguar itself. The large numbers of meat-eaters, whether hovering in the sky or living on the ground, showed that a lot of food existed for those who knew how to find it. The rivers and lakes had fish, and all the fish-eating birds, otters and caymans merely emphasized this point. Other birds ranged from the flightless *ema* to the heavy *mutum*, from large macaws to the smaller parrots. Different tribes had different prejudices and preferences, for food is largely a matter of custom, but the forest could supply wildly different diets, from the growing point of certain palms to the trees, such as a *Phimeria*, that can be milked for their edible sap.

The Indians were the first possessors of all this land, but large numbers of their communities had been overrun. The inexorable effects of the Old World's discovery of the New, which had so remorselessly transformed Brazil's population from millions of

31

Indians and relatively few Europeans and Africans into millions of Brazilians and a few thousand Indians, were all-powerful and all-destructive, save in a few remarkable areas. Quite the largest of these regions, west of Goiás and well to the south of the Amazon, was an area of about half a million square miles. Right into the twentieth century, more than 400 years after Brazil's first settlers had landed, the huge unexplored silence in the centre of the country remained an enigma. The more the other continents yielded up their secrets, as Africa unfolded, as Australia showed her emptiness, the more remarkable and enigmatic became the South American situation. The unknown area in the heart became a source of speculation; there had to be a name for this place, and the name became the *Mato Grosso*.

Mato is a word with many of the connotations of bundu, bush, outback. It means an undeveloped place of thick scrub and in Brazil this name became attached to the biggest piece of undevelopment of all, the Mato Grosso. It also became the name for one of Brazil's largest states, the westerly region enclosing Campo Grande, Cuiabá, and the headwaters of the Xingú river. People today readily talk of *the* Mato Grosso and thereby blunt the edges between the defined borders of a state and the indefinite precision of a type of world.

Mato Grosso is therefore both an entity and a remnant from the past. The state itself is enormous—390,000 sq. miles. Its borders meet the frontiers of Amazonas and Pará (two of Brazil's other large states), of Goiás, Minas Gerais, São Paulo, Paraná, Rondônia (a more independent territory within Brazil), and even two other countries, Bolivia and Paraguay. Mato Grosso is also a legend. The name has a ring to it, much as Timbuktu or Mongolia, full of implications, packed with pre-convictions. To see 'Mato Grosso Barber Shop' painted on a sign makes the visitor realize the lustre and reputation of the name. 'Pará Barber Shop' does not have the same effect. Confusingly there is even a town called Mato Grosso, admittedly a modest place in the west of the state, hardly more than a large village, but it exists as well as the area with all its past and present associations.

The more the Indians held firm to part of the Mato Grosso the more renowned it became and the more legendary its facts. 'I know of no part of South America about which so little authentic information is available as this central plateau; fact and fable are so interwoven that it is impossible to say where one begins and the other ends,' wrote Commander George M. Dyott in 1928. In the absence of information anyone was entitled to weave his own tales. Colonel Percy Fawcett convinced himself of a whole civilization—'Whether we get through, and emerge again, or leave our bones to rot in there, one thing is certain. The answer to the enigma of Ancient South America, and perhaps of the prehistoric world, may be found when these old cities are located and opened up to scientific research. That the cities exist, I know . . .'

The Xavante Indians did not kill Fawcett but this tribe achieved fame as the principal defenders of the Mato Grosso citadel. They were nomadic, and this had helped them in

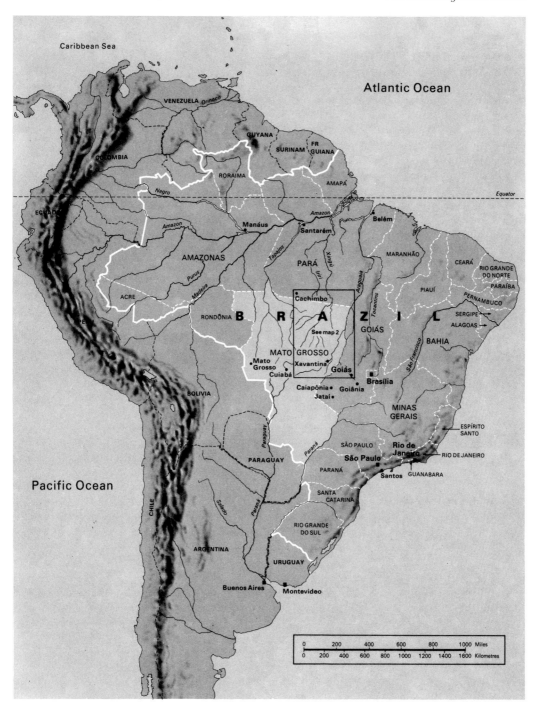

The map shows South America with the following labels:

Caribbean Sea

Atlantic Ocean

VENEZUELA — Orinoco

GUYANA
SURINAM
FR GUIANA

COLOMBIA

RORAIMA

AMAPÁ

Equator

ECUADOR

Negro

Amazon

Manáus

Amazon

Santarém

Belém

AMAZONAS

Purus

Madeira

Tapajos

Xingu

PARÁ

Araguaia

MARANHÃO

CEARÁ

RIO GRANDE
DO NORTE
PARAÍBA

ACRE

PIAUÍ

PERNAMBUCO

RONDÔNIA

B   R   A   Z   I   L

Cachimbo

SERGIPE
ALAGOAS

See map 2

GOIÁS

BAHIA

São Francisco

MATO GROSSO

Mato
Grosso

Xavantina

Cuiabá

Goiás

Brasília

Caiapônia
Jataí

Goiânia

MINAS
GERAIS

ESPÍRITO
SANTO

BOLIVIA

Paraguay

Paraná

SÃO PAULO

Rio de
Janeiro

RIO DE JANEIRO

São Paulo

GUANABARA

PARANÁ

Santos

PARAGUAY

Salado

Paraná

SANTA
CATARINA

Pacific Ocean

CHILE

RIO GRANDE
DO SUL

ARGENTINA

URUGUAY

Buenos Aires

Montevideo

| 0 | 200 | 400 | 600 | 800 | 1000 | Miles |
| 0 | 200 | 400 | 600 | 800 | 1000 | 1200 | 1400 | 1600 | Kilometres |

The central rectangle, crucial to the content of this book, is shown in greater detail on map 2, page 57.

33

their long retreat from one river to the next, first back from the Tocantins, then to the Araguaia and the Rio das Mortes. For years this tribe had killed every white man who crossed that 'river of deaths,' and mineral prospectors and other frontiersmen who had stayed too long even west of the Araguaia were likely to be attacked. With every death the Xavante reputation grew. According to one report, they even ran with their feet pointing the other way to mislead their trackers. They had a chief, Apewen, who was quick to reject all the invaders' gifts. The traditional habit of leaving presents for the Indians, thereby acquiring their trust, had been generally effective with other tribes and disastrous to their independence. Pacification in this fashion had frequently led to sub-jugation or to death, and Apewen had seen too much. The salt bags left for him were ripped open, the gifts scattered. Apewen's message was clear, and so were those of the Kayapo in the north and Kajabí in the west. The Indian was holding his own.

It is extraordinary that there should ever have been doubt over the manner of Faw-cett's death, but the various legends surrounding his fate, all the tales of old white men and half-white families, help to explain the greater legend of the place itself, the wilder-ness where fiction tramples on fact. It was all very well to postulate a civilization, and fairly well to dream up a Lost World (as Conan Doyle did when he too was fired by the obvious mysteries of the hole in the map) but it appears entirely unreasonable to be amazed that Fawcett, his son and his son's friend did not emerge from the forest. That fortress of the Xingú headwaters, even when approached from the west to avoid the traditional Xavante frontier, was full of Indians. Stories of white men's activities must have had considerable currency within it, thereby fanning the flames of hostility. More-over internecine warfare between one tribe and its neighbours was common and three more killings were extremely likely, whoever the victims. Fawcett had pulled off some formidable journeys in his time, and had previously returned unscathed, but the kind of roulette involved did not guarantee permanent success. Three men, therefore, laden with gifts, some for the tribes first to be encountered, some for their neighbours along the way, had only to meet a little opposition, a cantankerous chief, a warrior jealous of the gifts he did not get, and the three Englishmen would be only too easy to ambush. Arrows or clubs would quickly deliver the vengeance.

'If we should not come out,' said Fawcett, 'I don't want rescue parties to come in looking for us. It's too risky. If, with all my experience, we can't make it, there's not much hope for others. That's one reason why I'm not telling exactly where we're going.' A search party, if not a rescue party, did cover the same sort of ground a couple of years later. Its leader, Commander Dyott, wrote after the expedition: 'That Colonel Fawcett and his companions perished at the hands of hostile tribes seems to me and all my party beyond dispute.'

Which tribe was hostile, or how, no one will ever know. The Kalapaló have been generally credited with Fawcett's death by clubbing Fawcett, so one story goes, when he was helping his son Jack and Raleigh Rimmell up a river bank shortly after they had

34

In the Vale dos Sonhos it was easier to understand the belief in lost cities. The rocks stood up like buttresses and from afar looked like huge structures fashioned and shaped by men.

left a disgruntled village. The two lads were then quickly dealt with, the gifts dispersed, and all three bodies buried. According to Dyott the killing probably happened some four days' march east of the Culuene river (or within a very short distance of the new road whose existence forms the backbone of this book).

In a sense Percy Harrison Fawcett did not die, and never will die. 'The Dyott expedition returned with no proof of anything,' wrote Fawcett's son Brian, a good many years later. 'It did not even prove that the Fawcett party had been there. . . . It was Commander Dyott's belief that my father had been killed. . . . We of the family could not accept (his argument) as in any way conclusive.'

A more light-hearted party left for Brazil in 1932 in the company of Peter Fleming. 'Room Two More Guns,' he had read in *The Times*, 'for exploring and sporting expedition, if possible ascertain fate late Colonel Fawcett.' Later on, when he and the others had paddled this way and that around the Araguaia, he wrote: 'In London I was inclined to be scornful of Dyott's failure to bring back final and conclusive proof of Fawcett's fate when it was so nearly in his grasp; I am not scornful now that I have seen something of the difficulties with which he had to contend.'

Fawcett disappeared in 1925. At that time the world had been largely explored. Nowhere else on earth could have concealed a lost living civilization except the Xingú enclave, and Fawcett had only emphasized the drama by disappearing himself. The world has been eternally loath to have emptiness on its maps, and its abhorrence of these vacuums has meant that they are either filled up with extravagant tales or subjected to increasingly intense exploration. The Xingú could not last any more than any other citadel. The most surprising aspect was that it had survived so long. People were flying the Atlantic while the Xingú was still intact, but it was this very fact of the aeroplane that led to its collapse.

In the 1930s General Rondon, a man who was full of compassion for the Indians, being a *mestizo* with half their blood in his veins, began opening up the closed area of north-eastern Mato Grosso state. He had been doing this kind of work all his long life, having been the main force behind the enlightened founding of the Indian Protection Service in 1910, and his name is perpetuated in Rondônia territory, the huge piece of land to the west of the Xingú. With him in those early days of the Xingú collapse there were three brothers, part of an enormous São Paulo family called the Villas Boas. These three were in their twenties when they first came to the region: Orlando was the oldest, then Claudio, then Leonardo and, after 1946, virtually every expedition around the Xingú headwaters has been led by one or other of these three men.

The brothers have worked principally by cutting *picadas* and then creating airstrips for the delivery of supplies. The picada is a pathway entirely suitable to the forest and savannah country, and it can be as wide or as narrow as one chooses to make it. Essentially it is a matter of proceeding in a straight line and of cutting down the trees, bushes and saplings in one's path, a labour that varies precisely with the type of vegetation in the area. The subsequent picada provides security, and a safe and speedy route back to base. The Villas Boas expedition to the heart of the Xingú country in the late 1940s hacked out 650 miles of picada, a fact still spoken of with a kind of affection by Claudio. Within this heart they made yet another airstrip, they created an outpost of a few huts and called it Capitão Vasconcelos (after a man who had dared to explore the Xingú in 1924). 'The jungle was then almost conquered,' said Orlando, 'but remember that it was conquered by the aeroplane.'

Soon afterwards Leonardo died and, following the tradition of an area steeped in legend for so long, every kind of exotic tale is told about his end. 'It was nothing,' says Claudio, 'but a calcification of the mitral valve. He was operated on successfully in Goiânia, and sewn up, but 30 minutes later he collapsed and died.' They then named the central Xingú outpost after him, and today it is Posto Leonardo. Ever since its foundation the two other brothers have worked to transform this place and the rich region all around it into a refuge for Indians.

With increasing pressure from outside such a retreat became vital. The plight of the Indians was being intensified almost everywhere. Bullets and epidemics were continuing to take their toll, and the resistance of the formerly invincible tribes seemed to disintegrate the moment their vulnerability had been proved. They would die without effort,

His name was Matampó. He was a Txikão, and in his late twenties. He was heir-presumptive to the chief- ▷
taincy, but of his tribe only fifty-three remained.

or would cease breeding, or just vanish. In theory their fate was still being cared for by the Indian Protection Service, the Rondon organization whose motto had been: 'If necessary die, but never kill.'

In 1967 the I.P.S. was abruptly dissolved, and the reasons given for its dissolution helped to explain the Indian demise. An investigating commission, set up by the Brazilian Ministry of the Interior, disclosed some of the facts in a 20-volume report. It found evidence of wholesale slaughter, whether by dynamite, machine guns or sugar laced with arsenic. Of the 700 employees of the Service 134 were charged with various crimes and 200 were fired. In a mere two years of service, from 1964–6, the director had committed 42 separate crimes against the Indians, including collusion in several murders, torture and the illegal sale of land.

The man in charge of the investigation, Jader Figueiredo Correia, estimated that hundreds of Indians had been killed and thousands more had died as a result of mistreatment. It was not so much any casual neglect of the Indians and their problems that so shocked readers of the investigation's report as the hideous and blatant brutality. How could a Cessna fly over an Indian village, drop gifts to encourage people from their huts, and then land a bundle of dynamite with the next consignment? How could anyone inoculate Indians with smallpox virus in order to get their land?

In 1823 José Bonifacio had said in Brazil: 'We must never forget that we are usurpers in this land, but also that we are Christians.' Forgetfulness, and murder, were rampant both before and long after he pronounced his forthright dictum. The Indians had been usurped again and again and then, within their all-powerful Mato Grosso stronghold, they also suddenly collapsed. There was no pitched battle for the historians to record. There was nothing, save for the aeroplane, and disease, and various perfidies, and a kindly but firm exploration leaving picadas in its wake. There was no big bang to end it all. There was a sudden pointlessness, and the powerful Xavante nation became a lot of powerless Xavante misfits, like the rabble from any fallen army.

With the end of the Xingú citadel, and with the speed of its demise, few people could fully or immediately appreciate the changed situation and its implications. Besides, Brazil in the 1950s was in the throes of building her third capital. The first had been Salvador, the second Rio de Janeiro, but suddenly political reputations and much of the country's finances were being staked upon a gigantic, lavish and vigorous move into the interior. For years there had been talk of disrupting Brazil's permanent loyalty to the coastline, and for quite a time even the site of the new capital had been selected. In the outside world there existed many precedents for building brand-new capitals, such as Washington, New Delhi, Ankara and Canberra, and suddenly Brazil decided Brasília

◁ *Protectors of the Indian, founders of the Parque Nacional do Xingú, gold medallists of the Royal Geographical Society, the brothers Claudio* TOP *and Orlando Villas Boas have been indefatigable in their efforts on behalf of the surviving tribes.*

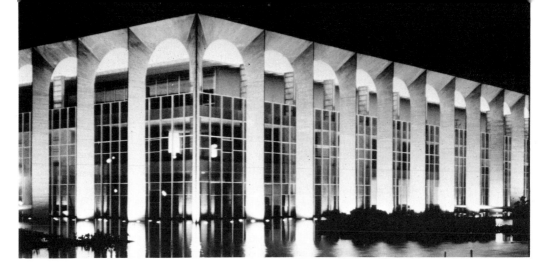

Brasília, the new capital, was a bold leap 600 miles into the Brazilian interior. Its existence has undoubtedly stimulated enthusiasm for the country's enormous hinterland.

would be a fact. The mood of the country was right for the change. Money was available and a man, Juscelino Kubitschek, was there to provide the necessary impetus. On 21 April 1960 the new capital was formally established.

Brasília lies some 600 miles north-west of Rio. It is nearer the presumed death place of Fawcett than it is to the former seaside capital, and its sudden existence undoubtedly stimulated interest in Brazil's colossal interior. A scheme for opening up Brazil's empty quarter by driving a road from south to north was greatly helped by the fact that the new capital had occurred. It is possible to drive from Rio to Brasília, and even to drive for three weary days from Brasília up to Belém near the mouth of the Amazon, but it is not possible to travel overland, except with considerable hardship, from the developed lands west and south-west of Brasília up to the more westerly towns on the Amazon, such as Santarém or Manaus, that dowager of a city with all its flamboyant rubber-boom past so curiously a part of its present. The new scheme planned to drive a road from a spot on the central belt of Mato Grosso state for some 1,200 miles until it reached the colossus of the Amazon. It would start from the place where the Araguaia was met by the Garças river, and it would first travel north to the famous Rio das Mortes, that old frontier waterway. Then it would continue northwards along the Serra do Ronca-dor, the range of slightly higher ground always said to be the principal home of the formerly fearsome Xavante.

Thereafter, and to reach Manaus, it would have to evade as many rivers as possible but would inevitably become involved with a few. All the major rivers in this area flow north in their obeisance to the Amazon, and the first such river to cross would be the Xingú. Its headwaters are a maze and therefore too much of an obstacle course for any road engineer, but at least the problem becomes united where the Xingú has collected all its early tributaries together, even though it is then a wider jump than ever before. The planners thought that the von Martius rapids looked a good spot for a bridge

The new road, spawning such towns as Xavantina LEFT, *will eventually link the capital with Manaus, that dowager of a city whose opera house on the Amazon is still a source of wonder.*

crossing, and so the dotted line on their maps went north-west from the Serra do Roncador to reach this point.

Thenceforth the dots became more vague, and wandered up towards Cachimbo. Quite what happened after that, and whether the road went further west, over the Tapajós and the Madeira to reach Manaus, or whether it took a smaller bite out of the unknown and went instead directly north towards Santarém, was itself uncertain at the southern end. Cachimbo was over 600 miles from Aragarças even along the straightest route any road could take, and it would be time enough to decide about Cachimbo-northwards when Cachimbo-southwards, a sufficiently formidable task in itself, had been satisfactorily accomplished.

Anyway, with Brasília securely launched and with the country's available finances still fairly sound, the Central Brazil Foundation could continue with its scheme for the great north road. This organization, founded by President Getulio Vargas in 1942, was responsible for all major developmental projects in the area, and it had started upon the road even before Brasília had formally taken over the reins of office. The 90-mile section from Aragarças to Xavantina, the first hesitant leap northwards, had been finished in the 1950s, but the old frontier of the Rio das Mortes had held things up for a time. The town of Xavantina, built by the side of this river, and equipped with a hospital, a church, an airfield, electricity and a central football patch, is no Brasília, but it is a new planned community, albeit in its humbler fashion. Around the square are the neat bungalows and the straight streets but not too far away is the even humbler shanty town. Here there are no streets, but pathways on the earth. Here the houses have walls of mud and wood, and the roofs are mainly thatch. Here the people and not the planners have been in charge.

Further down the river is an encampment belonging to some of the remaining Xavante. They occasionally wander into Xavantina, the place named in their honour,

41

to see what is happening, to beg, to pass the time of day. They print their broad feet into its dust, and look unkempt in their aged European clothes. They still have their hair cut Xavante style, a fringe in front, very short at the crown and long at the back, and they still have the powerful barrel physique of their warrior forbears, but the Xavante are out of place in Xavantina. One of them has taken a job as a mechanic in a workshop, and has had his hair cut to an even length, but for the main part they have no part in this brand new place on their aged soil.

The Indians used to say that they shot macaws to pluck out their bright feathers, and jaguars to acquire claws for a necklace, and rubber-tappers to find fish-hooks, for hooks were as inevitable in the pockets of a rubber-tapper as were claws on the feet of jaguars. Now the Xavante just ask for fish-hooks, or torch batteries, or *fumo preto* (a tobacco sold by the yard) and then they go back to their village. They leave the town of Xavantina to its own perplexities and Brazil, having overrun them, is now passing them by.

In the 1960s the Central Brazil Foundation started upon the task of taking the next leap northwards. It had built two bridges at Aragarças, one crossing the green waters of the Araguaia and then another, almost immediately after it, over the browner waters of the Garças, but they built no bridge at Xavantina. Instead they constructed a ferry, and took everything across on that, before heading further north. There was one more substantial river to cross, the Areões, a tributary of the Rio das Mortes, and they built a small bridge over that, but thereafter they tried to keep to the watershed. This meant, insofar as it was possible to do so, keeping to the west of any more streams leading east-wards to the Rio das Mortes but east of anything leading down to join the waters of the Xingú system. Due north from Xavantina the Serra do Roncador, the snoring mountains, provided the ridge for the new road. They were to be woken up at last.

To begin with, the road on the far side of the ferry carved its way through the scrub-land of cerrado, that world of gnarled and modest trees. Every now and then, wherever there was water to support a more luxuriant growth, there would be taller trees taking advantage of the changed situation. Progress would then be slower, but the bulldozer, the axe and fire would effectively destroy all growth and prepare the barren roadway. The central track of the road would be paved with the most suitable kind of earthy surfacing quarried from any convenient spot nearby. The small bridges over minor streams were mainly made from available local materials, with laterite rocks forming a compact foundation to resist each summer's surging water and with long logs making the bridge itself. The round trunks of suitable trees were chopped first into rectangular trunks, and then cut to length to fit over the stream. Two trunks on one side and three trunks on the other, so that any vehicle could conveniently straddle any gap in the

The Xavante, former warriors, now wander into the towns, beg for tobacco, and watch the transformation of ▷
their former world. OVERLEAF *The odd patterns of the forest, here caused by insects chewing furled-up leaves, are yielding to modern shapes no less strange, such as Brasília's giant coronet of a cathedral.*

middle, was the accepted pattern (although one wondered at this lop-sided economy as heavy vehicles skidded down the slope in their attempt to hit the unevenness evenly).

About 170 miles north of Xavantina the roadmakers abruptly encountered forest. The eternal scrubland became, thenceforth, eternal forest and the work slowed down accordingly. On either side of the central road two rather broader swathes had to be cut to protect the road from falling trees. The forest community normally protects its individual trees from storms and from having to stand upright on their own. Consequently, when the road strip had carved its way, the borderline trees were suddenly unprotected on one side. They fell easily and the gentlest of winds would send them crashing over with a simplicity that would be unthinkable for trees accustomed to receiving several gales a year. Therefore, as the road engineers moved on, they left behind them a smooth brown (or reddish, or yellow) surface of brand-new road flanked by a less orderly piece of marginal destruction. These borders did not have to be cleared so precisely and they became a dumping ground for roots, for half-consumed timber left from giant fires, and for the expired parts of various machines. On to this no-man's-land the trees could fall with impunity, and frequently did so.

It was in 1965 that the Brazilian government, conscious of the unparalleled opportunity for scientific work as the road carved its way through such new land, issued an invitation to various other governments. It explained that a vast area in the north of Mato Grosso and in the states of Pará and Amazonas was being opened up, and countries were welcome to co-operate in a programme of research along the new road. The scientific investigation would be an expedition into hundreds of miles of virgin territory, but without the hideous logistics such an expedition might normally entail. The road, the brand-new road, would always be there to provide effortless access to and from the particular piece of virginity being investigated at the time. Food, transport, fuel and the other demands of a major piece of exploration would all be present at the road-head.

Such an offer of assistance through the last really large portion of unexplored territory on earth was of paramount importance. Britain received its invitation via the British Embassy in Brazil who had forwarded it to the Royal Geographical Society in London. The Royal Society was then informed, and it too expressed great interest in the project. Its expeditions committee pointed out that the road was cutting through 'one of the few remaining areas of the world which has not been available for scientific research and which offers opportunities for original research not available elsewhere.'

The Royal Society and the Royal Geographical Society arranged for a reconnaissance party to be sent to Brazil in May 1966. A. F. MacKenzie, a former agricultural adviser to the Ministry of Overseas Development, and Iain Bishop, a young zoologist

◁   *The Xingú headwaters are a plethora of rivers, all heading north in their obeisance to the Amazon a thousand miles away and all part of the greatest river system in the world.*

47

from Leicester University, then spent six weeks in the country and were joined out there by David Hunt, a botanist from Kew, and H. S. Irwin of the New York Botanic Gardens. The team travelled from Rio to Brasília, then further west to Aragarças via Goiânia and Rio Verde, and then up the famous road. They reached Xavantina, crossed the Rio das Mortes on its ferry, and drove up to the road-head, still a thousand miles short of its destination at the Amazon.

This reconnaissance party reported back enthusiastically. They said it was extraordinarily exciting country and, as the road continued northwards, it would continue to be exciting, possibly even more so. On the other hand the very convenience of the new road meant that development would rapidly follow, and the area would soon be trampled on by the twentieth century. Extreme urgency was therefore necessary. The place had to be studied *before* development took place. As a further inducement for study there were the Indians, wherever and however they were living. Development was going to hit them a further blow just as it would hit their forests.

Back in London decisions were taken, and Iain Bishop, now leader of the main expedition, was despatched as advance guard for the scientists, with the first batch due to arrive two months later. With Iain went Angela, a nurse who had become his wife shortly beforehand. Both Royal Societies, mindful of all the famous expeditions their societies had despatched in the past, when the idea of a leader taking his wife along had been entirely unthinkable on all sides, were not daunted by Iain's marriage after his appointment as leader. In any case, he was insistent; his new wife would not be left behind in England.

Iain's initial brief was to spend time in Rio and Brasília seeing relevant people, to check on the problems of clearing equipment through customs, to establish a system so that future scientists would follow a simple route to the destination, wherever that was, and to decide upon that suitable destination. To send an expedition to Antarctica or to some uninhabited isle, despite the physical disadvantages of those places, is to encounter only one set of problems—those presented by the environment. To mount a research unit within someone else's country, despite the ease of flying into airports, catching buses and so forth, is to encounter quite a different set of obstacles. To go west from Brazil's seaboard is to exchange, for every mile travelled, the hazards and difficulties of any Western bureaucracy for the hazards and difficulties of an increasingly harsh environment. Some people prefer arguing with a customs official to dealing with a savage habitat. Others would welcome a swamp or a bee swarm any day to governmental impasse. Brazil was to provide much of both kinds of difficulty in her own particular fashion.

The Mato Grosso venture was initially described by its parent societies as the

◁ '*The resistance of the formerly invincible tribes seemed to disintegrate the moment their vulnerability had been proved. They would die without effort, or just vanish.*'

49

'Expedition to Central Brazil'. Later on the vagueness inherent in this particular definition was removed and the endeavour became the Xavantina/Cachimbo expedition. Although Xavantina is in Mato Grosso state, the more modest community of Cachimbo is in Pará, but the new road would eventually be linking the two places. Xavantina was already thriving in its planned and unplanned fashion whereas Cachimbo was little more than a name and an airstrip. It was waiting for the road to reach it before it too could thrive, and grow, and start earnestly upon its existence. Xavantina/Cachimbo therefore stretched from reality to intent, from the present to the future, and summed up the aims of the expedition even though not one of its members would come within a hundred miles of Cachimbo, except fleetingly in transit. The road did pass through one, and would be passing through the other, and it was the creation of this road that had caused the venture to occur, the Xavantina/Cachimbo expedition.

Nevertheless both places are only dots on the map and the road between them, when it is eventually completed, will only be the faintest scratch in that enormous piece of land. From Xavantina north just to the boundary of Pará is 400 miles. From the Araguaia to the Xingú is some 200 miles, and the famous headwaters of that river occupy a square whose sides are all more than 200 miles. To arrive at the frontier with Pará or at the river Xingú is not to reach an entirely different country, a developed land bordering upon the remoteness of the Serra do Roncador, but just to encounter more and more of the same kind of territory and to realize the vastness of this unexploited zone. The Xavantina road is like a single lonely track across Europe. It is awesome to stop, say, a hundred miles along its course and to know there is no other road for hundreds of miles either to the west, to the north-west, or to the north. It is even more forbidding to fly above this solitary highway and to see its pathetic size in its true perspective. Driving along the road makes it seem of tremendous importance. Flying above it, and even losing sight of it with remarkable ease in that sea of green, is impressive. The scale of this particular portion of the planet is hard to absorb.

The human emptiness is also difficult to appreciate. To travel in Africa, and to choose some empty spot for a camp site or even a picnic, is to understand the relative density of its population. People emerge from the nowhere of their home and instantly curtail any feeling of loneliness. To drive across the Syrian desert, and to pick up hitch-hikers standing on one sand dune who wish to be transported to some further desolate piece of sandy emptiness, is to realize that the landscape is far from stripped of humanity. Not so with great tracts of the Mato Grosso.

It has been said by the space travellers that it is difficult detecting any proof of this planet's human occupation. The big cities tend to be hazily shrouded in their own effluent, and most other man-made things are too small to be distinguished from an orbital altitude. Therefore, by this token, the green area some 800 miles north-west of

The new road would carve through the forest, a neat incision of the twentieth century. ▷

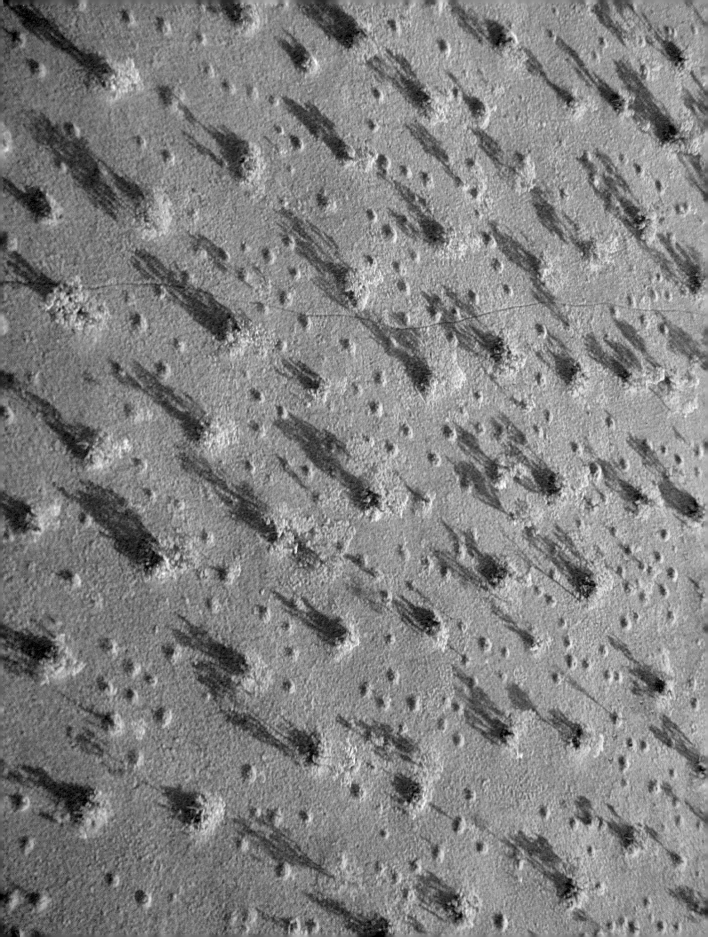

Rio de Janeiro does not appear greatly different to other large planetary areas with their varying hues of brown and green. Had such a high flier descended even when the Indians were still in full possession of this land he would still have seen mile upon mile of forest and scrubland with scarcely a sign of the inhabitants. The Indians had their invisible pathways, but they did not change the face of the Earth. They hunted in it. They picked its fruits. They selected wood for their bows, for their homes and for their canoes. They only made use of the world around them and they did not transform it. Certainly they did not, as Genesis instructs, first multiply and then subdue it. Therefore neither their coming nor their going had been disruptive. For this reason alone it is possible to refer to the place as an untroubled Eden, a piece of the past, a world on its own.

The Royal Societies' expedition initially took, as its brief for investigation, all the land lying within the vicinity of those completed portions of that north/south highway. This road, despite the faintness of its scratch upon the Earth's surface, would eventually lead to the transformation of tens of thousands of square miles, and the expedition's various camps would be gobbled up in the change as surely as hundreds of other as yet unnamed and unnoticed specks on the map. There are still no valid ground-based maps of the region, but there are air photographs and some maps have been made from these with their inaccuracies being further signs of the remoteness of this ancient world. The road, in time, will change all that. Eventually there will be maps, and a pollution problem, and erosion, and a conservation policy. The road, by permitting access, will have been the cause. Like a hairline crack in the dam it will surely lead to a particular kind of deluge, the kind that modern man has been making so inexorably almost everywhere else.

However, as Iain and Angela Bishop left London for Rio, the road was still new, and the Garden of Eden they and the others would be investigating was still untouched, unharmed. The unexplored territory, empty for so long, then the home of Indians, but then so sadly drained of most of these earlier invaders, formed a fantastic dividend from the past. The road was carving through it, a surgical incision of the twentieth century certain to spread its kind of infection in every direction. There was no time to lose. The land would so soon be in the hands of the second wave of inheritors, and this new invasion would be nothing like so gentle with its inheritance. In fact they would transform it, totally.

◁   *Large rivers like the Araguaia often have great borderlands of pantanal on either side. Frequently flooded, these can form into a pattern of evenly spaced clumps, each consisting of a termite mound and a few trees.*

53

2 JOURNEY TO EDEN

Air travel has totally upset the time scale of the modern expedition. The profusion of ludicrous accoutrements belonging to another world, scarf, overcoat and so on, emphasize that haste of intercontinental travel which permits so little time for readjustment. Voyages by sail must have been ideal. Today one suspects that a man may even die of thirst in some remote spot while still clutching his final boarding card.

Fortunately Brazil quickly injects its own sense of time into the visitor's schedule, and therefore permits him to catch up with his thoughts and the right kind of clothes. When the Xavantina/Cachimbo expedition was under way, from the middle of 1967 until its closure two years later, its members would arrive at Brasília soon enough, but then have plenty of time to catch their breath while travelling the final 340 miles, the straight distance from capital to camp. One day for the first 6,000 miles was fair going. Four days for the final leg was not at all bad, but longer times were plentifully recorded. The delay did impart to the new arrival some kind of respect for the terrain and its peculiarities, an awareness totally missed when flying high. Moreover, the various minor setbacks inevitably encountered en route gave everyone a chance to practise their Portuguese as the days passed by.

Those invited to investigate part of another country assume everything will be made somewhat easier for them, and they therefore lose precious time before realizing that nothing will be simpler just because of the invitation. In Brazil the port of entry itself was a suitable spot for disillusionment because it harboured a department of the Brazilian customs. All the world has tales to tell about its customs authorities but, even with so much belligerence and bureaucratic officialdom at all these other frontiers, the customs authorities of Brazil have managed to carve a name for themselves, despite world-wide competition. Seasoned travellers, experienced in *douanes* of every denomination, are happy to give more than an accolade to Brazil. In this competing world it takes the biscuit, and retains the goods for month after month after month. Many of the invited British scientists left Brazil long before their incoming equipment had left the customs warehouses. Others, having replanned their work in the absence of their equipment, then planned it back again when their packages were mysteriously re-leased. The facts of the Brazilian customs need not be reiterated excessively, for the word is already abroad, but it should perhaps be said once more that anyone planning any kind of venture into Brazil, which involves anything more than the most ele-mentary baggage and who then forgets about the Brazilian customs, does so at his peril.

With or without equipment, with or without a tale or two to tell ('I had to swear I would expose none of the unexposed film I had brought with me'; 'I could not explain why a thermometer—scientific equipment—was wrapped up in a shirt—personal clothing—and they kept both'), the scientists arrived at Brasília. On average the British visitors each spent less than three months in the field, but in total 46 people from Britain were able to take advantage of Brazil's offer to investigate this other Eden. Either for a short time or a longer period, either young or old (the youngest was 21, the oldest 66), either male or female, and either with equipment or thwarted by the system, the British scientists left their home laboratories to work in Brazil.

A need to visit colleagues or laboratories or museums delayed a few of them en route at Belém, Rio or São Paulo, and there were further colleagues at the University of Brasília. Consequently the journey to the Mato Grosso camp site began in earnest the moment each member of the expedition left Brasília. Until the final moment of de-parture from the capital each member was cared for by the British Council, met at Rio, transported to hotel or airport, inveigled through bureaucracy, calmed when need be, introduced to appropriate people, and then issued with the bus ticket to Goiânia, the important town west from Brasília. Everyone's schedule and itinerary before reaching the capital tended to be individualistic, and according to his or her wishes. Everyone's journey from Brasília tended to be equally unique but for a plethora of reasons. In one way or another, whether by cancelled aircraft or punctured buses, the country's interior added that necessary dimension of time so crudely vanquished by subsonic travel from one capital to the next.

The Brasília-Goiânia bus either left on time or even before it was due. Brasília's lower level bus station, centrally placed but burrowed out of sight, is a small piece of reality in all that surface landscaping. Above, there are planned views and the silence of the buildings. Below, there are drivers trying out their engines, there are beggars, and there are shoe-shine boys. There is also coffee. At seven in the morning, a popular time of departure, this is the most pertinent requirement, and Brazil excels in it. Small, sweet and strong, its *cafezinhos* have everything to commend them, and the passengers fortify themselves at 250 old *cruzeiros* a time.

Leaving Brasília by road is complex. One might have thought with this new city built on nowhere that its exits would radiate, spoke-like, in all important directions. Instead they circumnavigate, maze-like, around roundabouts, loop-roads and the like before settling down on a more positive course and letting the sun burn more consis-tently through just one side of the bus. Viação Araguarina's service to Goiânia then eats up the miles as the red-earthed countryside travels by. It is undulating country, plainly with fewer trees on it today than beforehand, and the driver hurtles down each descent to make up for the more laggardly sections up the slopes. It is a tarmac road, with rough and well-eroded edges to it. A line of wispy poles, whitewashed in part and carrying a telephone wire or two, keep the road company for part of the way, and occasional groups of zebu cattle wander through the cerrado scrubland on either side. To begin with there are large hoardings all facing those driving towards Brasília, whereas nothing faces those who are departing, but every gate, or so it seems, and every large rock has been whitewashed with the names of department stores and their products existing somewhere, presumably, in the vicinity of all this emptiness. *Casas Pernambucanas, Casas Buri:* the whitewash men have been diligent, but who is there to buy?

It is developed land, but thinly populated. There are barbed-wire fences travelling in straight lines between the trees and shrubs of the cerrado, but with identical vegetation on either side of the wire. A European's eyes equate a fence with a change of scene, with a crop or at least bare earth, but these wired barriers south-west of Brasília march regularly through that even landscape, much like that old rabbit-fence of Australia with rabbits hopping about on either side of it.

After less than a couple of hours hurtling down and clambering up this dusty land of gently rolling hills, the bus pulls into a modest settlement providing a convenient staging post on the journey. It is 1 hour 40 minutes since the last cafezinho, and everybody crowds into the Posto Mocasp Bar for the crucial restoration. The Bar also sells sweets and buns, but the small coffees are paid for by the bus company. The town of Alexânia has no building in it of any stature, and has a Western appearance with its twin rows of modest establishments, but it smacks mildly of Brasília because there are at least 70 yards from one side of the street to the other. The road itself is a mere strip along this greater causeway, and is therefore sensibly distant from the shack fronts where the people sit, talk, lean, examine a well-ribbed horse, kick an even thinner dog, and the children play within the bare bones of a truck, long since dead.

The hooter hoots and the journey continues. More and more of Brazil unfolds itself. Every now and then there are small plantations of bananas and fruit trees grouped casually around the basic tropical hut, that rectangular simplicity of a home whose general design and comportment are a feature around the world. Its doorway is a simple three-sided frame of wood. Its windows are lesser frames, but four-sided, and the house's walls are of mud, or sticks, or brick, or a bit of each. Its roof is thatch, or iron, or even tile, and its slopes are as conformist as that rectangular shape. The rain has spattered the earth so that the walls change colour near the ground, and these houses

Map 2. Base camp was built at the end of a cul-de-sac off the new road, halfway between Xavantina and São Félix. It lay within the marked square shown more clearly on pages 84 and 85 (map 3). The projected route to Cachimbo (broken line) was plotted before the Xingú Park became a reality. The two must not overlap. ▷

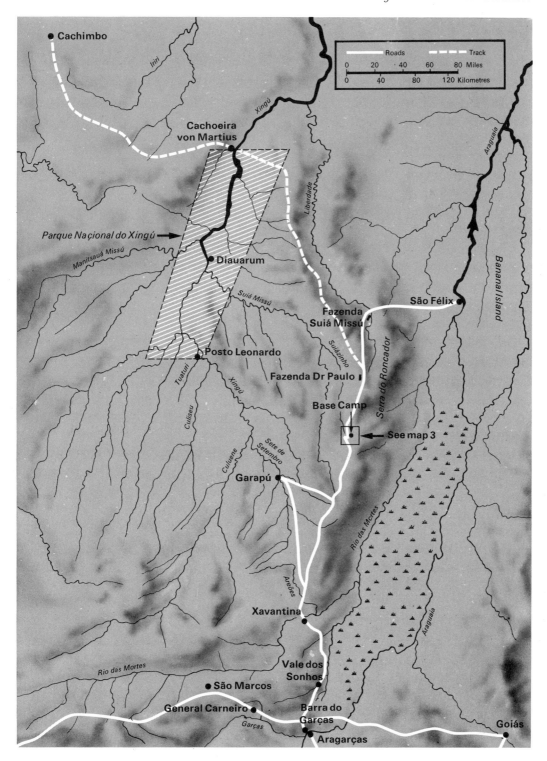

Cachimbo

Irìrì

Xingú

Cachoeira
von Martius

Liberdade

Parque Nacional do Xingú →

Manitsauá Missú

Diauarum

Suiá Missú

Araguaia

Bananal Island

São Félix

Fazenda
Suiá Missú

Posto Leonardo

Suiazinho

Tuaturi

Xingú

Fazenda Dr Paulo

Serra do Roncador

Base Camp

Culiseu

← See map 3

Culuene

*Sete de
Setembro*

Garapú

Rio das Mortes

Areões

Xavantina

Rio das Mortes

Vale dos
Sonhos

São Marcos

General Carneiro

Barra do
Garças

Garças

Araguaia

Goiás

Aragarças

Roads	Track

0 20 40 60 80 Miles
0 40 80 120 Kilometres

look an age the moment they are built. The chickens scratching around them look no less ancient, and they are everywhere. Quite suddenly, whether by cart or bus, or even train or taxi, people have chickens as inevitable accessories. The animals seem dead, and really ought to be dead, but they give slow nictitating blinks to confound anyone who cares to check.

Brazil, it has been said, could well feed a thousand million people because of her rainfall and her enormous size. As it is, the country imports food, and many north-easterners in particular are often hungry, sometimes starving. To travel straight from Europe, to catch that Goiânia bus, to travel past miles and miles of partially developed land is to realize, however poor the soil's fertility, that Brazil has only begun to scratch at the land's potential. The easy exploitation has been achieved, and is about to be achieved in so much of the Mato Grosso, but the large-scale development of the land is still for the future. Where are the dams? Where is the water power being used? What will feed the 3·5 per cent more mouths every year? Where are all the people anyway, the hundred million already living in this fifth largest nation of the world? The cerrado certainly does not house them, the empty zone of this empty land.

The hoardings supply the answer with increasing size and vehemence. Another town is approaching: 'Beba Coca-Cola', 'Pneus Dunlop', 'VW Serviço'. The towns contain the people and the town population is increasing over twice as fast as the total community. South America is a wilderness pock-marked with cities and towns. It is an urban society in a rural scene. It is an emptiness with occasional crowds. It is the cerrado and then, round a corner and spread like a carpet over the land, it is Goiânia.

Driving down into Goiânia, with its white-walled sky-scrapers and its leafy streets, means seeing the place at long range before becoming enmeshed in the more short-sighted complexities of its traffic, its pavements, its shops with their salami-shaped nets of apples and all their produce bulging into the streets. Like Brasília, the development of Goiânia is a planned governmental stride into the interior, and its streets are excessively rectilinear, but the citizens have also put their own more human marks on the well-designed formality. The result is a warm, friendly, hurly-burly of a town, far easier to shop in and with better produce than—as yet—Brasília. The bus manoeuvres into its *rodoviaria* and then decants its passengers, now eager for yet another cafezinho.

Those who have not been to the place before have time to ponder upon Goiânia's peculiarly crowded isolation as a staging post to the west. The city has close on a million people. It is well placed for a further hop into the interior, and there are hundreds of miles of Brazil lying to the west of the town, but travel to the west has traditionally been of minority interest and maximum difficulty. The expedition members had to travel west, and they all encountered this curious circumstance. The rich, booming, sky-scraping stepping stone was more of an island than anything else, a self-contained bustle created by planners and then maintained by its own importance.

Throughout the period of the expedition it was possible to travel to Aragarças, a mere 200 miles further on as any crow would fly it, and the next stepping stone, by one of two means. The first was to emulate that crow, and acquire a seat on one of the two Vasp Dakotas flying weekly through to Cuiabá, the capital of Mato Grosso. These planes were excellent when they were there, but there is nothing quite so vacuous as an airport which, owing to bad weather or engine failure elsewhere, has no aircraft. To be told on Tuesday that the plane may come on Friday, or that a mechanic must first arrive from São Paulo, imparts a beleaguered desperation to this information, and soon sends the traveller off in search of other transport. (The Brazilian passengers, of course, have always known unerringly that no plane would be arriving that day and have sensibly failed even to arrive at the airport, thus giving the place an additionally forlorn appearance. To see only foreigners is to know at once that no plane is imminent or due.)

The alternative route west was south-west and then, after this major detour in a contrary direction, north-west to make good the error. This lengthy diversion, taking 20 hours by bus to cover those 200 crow-fly miles, had historical events to explain its contrariness. Firstly, there had been earlier boom towns along the more direct route, such as Goiás, but they had fallen on bad times and the road had fallen with them. Secondly, the incentive to travel west, to reach the Araguaia and the das Mortes, had always been much reduced by that former presence of the Indians. People build roads, even unpaved, fair-weather-only and fiercely twisting tracks, from A to B and are much less enthusiastic about building them from A to nowhere in particular or from A to Indian country.

Therefore the scientists either climbed into the twice-weekly plane to Aragarças, or clambered aboard various buses and drank deep of countless cafezinhos as they travelled overland via Jataí, Caiapônia, Piranhas and Bom Jardim de Goiás to reach the same Aragarças either 20 dusty hours later or, if the connections had failed to connect, three days later. Those who travelled by bus had both a seasoned look about them when they arrived and a full appreciation of the roadside development. Those who came by air, having experienced low-level buffetings for a couple of hours, often had a hideous green-gilled look about them but may also have had a chance to gaze out at the long zig-zag roads beneath them, the scattered houses, the straight lines of cut-down forest and scrub, the deep gullying of erosion.

The air travellers had a better chance of seeing the geographical siting of Aragarças. They could observe that it is two towns at the junction of two rivers, the deep green Araguaia and the brown-green Garças. Dolphins, pink and fat, were always at the precise point where these two rivers meet, and human beings have a similar affection for existing at the union of waterways. Officially Aragarças was founded in the early 1940s as part of the great south-north network planned by the Central Brazil Foundation. Unofficially there had been a shanty town on the spot beforehand, partly because the river junction had some minor fame as a profitable site for panning gold, and on to

59

this former dwelling place the C.B.F. grafted its own nobler ideas, a resplendent avenue of trees, an airport, the Grande Hotel, and wide streets with street lights down the centre. Instead of the ferry, which used to hang on a wire linking the two banks of the united rivers, the new developers constructed a bridge that leapt, slightly further upstream, across the two rivers. Major bridges are an infrequent sight in Central Brazil and this one is deservedly famous. It was built to join the new Aragarças in the state of Goiás with all the new land over the river in the state of Mato Grosso. It was a crucial crossing point on that great north road.

On the other side of the river, stimulated by all this construction, the town of Barra do Garças has also leapt into substantial being. It is more casually built than the formal development on the other side, and is more a creation of private enterprise, but it is the principal headquarters of a gigantic administrative department, or praefecture, that includes all the Serra do Roncador area right up to Cachoeira von Martius in the north-west and to São Félix in the north-east. England and Wales could very easily be fitted within its single administrative compass. The praefecture controls the land of this enormous domain, and does so from a couple of rooms with half a dozen people. Governmental control may seem to lean somewhat heavily in various sectors of the Brazilian administration. In the praefecture of Barra do Garças its lightness of touch is incredible.

The principal decoration within its office is a map of all its huge territory, neatly compartmented into straight-sided plots of land. Within each rectangle is a name, the alleged owner, following governmental sale of this jungle estate at peppercorn prices of a penny or two an acre. However, to jump ahead in this particular story, no name on the map matched up with the name or names of any owner actually in residence within any one of those rectangles that we were to visit. The selling and re-selling of the plots, as and when owners felt a deal could be profitable, must have been prodigious. It is also certain that some areas have more than one claimant to their ownership because sales of Mato Grosso plots, both correctly and otherwise, had been customary and remunerative long before the Indians were cleared off the land and long before there were effective aerial photographs in lieu of maps. Disputes were inevitable, but these are early days on that score.

Barra do Garças itself, to return to this further stepping stone northwards to the Amazon, is a pleasant motley of shops and houses. The commerce is almost entirely in the hands of Arabs, a loose name for all the modern Phoenicians who find it rewarding to open up stores in primitive areas, whether in West Africa or Central Brazil. Their style is universal, operating from the packing case direct to the customers with credit,

The river Araguaia had once been a barrier. Now at its union with the Garças there is a bridge and two ▷
busy towns. In those old days travellers must have come this way, talking of Indians, and of discomfort, of
huge spiders OVERLEAF *and biting attacks by tabanid flies.*

all-powerful credit, playing a vital intermediary role. The most exciting, well-stocked and prosperous shops in their appearance were the pharmacies, catering for needs both imaginary and genuine. The place may be Central Brazil, sorely in need of so many trappings of civilization, but a man is likely to have a higher level of antibiotics in his bloodstream in Barra do Garças, following careful and continuous self-administration, than in the antiseptic wards of western Europe. Whereas the pharmacists cater happily for the multicoloured whims of their clients most other stores were far more functional and restrained, serving axeheads, sewing machines, two kinds of hat, one kind of hammock, exceptionally few varieties of food and nothing that was not a positive need for most of the people for most of the time.

Two establishments were patronized extensively by every member of the expedition on their shuttle north and south because they were excellent of their kind: the Hotel Kanaxue and the restaurant Vera Cruz. The former boasted simple accommodation and lavatories at the end of a cool courtyard with lines of washing and banana trees, while the restaurant produced food almost the moment a customer sat down and long before he had detailed any particular requirements to the pubescent waitresses. Plates appeared heaped with rice, with beans (the principal gastronomic currency of Brazil), with meat, tomatoes, fried plantains, eggs and raw onion.

All places—and not just a town like Barra do Garças—should be seen, and observed, both on the journey into some hinterland and then on the return: they change immeasurably in the meantime. The rather suspect sanitation becomes highly laudable, if only for its spasmodic efforts. The poorly-sprung bed becomes a bed with genuine springs, and the five watt bulb, waning and waxing with the load imposed nearby, is transformed during one's absence into something wholly admirable. To arrive in Barra do Garças was to be amused by the Kanaxue and the Vera Cruz. To return was to fall upon these fragments of better things with both appetite and gratitude.

The road north from Barra do Garças had been started in the late 1940s. Once an airport had been constructed at Xavantina on the Rio das Mortes, 90 miles to the north of the outpost of Aragarças, the logical step was to connect these two frontier establishments with a road. That done, having curled round the Vale dos Sonhos and having side-stepped, insofar as this was possible, the low-lying and swampy areas rich in bamboo and black marshland soil, the Central Brazil Foundation paused at Xavantina to regain its breath. Settlers moved in to the area, whether legitimately as proven owners or casually as squatters to make temporary use of the land, and the place almost instantly acquired an ancient look, as if time immemorial rather than a handful of years had leaned upon that fragment of development.

Ancient carts, with round table wheels devoid of spokes, lumbered along the road. A

◁ *The hills that had helped the Indians defend their territory now provide an excellent look-out point over the country through which the new road has already made its way.*

bus, with faded lettering, made the journey either south or north or both ways almost every day. Other cars of different sorts lurched or sped or coughed along the road, once every hour or so. From the straight line of the engineer the road acquired new twists as the drivers wheeled round obstacles and took increasingly wide curves to avoid the rutted tracks of their predecessors. The halfway stopping point along this instantly ancient road sold cool beer and also *guarana*, a sweet and harmless concoction containing a bubble or two of taste, but the commonest form of refreshment was an orange, peeled with a knife as if it were an apple and then sucked dry of all its juice. The discarded remains, puff-ball white and something to kick, are a major form of Mato Grosso flotsam, along with bottle tops and the filter tips of cigarettes. Look at the ground almost anywhere that there have been people and there are these things, seemingly indestructible and pecked at with the perpetual hope of the omnipresent chicken.

The township of Xavantina also tended, when the expedition was in full swing, to have an omnipresent Englishman, someone heading either north for the camp or south for home. It was another staging post, and different yet again from all the others. There had been nothing at Xavantina before the C.B.F. had arrived there, first to build that airstrip, then the hospital, the school, the church, the town square with its Xavantina Hotel, and the few streets with neat and even houses on either side. The population had reached a thousand by the time the Englishmen arrived to see the place. The visitors could bathe in the cool green water of the Rio das Mortes, watch the fabulous sunsets, test the rival merits of Antarctica or Brahma beer, and see their first Indians. The Xavante were happy to ask for gifts, to smile at some blatant mishap, to laugh deeply at some obvious disaster. A few of them spoke Portuguese and did so very close at hand, as if it helped for the two participants to be out of focus.

A house in Xavantina was loaned to the expedition by the Brazilian authorities, and the members stayed in this when waiting for transport north or south. For most of them work could begin almost the moment they left its door. The river was full of fish, and the children were only too eager to catch them. More bird species could be seen in a short space of time than at any equivalent European viewpoint. And all around, beyond the mango plantations, and beyond that inevitable shanty town grafted almost immediately on to any piece of Brazilian planning, there was the cerrado with the trees and shrubs taking their own time and season to come into flower and fruit.

At most times Xavantina itself was an empty place, with the hospital quite empty— both of nurses and patients—and the streets strangely bereft. A few horses either nibbled the dust in the places where it was flecked with green or they hung their heads heavily in the hot sun. Every now and then a vehicle lumbered into town and either stopped or went down towards the ferry and blew its horn. The road through Xavantina was undeniably the major highway northwards from Aragarças, but each and every crossing of the ferry was something of an event, rare and worthy of time. The drivers put chocks under the wheels, and waited for the ferryman to emerge. Sooner—or later—he came.

Once the Rio das Mortes had been a formidable barrier to invasion of the Mato Grosso. Now there is a leisurely ferry for everyone crossing the river on their way north from Xavantina.

He helped the vehicle on to the ferry, and then he pushed the device over to the other side with a 12 h.p. outboard attached to a dugout canoe. He charged 10s. for a trip in daytime, or £1 for a night trip, and in this humble, leisurely, casual fashion the famous Rio das Mortes was crossed. To cross it before that Xavante pacification in the 1940s was to invite disaster, and probably to be dead very shortly afterwards. To cross it when Xavantina had been built was to be mildly irritated by the inevitable delay, to be enchanted by the groups of black cuckoo, by the kingfishers called *martim pescador*, by the rows of martins sitting on the cable wire, and then to saunter up for a final coffee, this time at the Bar Gloria and to look back at Xavantina. As at Aragarças there is formality on one side of the river, and a less disciplined development on the other. From this more northerly and simpler portion of Xavantina the road again heads north along what, for the visiting scientists, was the final portion of their journey.

There was one more major river to cross, the Areões. Of no great stature in the dry season, being deep down at the bottom of its gulley, it could rise by 20 feet or more when the rains gave it substance, and the C.B.F. built a respectful bridge over its seasonal turbulence. Thereafter the roadmen first aimed their efforts in the direction of Garapú, yet another of the crucial bases en route to the Amazon. The original purpose of Aragarças, Xavantina, Garapú and all points further north was, to reiterate this important point, to provide *aerial* stepping stones for the great air route northwards. If a road could be built between the outposts, all well and good, but the places were primarily air bases. It is for this reason that Garapú, the next stone north, was built in a bridge-builder's paradise, assuming he received both money and the go-ahead. The Rio Sete de Setembro, the Culuene, the Culiseu and dozens of minor streams all demanded major bridges to cross them for any road leading even further north than Garapú. Consequently they built a road to Garapú, and there it stopped: no one in his right senses would attempt to drive a road any further into that broad aquatic filigree of the Upper Xingú.

This particular and frustrating obstacle was to pay rich dividends later on with the establishment of the *Parque Naçional do Xingú*. The creation of a reservation for Indians was inevitably simplified when the territory marked out for it had few other claimants, and the very inaccessibility of the Xingú network now kept would-be developers at a respectful distance. Therefore it was possible to mark out 8,000 square miles of Xingú territory, to proclaim and ratify it as a reserve (in 1967), and to have this Parque Naçional as a going concern before any individual had staked a positive claim on the land to which he had the title deeds.

It might have appeared paradoxical, particularly to the early explorers who made such full use of the rivers, and to the Indians themselves who looked upon them as convenient causeways, that a profusion of rivers could be an impediment; but such was the case. There is nothing quite like a road for opening up a country, for bringing in the developers, by foot, by horse, by station wagon. Consequently the land developers reached Garapú, and made quite a large community there, but they went no further.

The invaders reached Garapú first by air, then by picada and finally by road in the late 1940s. Only the picada went on—on to the north, linking further airfield outposts along its path—Vasconcelos, Diauarum, Jacaré—but the road itself stopped emphatically at Garapú. The area around the next post in line, Vasconcelos, was well inhabited by Indians, and it was this area which became the world-famous Parque Naçional do Xingú. Its air base, after it had been renamed Posto Leonardo, served both as a base for the Air Force and as the headquarters of the new park. It received a Dakota with supplies roughly once a week. It had an efficient radio, various buildings and a clinic, but it had no road. For this omission it has every cause for thankfulness. Even today a road to that area could kill the place.

In any new plan to drive northwards the Xingú would have to be crossed, and would be more simply crossed after it had coalesced into a single river. The rapids of von Martius, named after an early nineteenth-century botanist/explorer from Bavaria, were an obvious crossing point because the firm rocks of this *cachoeira* would provide suitable support for the striding bridge. In 1965 the roadmen set out from Xavantina once again, but this time they disregarded the old cul-de-sac of a road to Garapú, and aimed more northerly along the slender ridge of the Roncador.

In 1966, when the reconnaissance mission from London was in the area, the engineers were 130 miles north of Xavantina. In April 1967, when Iain Bishop left England to act as the expedition's spearhead, they were some 300 miles north of Xavantina and deep in the forest zone, having left the easier cerrado to the south of them. All, apparently, was going well, and the road was about to swing round in the general direction of the Cachoeira von Martius when everything stopped again. The government was new; it had a change of heart. It disbanded the C.B.F., the pioneer organization that had done so much, and it recalled both men and machines. At the same time it withdrew financial support. The sound of the axe, carving its way through the huge undeveloped world, suddenly became once again the age-old sounds of the virgin forest, untouched, untarnished, and as they had always been.

This volte-face was, of course, a total surprise for the British expedition, and Iain Bishop sent word of it at about the same moment as the first batch of four scientists was about to leave England. It was decided that the road had already gone through country exceptionally worthy of study and that there was more than enough to be investigated. A camp should be constructed somewhere along its track, and the scientists would operate from that vantage point. After all the empty and undeveloped dimensions were still fantastic. The 300 miles of new road, having invaded the precincts of so much new territory, meant that any camp would be within easy reach of tens of thousands of square miles of an empty world.

The camp was eventually built to gain in every possible manner. An old site of the roadmen, built by them a mile off the main road at the junction of two small but permanent streams, happened to be on the border line between the cerrado that stretched away to the south and the forest that led right up to the north. It was both a site in a wilderness and at the union of these two vegetation zones, precisely what had been required. One of the C.B.F. roadmen knew of such a place, and showed it to Iain Bishop. It had everything he was looking for, and he brought up a recently-recruited gang of Brazilians a couple of days later. They set to work to transform the decayed remnants of a temporary construction camp into a place where a score of scientists could work, eat and sleep with reasonable ease in the middle of the Mato Grosso. The month was September 1967. The season was just before the rains. The initial complement of people was Iain, his wife, some fifteen Brazilians, and four scientists from Britain. They moved in to that clearing, within its two arms of gallery forest, and the place henceforth was always referred to as base camp.

It was to this base camp that every successive visitor from Britain was travelling when he headed north from Xavantina, crossed the Areões, disregarded the old road to Garapú, and took the new road along the ridge. One man reported that it was a journey 'fascinating to the geomorphologist, but uninteresting to the layman.' Being bereft of anything save the gentlest of hills, the most modest of tiny streams (save for their occasions of spate), and being covered with the eternal scrubland of cerrado, it was a world that also gave particular pleasure to the botanists, but it provided a kind of pleasure for everyone. Occasional animals appeared from nowhere—a maned wolf with its long, thin legs, a giant anteater, a deer or two—before disappearing into the sparse but entirely effective cover on either side. Parrots shrieked overhead and sometimes flew alongside the dusty vehicle speeding beneath them. Macaws shrieked louder, but flew more ponderously, and looked best when a sinking sun could pick up their most extravagant forms of colour. A toucan would fly by, awkwardly and hesitantly, as if uncertain of flight, but with the sun glinting from its beak as from the high-flying fuselage of an aircraft.

Of people there were few, particularly in the early days, but there were some adobe huts along the road almost the moment its makers had created it. They had people in them, and in fair numbers once your eyes had grown accustomed to the darkness within. A man named Geraldão, half-way from Xavantina to the base camp, owned one such modest settlement beside a stream and regularly transformed some of it into coffee for us at this convenient staging post. He organized his life, or so it seemed, from his hammock, and he sold a cow or two from time to time. He also owned a few black-grey pigs, some feather-free hens, a couple of huts, and a large smooth paunch always allowed to feel at liberty beyond his unbuttoned shirt. In his mud-floor world of poverty, and swinging from a hammock above those scratching chickens and dusty pigs, he somehow exuded prosperity. Moreover, he always refused payment for the coffee.

The occasional *seriema* might cross the road as the truck hurried on, a bustard of a bird reluctant to fly. Or an ema might run away, an ostrich of a bird totally incapable of taking to the air. Sometimes there were locusts, plainly able to fly and to maintain direction, but far less able to alter that direction. Their flapping leaps were rarely finished with finesse, as they clutched on to the branch into which they had flown. Frequently their flights ended in death when they and the truck collided. Their reluctance to leave the road or to leave time enough for escape was matched only by the nightjars who crouched low, with their eyes glinting back the headlights of the truck, and who then sprang up to twist aside with bat-like flight. Other eyes in the night sparked back with reflection, but their owners disappeared before they could be identified.

Mainly owing to the nightjars, but partly to the nocturnal habits of other animals, the road seemed a livelier place by night than by day and the daytime sightings could be disappointingly few. Central Brazil does not abound in large numbers of readily conspicuous animals, a fact which made the few such observations so much more distinctive and memorable in any day. Visitors familiar with the visibly dense assortment of wildlife pounding about on, say, the East African plains had to adjust their values, and take pleasure accordingly from the sight of one fox or the four-by-three arrangement of toe-prints left in the wake of a tapir. They had to look rather more searchingly and be rewarded on a different scale.

At length, some five hours after the Xavantina ferry, and two hours after Geraldão's brand of hot, gritty coffee, there came the turn-off. The last nightjar leapt swervingly out of the way, and another consignment of scientists had arrived at their destination. Each visitor could be exonerated for feeling that he had indeed come a very long way. He would creak his joints out of their final position and relish the thought of having arrived. Only later on would he realize quite how near he was to Brasília, that point of departure he may have left the best part of a week beforehand. Even a small plane could have flown the distance in less than three hours.

Within an unbelievably short time, once the site had been chosen, the camp was a going concern. Basically its construction followed the time-honoured rule that it is best to abide by the local customs, that it is simplest to do things their way. The *caboclo* of Central Brazil, the half-breed who is part Negro, part European and probably part Indian as well, has generally lived much of his life in buildings of the sort they constructed at camp. Corner posts, suitably shaped to have a V at their apex, are cut from the forest and sunk into the ground. Horizontal poles are lowered into those V's, and the bare bones of a roof are similarly notched and nailed together. The carpenter in charge, a man named Arjimeiro, was an expert with logs and three-inch nails, and one wondered if his carpentering career had ever led him to areas of greater finesse, say to planks and one-inch nails. Within a few hours he had each house, each store or future laboratory as firm as a rock and ready for its thatch.

The thatching took more time because it involved finding *Buriti* palms, chopping them down, cutting off their huge fronds of leaves, removing each tree's growing tip (good for making lashing material) and then transporting everything back to camp, save for the naked trunk now left where it had fallen. Essentially the thatching technique, the dividing of each frond, the way in which they were lashed in sequence, was an Indian method as we each realized later on, when walking or ducking into our first Indian house. The system stood all of us in good stead at camp, keeping out the sun and the rain, and changing from fleshy green to brittle brown as time passed by.

There was an idyllic side to this camp. The first sound in the morning was often the shriek of parakeets, flying in tandem at great speed, or the three notes of a screaming piya, two up and one down. Sunrise in a forest does not have the immediacy and precision that it does when horizons are visible. Instead it was insidious and gentle, and the day became warmer unobtrusively. A great sense of timelessness hung over the place, hot and steady. Enormous clouds bulged into the sky, and the sky itself always looked larger than normal. At every level, as your eyes adjusted their focus, there were the dots of hawks, suspended without movement, and yet gone so soon. On the ground there were always new things to see, provided the onlooker took time to look. That ripple was a snake's head, moving back and forth. That twig became a stick insect, swaying gently in its walk.

At all times it was noisy. The cicadas wound themselves up at their appropriate hours, and then maintained their specific forms of racket. A humming bird swept in from nowhere, stopped upon the instant before a bright red flower, fed from it, and then flashed off in a flurry of green. A group of ants, shiny and brown, chumped through a plant, severing its leaves and stems into portable sizes, and letting these pieces drop to other ants who carried them along their positive pathway, over logs and beneath leaves, before diving down through the quite diminutive hole at the entrance to their subterranean community. A nearby hole, equally small for its importance, would give out a steady stream of winged termites, leaving their homes in lemming-like fashion, and flying away with identical speed in an identical direction.

Eventually the sun descends from its position of dazzling power, too bright and too high to see, and appears briefly as a fiery ball close to the leafy horizon before disappearing to create the lengthy tropical night. The broad band of the Milky Way, so much more dominant in the southern hemisphere, then stretches like a rainbow while the familiar Plough, up-ended and undignified, points down to the northern hemisphere lying somewhere beneath that encircling horizon of trees.

There was also another side to camp life, infinitely less idyllic, and more in keeping with the reputed belligerence of the Mato Grosso. It was almost possible to know the time of day, and also your location with respect to forest or open cerrado, by taking note of the insects that were rampant at the time. Easiest to take note of, in that they had a proboscis like a hypodermic, were the tabanids. They liked shade and, of course, blood. They were about half-an-inch long, related to the clegs, horseflies and gadflies known elsewhere, but not to the tsetses who lead a similar existence, and the best defence against them was either to wear thick clothing or move into the bright sunlight.

Thick clothing makes a man sweat and the sweat bees, small but similarly proportioned to honey bees with their third pair of legs dangling down, would cluster all over him. Fortunately they did not sting, and neither did many other even smaller species of bee that liked crawling up nostrils, but there were plenty of bees that did sting. The brushing away of an armful of sweat bees could include the disturbance of a standard honey bee that would instantly give away its sting and its life as it pointed out the error. There was a wasp that could—and did—produce sizeable amounts of pain as it bit through one's skin and, if brushed thoughtlessly away, changed from biting to stinging with little hesitation.

To sit still, and to reduce the effusions of sweat, was to invite the attention of minute little fruit flies, or acolypterae. They did not get into anyone's eyes inadvertently; they were attracted to them. While one was extracting their tear-sodden bodies from one's eyelids other flies of the same type would surmount the hairy, waxy defences of one's ears and then make great fluttering noises either on or near the tympanum. Such a dual invasion could turn sane men into flailing idiots, as their eyes drooled, their ears hummed, and nostrils and mouth proved just as accessible to the invaders. Of course this flailing and all other energetic gestures of displacement activity brought on the sweat, and then further contingents of sweat bees. Fortunately such destroyers of contentment tended to be local, or rather they were not totally ubiquitous, and it was possible to walk out of their area.

Geraldão lived with an indefinable opulence in an adobe hut with a hammock. His offer of hot, gritty coffee was ▷
entirely welcome after hours of travel on that hot, dusty road.

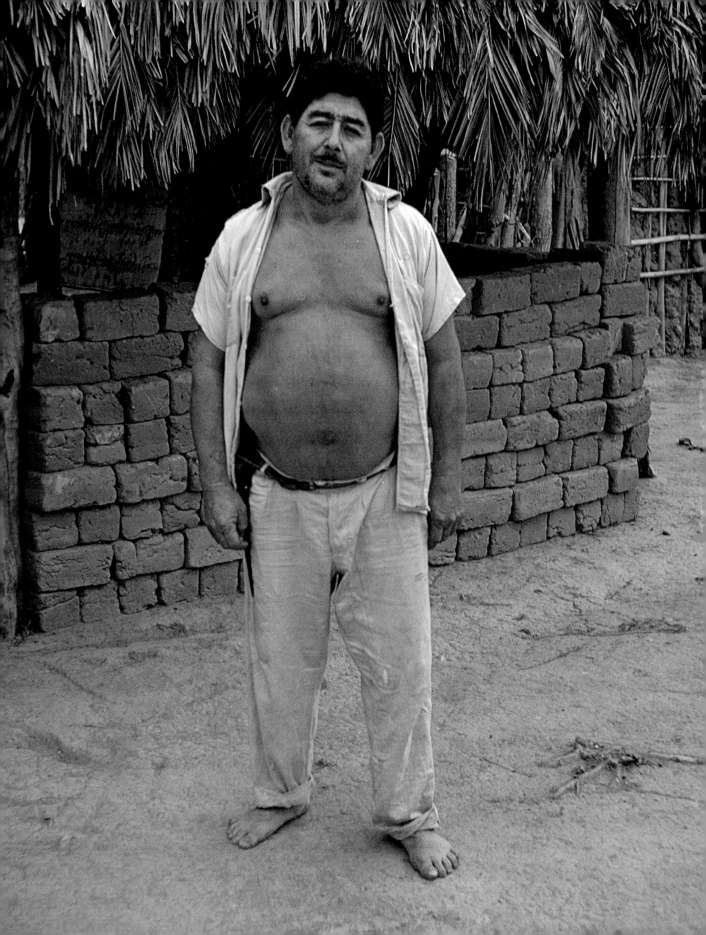

As the price to pay for such relief, it was entirely possible to walk into the world of the voracious *pium*. Their larvae are produced in running water, notably in the larger rivers, and the adults are capable of moving a considerable distance from their birth place. In other words, as the area is rich in streams and rivers, it is also inordinately rich in pium, the members of the Simulidae whose relatives are the famous buffalo gnats. They bite on any exposed surface, they live only in sunlight (and so can be escaped by ignominious retreats into the darkness of a hut) and they can produce lumps hundreds of times bigger than themselves if one's body happens to react violently and irritatingly against their injections. Even without such a major reaction they produce itching spots which become, some four days after the bite, a small black point of clotted blood to remember them by.

Fortunately, as the sun goes down, the pium also retreat. Unfortunately they are simultaneously replaced by the *maruim*. Other people in other places may know these midges of the genus *Culicoides* by other names, and Scotland just calls them biting midges, but they are nearly invisible in most cases and their bite is undetectable. It is the effect of their bite, traditionally an evening event, and the reaction of the body to this other antigen, that is so itchingly unpleasant. A new arrival to camp, bare-armed and relaxed, would suddenly be amazed to see what a pox had struck him on his forearms. Innumerable red spots, a quarter of an inch in diameter, would be densely plotted and the irritation would follow a short while later. Thereafter, at the maruim hour, it was customary to roll down sleeves, put trousers into socks, button up collars and apply insecticide to the remaining skin surfaces. A disadvantage to such cowardice was that the repellent not only quelled the insects but would soften the plastic of any ball-point pen. This made writing a messy business but increased one's confidence in the virulence of the lotion. The body's violently sensitive reaction to the insect's bite happily abated after a few weeks or months, and it was possible not to spend the evening hours muffled against the invaders while putting a drooling, flaccid pen to paper in writing up the day's events.

At night, as is customary in the tropics, droves of insects would batter and burn themselves to death upon the paraffin lamps. Large moths would perhaps burn just one wing and then cavort concentrically about the table, only coming to fluttering rest when someone's coffee or beer drowned their energies. To escape from the light, and to wander into the immediate forest, meant encountering Psychodid sand-flies. They are small, and can fly through the mesh of most mosquito nets, but they bite convincingly enough. To sit in the forest at night, perhaps waiting for an animal or taking a photograph by time exposure, was to become increasingly aware of the sand-flies and less and

◁ *The cerrado on either side of the road from Xavantina could be both beautiful and forbidding. It was possible to watch ants neatly attack a shrub, chop it into convenient segments, and carry it all away down their hole within a matter of minutes.*

less convinced of any value in waiting for either animal or photograph. At night there were also mosquitoes, but only a few. For much of the year it was not even necessary to have a net against them.

For such relief much thanks, but not all attacks were airborne. A naturalist from Europe happily parts the grass with his hands, if he thinks something of interest might be within it. Naturalists from South America take no such risks, and part the vegetation with a knife or a stick. Anyone from Europe is happy to lie down upon the ground when he is weary; such bliss is short-lived in the Mato Grosso. The insect life retaliates at once, but it was not necessary to lie down to suffer ticks.

They were of three main sizes. The largest were flat, much like a bed bug, and about three millimetres across before they had gorged themselves and swollen their bodies. The medium and commonest kind were about one millimetre across, exceptionally adept at finding their way into the soft recesses of passing bodies but fairly easy to pull off. The smallest kind appeared, when they did so, in their legions and congregated in patches rather than individually. They could initially be brushed off but were far harder to remove later on. It was fascinating and macabre to sit on a bare log within the forest, and then to observe the ticks crabbing along from both directions. To begin with, the attackers were meticulously killed, between one finger-nail and another, but such puny revenge was of no consequence, and a man was considered to be well covered with them when he was content merely to pick them off and throw them away with all the hasty repetitive action of a man plucking a chicken. Ticks are thought to detect prey either by smell, by warmth or by vibration, and presumably not all ticks are the same, but each one of us was overtly impressed with their skill of detection, whichever system they chanced to use.

To live in that camp, with its mile-long road leading up to the main highway, with—eventually—its 22 huts of living quarters, sleeping rooms and work huts, with its dammed-up stream of a swimming pool, and its meteorological site, water tower and parking area, the place seemed an impressively large establishment. After a time, with its compound and its paths firmly trodden down, and with the routine well established, a sense of familiarity with the place helped to increase its stature. From time to time people had a chance to fly over this *acampamento inglês*, and then they were shocked to see the place in its actual setting, a minute dwelling place in a world of trees, much like a small boat upon the ocean. It was humbling and entirely right to see the camp that way.

It also gave a sense of proportion to the camp's chosen working area, a zone whose sides were 20 kilometres long. Camp was almost at the centre of this square and it was felt that such a chunk of land was neither too formidably large for any detailed study nor excessively small and unrepresentative. From the air this study area, 400 square kilometres or 156 square miles, still looked minute in its setting of thousands upon thousands of square miles of a similar world. From the ground, and when walking to

Base camp, set at the union of two rivers, was surrounded by cool gallery forest. With the brooding Buriti thatch keeping out both heat and rain it was a civilised place to work in.

some further point of the square, it seemed quite large enough. A lace-work of picadas eventually made much of it fairly accessible but, especially in the early days, it was always heavy going. A compass and a good look at the air photographs beforehand were both essential to those preliminary forays.

It was quite extraordinary, certainly for those unacquainted with virginal forest land of such magnitude, to be able to lose one's bearings quite so rapidly in that particular wilderness. There were various exacerbating factors. In the first place there was no view and, on cloudy days, no visible sun. Secondly it was generally impossible to walk in a straight line, and usually difficult to walk without stepping over obstacles, cutting away others and being diverted from single-minded attention to the problem of navigation. To fall over, to be stabbed by a spiny palm, to walk through a swamp, was never helpful. A better compass sense was maintained by the second man because he did not have to hack at a bush, then discover it was full of ants, rid himself of them, find his knife again, restore his equilibrium, and finally prove to all observers that a particular tree trunk lying along the ground was so entirely rotten that anyone climbing on to it would assuredly fall into it, just as he had done.

The second man was better able both to stand up and to keep his bearings. Nevertheless a compass was essential. To put it away for a while, to thrash along further in a supposedly straight line, and then to check its straightness with the compass was always to be dumbfounded by its message. The assertion frequently arose that the compass must be at fault, that something in the land must be rendering it inaccurate. Equally frequently, but less rapidly, the admission was made that the compass was entirely correct and the human senses were wildly astray. Within a hundred yards a man could be wrong by 90 degrees, particularly if the going had been unduly tough and, which was more important, if the man in question had a kind of conviction that it would be better for him to be one side or other of his compass course. To know that there was a stream over to the left, and that there was nothing to the right, would almost inevitably act as an irresistible pull, however much it might be fought against. Pilots lost in the air tend to fly, if nothing else can act as a lure, towards the sun. Ground travellers equally lost will tend to walk or drive towards something rather than nothing, however pointless that something may be. So too in the bewilderment of the Mato Grosso. It was extraordinarily difficult to maintain a straight course whatever the vegetation, uniform or otherwise.

After some early investigations, partly in order to get a measure of the problem, and to confirm that picadas were entirely necessary, it was decided to create some definite routes across the square. These would serve both as access pathways and as transects, the straight lines through differing areas along which precise information could be obtained about soil changes, plant types and so on. As pathways they made all the difference to travel because normal walking speed became possible. Even so discretion was necessary. To cut a picada meant cutting and removing the small trees and plants along the narrow band of that chosen route. Cutting everything near the ground and at a convenient angle meant that the picada was effectively armed with severed staves pointing upwards, the sharp remains of the earlier obstacles. To receive one of these daggers in an ankle was bad enough. To fall over or, at worst, to fall backwards and then sit down could be lethal. The anus is a weak spot, highly susceptible to such damage. To sit on a point heavily, and to have that point aimed at this weakness, is possibly to suffer mortal injury. Such an intestinal stab was an even greater possibility when the picada travelled through a zone of bamboo. This member of the grass family, with its hard and rigid stems, was responsible for the most dangerous sections should anyone chance to fall.

The picadas were always a compromise between having no path and having clear routes entirely without obstruction. To have levelled everything flat would have taken excessive time. It was up to the expedition members to be grateful for these severed passages but always to beware, particularly when the path went through the disarrayed, slippery and towering stems of a stand of bamboo.

To begin with, incidentally, the British cut the picadas. With compasses they plotted the course. With compasses they checked its alignment. The Brazilian employees

---

A tick firmly entrenched in a scientific arm. Whereas these parasites were most adept at locating humans and ▷
making their presence felt, it was never easy for the humans to see the animals watching them, OVERLEAF,
whether coati, snake, deer, or one of the exotic multitude of insects.

watched. When the British were tired of all this activity the Brazilians took over. Without compasses, and merely with a backward glance from time to time, they cut the picadas far more rapidly and with much greater precision. The British now watched, and thereafter took it emphatically to heart that the dark-faced, scruffy, illiterate bunch of Brazilians standing in front of them knew more than a thing or two about this special area. After all they had been living and hunting in the rougher parts of Brazil throughout their lives and had much to teach the visitors. It was up to the visitors to learn at least this fact as soon as possible.

The caboclo of Central Brazil is someone about whom it is both easy and impossible to generalize. Racially, and therefore facially, he can be from white to black with his genetic background being similarly complex. Whether mainly Negro or mainly Indian or mainly Portuguese he can be a unique blend, with perhaps Negro hair and Indian features or the other way about. The Indian population has undoubtedly been reduced from millions to thousands, but the Indian genes within the Brazilian population of today represent a sizeable proportion of the whole. If one were to add together all those fractions, whether one-eighth, one-quarter or whatever, the ratio of surviving Indians would be considerably greater. However, unlike the United States, where a man is adjudged a Negro if he is only partly Negro, an Indian in Brazil is judged to be a Brazilian if only part of him is Indian or if he wants to be a Brazilian. (Of course Indians could be argued to be Brazilians, but no one ever refers to *Indios* as *Brasilieros*.) One or two of the Brazilians at camp, judging by their faces, their general lack of body hair (Indians rarely grow any on their face or chest), their sleek black head hair and the colour of their skin, must have been almost wholly Indian, but they were as Brazilian as the President. Certainly their culture was entirely Brazilian.

Nevertheless as backwoodsmen they had much of the Indian about them, if only because they lived in and made use of the same area. Almost all the camp Brazilians could fish superbly well, albeit some more superbly than others. Without a rod, but with a line swirled round their heads and then cast out over the water, they could pull in fish with the necessary sensitivity to make a good strike and with alacrity. They could see fish in the water, and stop rigidly on seeing them. An Englishman, staring, squinting and peering, could entirely fail to see the same fish, however much it was being pointed out to him. The caboclos knew by how much they should aim beneath a fish to counteract refraction.

They would also get excited about particularly noble trees. To observe a group of Brazilians excitedly standing in the forest, and all looking upwards with much talk, would lead initially to an assumption that there were animals up there, perhaps a couple of capuchin monkeys, or a wasp nest four feet long. In fact features of the tree

◁ *For people living in the forest camp it seemed a large and important place. To fly over it was to see it in its true perspective, a small speck in an ocean of green, with its sliver of track leading up to the main road a mile away.*

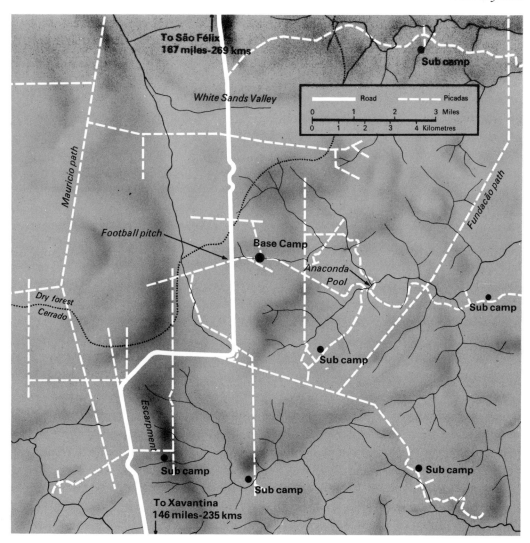

Map 3. Work was concentrated within a 20-kilometre square around base camp. This area forms the central portion of the aerial mosaic on the opposite page, made before either road or scientists had arrived. The scale units at the bottom each represent one kilometre.

itself would often be the object of admiration, either the straightness of the bole or the excellence of its flowers. Trees were known as much for their uses as for their names, those which resisted termites or damp, those which made good planks, which bent nails, and which burned well. The forest to these Brazilians, as to the Indians, was a super-market of differing goods, all there for the taking. At the botanical level several of them had an uncanny feeling for taxonomy, grouping plants correctly together merely because they seemed to be related.

It is often said that Brazil is a country without racial barriers. Instead it has to be said that barriers undoubtedly exist but with more of the class structure about them than the black-white straightforwardness existing in some other countries. The poorest sections of the community tend to be those with much Indian or Negro blood in them, those who have always been on the bottom rung. 'Could a dark Negro become head of state here?' we once asked. 'Oh, yes, there would be nothing held against him.' 'Will one ever become president?' 'Well no, because he wouldn't have the education.'

Negroes never did get any education in the old days and they were undoubtedly poor. The old rule still applies. Look around you in any office, and the hierarchy of jobs is a graduation from white to black. The sweepers are dark; the bosses are white. Only in those classless occupations, such as taxi-driver, will there be both but, generally speaking, the less desirable the post the less likely the face is to be white. The generalization also holds for the country as a whole. The desire for the east coast is almost as total as the enthusiasm for football, and with this nearly universal affection goes a corresponding disaffection for the undeveloped areas. Consequently the faces at Aragarças, at Xavantina and among the road gangs of the Mato Grosso, tended to be dark. It was from these communities that the men at camp had been selected. They were true caboclos, poorer than most and unacquainted with the big cities. (João used a knife and fork ever after the expedition sent him on a trip to Brasília, never beforehand.) The men were largely uneducated and therefore incapable of rising to much authority. They would be considerably out of place in the big cities and would probably be transformed into second-class citizens more positively because they would be misfits in that abnormal environment. Within the Mato Grosso, whether shinning up a tree to bring back an orchid they had spotted, or digging a soil pit, or making do when it was raining, they had much to offer. The barrier of language did not prevent the English from acquiring great respect for the majority of their sudden companions, or from realizing quite how much these possessors of nothing could give.

Instead of these 20 Brazilians learning any English it was up to all the English to learn some Portuguese. The daunting prospects of instructing the men to collect Compositae only, or to clean the plug of the outboard, or to buy two files or cook fewer beans all vanished because a lingua franca arose of exceptional brevity in vocabulary but of high articularity in conveying both noise and meaning. A scientist might go off for the day with his Brazilian companion, having half a dozen words in common, and both would return full of the talk from the other. The Brazilians themselves, although acquiring no English, became adept to a high degree at understanding Englishmen. 'Bom dia,' the Londoner would say, 'não tem what the hell's a spade aqui. Porqué não tem isto facão? E boa o ruin?' and the Brazilian would agree that it was better than nothing. The word 'ruin,' meaning bad or very bad, had to be said with a powerful conviction as if nothing worse had ever existed, and this helped understanding. Simi-

No other tropical country has as many spectacular species as Brazil. A climber of the Aristolochiaceae. ▷

larly 'muito longe' had to be pronounced lengthily, and took almost as long to say as the lengthy journey being described. 'Brab' (correctly bravo) meant nasty, and it was readily noticeable quite how many items in the Mato Grosso were emphatically, and to both parties, either 'muito brab' or 'muito ruin.' For days together, nothing seemed to be anything else. The new way of talking became infectious. 'Talk about brab. There was this serpente and there was I with my facão. The puim were ruin, and it was muito longe back to camp, so I left it.' With ten words a man was expressive. With a hundred he was fluent. The Brasilieros, skilfully, noisily and unerringly, interpreted the rest.

Anyway, it was at this camp, perhaps a week, perhaps more, after leaving England, that the British scientists arrived and were later joined by various Brazilian scientific colleagues. It was to this speck in the jungle, an oasis on its own, that they came, with or without their equipment, to do their work. There they experienced both the joy of the place and its entomological discomforts. There they were amused by and then hungry for the boiled rice and boiled beans, basic accompaniments of every meal. They learnt and enjoyed the structural vocabulary of the Mato Grosso. They cut and then walked along the picadas, carrying augers or traps, binoculars or plant presses, according to their discipline. Invariably they had a Brasiliero with them, intrigued by yet another kind of occupation. In the evening they either returned before it grew dark at 6.30, or else stayed in one of the sub-camps less luxuriously, but nearer to their place of work. The long tropical evenings were entirely suitable, save for those blundering insects and their self-immolation, for writing up the day's work and these notes will form the factual backbone of all the papers eventually to be published.

David Moffatt, soil scientist, and a group of Brazilian assistants, leaving camp along one of its many and most necessary picadas.

◁ *Many piranha species live in South America, and many a tall tale is told about them.*

3 THE INDIANS

A recommendation, issued early on by the Royal Society, that every foray outside camp should include at least six people as a precaution against Indians was soon dropped. It became obvious that there were none in the immediate area. In fact no one was to see an Indian, either pacified or still capable of belligerence, within 50 miles of that camp. Nevertheless, it was sensible that people should inform others of their planned where-abouts and should not become too greatly separated from each other. The countryside, rather than the Indians, was the danger and any mishap upon some solitary venture away from the beaten track of a picada could be severe. After all it was the tropics and physiological deterioration could happen rapidly.

I personally learnt the truth of this after electing to walk back to camp along the 30 miles of road that led from the Suiá Missú river. Not only did I drink well before start-ing, but I took a large water bottle, and knew that I would be crossing the very drinkable Suiázinho a couple of hours after starting. There again I drank well, and refilled my water bottle. All went well until I left the shady side road for the main highway, well exposed at that time of day to the heat of the sun. The water bottle was soon emptied, and my arms were soon no longer wet with sweat. The road passed over some streams of exceptional sluggishness that emanated from swampy foetid pools, left haphazardly by the roadmen. The water surface there looked oily and had a purple tinge to it, and the tree stumps in those pools were rotten and black as they lay on the sodden, muddy and bubbling earth. To drink from such squalor would plainly be foolhardiness of a high order. It was only too easy to stride past that stagnancy, and to consume instead a further five miles of road. Then it abruptly became impossible to disregard the next such supply of water. It was even less wholesome than the others, but it had become pathetically necessary. It was rife with mosquito larvae, gritty with mud, and un-pleasant in every way, but I drank deep of it and the sweat reappeared on my arms.

Later on, when even such unattractive backwaters had been absent from the road-

◁ '*Acting as a lure to the west of base camp was the Parque Naçional*'.

side, and when nausea and thirst were vying with each other, it was only too easy to lie down. The world span round on an uncertain axis, and time passed before I became conscious once again of biting ants and protruding lumps of roadway. To walk again was to be impossibly weary and to need more water. The distance between collapsing points became less and less until camp, that most welcome camp, became sufficiently close to be a lure.

The awesome reality of the previous hours then vanished as a couple of beers were quickly consumed, but it had been a stern experience. The swiftness between a contented metabolism and one failing so visibly had been its most impressive feature, even on a walk lasting for a mere 30 miles. Certain pedestrians, if that is the word for people walking for days along that road and knowing no other form of transport, were occasionally found by our vehicles in an extremely dehydrated state and lying by the roadside as I had lain. Water without salt for such cases can do them great harm for desalination would be a more accurate description. Water not in moderation can be dangerous and the men were treated with appropriate care. They too were positive reminders that the environment could be killing. They also emphasized, via their long-distance strolling, the lack of any danger from any other source. The Indians had all gone from the vicinity of the road.

Fundamentally the survivors were in three kinds of place. Firstly they were in traditional villages but leading lives whose wretchedness bore little relation to their former existence save for those still-uncontacted tribes whose lives, presumably, were virtually as they had always been. Secondly they were in the Parque Nacional do Xingú, the enclave formed by law and the Villas Boas team to maintain them in a manner to which, roughly, they were accustomed. Thirdly they were in the hands of the missionaries as, for example, were most of the Xavante nation. In all three kinds there was some form of paternal influence, whether governmental, autocratic or catholic. In all three there were white men acting as a buttress, stolidly or most casually, between the Indians and the world all about them. Around the Serra do Roncador there were no free Indians any more. Those days had gone for ever.

Part of the suspicion that there must still be free Indians in an area they had dominated for so long had its cause in the fate of an earlier British expedition. In 1961 Richard Mason, John Hemming and Christopher Lambert were investigating the area east of Cachimbo. They too had been partially financed by the Royal Geographical Society and they were assured, particularly by those who knew Cachimbo and who flew in regularly to the area, that no Indians lived there. These were not the Fawcett days when the Indians were acknowledged possessors of the Xingú and beyond. These were the days when the chain of air bases had been built, when Cachimbo was one of them, when the Villas Boas brothers were living equably with the tribes. In such modern times Richard Mason and the other two acquired both permission and encouragement to map the headwaters of the Iriri, and also to travel downstream to the Amazon. From

John Hemming and Richard Mason (with hat) at Cachimbo during the time of their Iriri expedition. RIGHT, *the dark entrance into the forest where the Indians made their ambush. Mason's body, wrapped in the cloth, had been surrounded by the objects in the foreground.*

Cachimbo, together with members of the Brazilian Geographical Institute and some employed Brazilians, they cut a picada for thirty miles until they reached a convenient tributary. There they worked, and frequently went back to the airstrip community of Cachimbo along that path either to collect more equipment and food or to arrange more details of their forthcoming journey.

It was when John Hemming was away arranging for a parachute drop of supplies to their riverside camp that Richard Mason, aged 26 and a medical student, set off early one morning to walk again along that well-trodden picada. Ten miles from Cachimbo there was a patch of campo, a bright and open space along the path. On leaving this, and then entering the sudden darkness of the forest, Richard Mason was immediately killed by a group of Indians who had been waiting for him. It was an excellent place for an ambush. The men had sat there for quite a time, they had rested packs upon the ground and, after firing arrows at Richard Mason and clubbing him, they then left arrows, clubs and a long bow by the side of the Englishman. Members of the expedition found his body, and brought it back to Cachimbo. Peace-making presents were left for the unseen Indians, and the arrows and clubs were taken to the Villas Boas brothers. These weapons could not be identified with any known tribe, but it was thought they might belong to the Kran-Acorore.

In any case, if the reason for the killing had been a warning for others to keep out of the area, the plan had been entirely effective. The authorities are now inordinately sensitive about those Iriri headwaters and permission to visit them would be difficult or impossible to achieve. The death of one Englishman helped to increase the sensitivity in general, although one more murder elsewhere, say in Rio of a white by a white, would cause no such trauma. It is to be hoped that Richard Mason's death did not cause further contacts with Indians to be even more dangerous to the Indians. At all events, whatever happened in that similar area in 1961, there were no such incidents along the picadas cut in 1967 and 1968 by a further group of Englishmen and it was not just a matter of no Indians being reported from the area. There were no Indians to be reported.

The Xavante who hung about Xavantina, eagerly demanding bullets and fish-hooks, had probably come from the local *aldeia*, a village at the junction of the Areões and das Mortes rivers, some 25 miles east of Xavantina. This community of roughly 200 Indians had originally been promised a large area for hunting, but this had been whittled down as each new landowner had taken a part of it. Every now and then a group of Indians from the village did go off hunting, particularly just before and just after the rains, as there is still some land to spare, but the animals living in it have also been extensively hunted by all the new invaders. On these expeditions the Indians always build small bee-hive dwellings, a few palm fronds thrown over a slender framework of wood. A couple of miles from Xavantina there was a permanent encampment of this temporary type, a useful vantage point for visiting the town, but the aldeia at Areões was their only real home.

It had been under the charge of the Indian Protection Service, the organization publicly discredited in 1968. There, and in a rough hut of the basic Brazilian adobe style, the resident protector had been an intensely sympathetic man living in a condition of poverty matched only by that of the Indians. He had five children, all inexpressibly beautiful, all shoeless, and all being manufactured by the elementary passage of time into illiterates. Perhaps the man did have a salary of as much as £10 a month, but it certainly did not appear as if he received that amount. There was a dusty stack of medicines in an unlocked hut, but none were of particular value or relevance. The protector was not in charge of them—in theory a nurse also visited the aldeia from time to time. The protector's job was to see that no one took land away from the Indians, to keep the peace among them, to report on their condition, to ask for help if need be, to act as the intermediator between Indian community and western world. All this, while his children hung silently wide-eyed in the shadows and then fell asleep on the floor.

The aldeia was on the northern side of the muddy Areões river while the protector lived on its southern bank. I first went there with John Guillebaud, the expedition's second doctor. He wanted to collect, of all things, a day's output of urine from every Xavante man in the village, and we had paddled downstream from Xavantina in a hired dug-out canoe of teak-like resistance to one's aching flesh but of modest capabilities at keeping out the water. From this irksome craft we eventually leapt with the agility of two-toed sloths to pay our respects to that sad protector, and then we clambered into it once again to cross over the Areões to the village. We had a Brazilian from camp, both to act as a guide and to interpret between the Indian kind of Portuguese and the English kind. He was sufficiently adept in both.

John and I had a certain timidity about visiting our first Indian camp and were prepared to pour forth whatever seemed right when we met its people. We would be silent if they were silent. We would let them call the tune. A few of them appeared ahead of us along the path, but it was our party who, as it happened, first called them. Our Brazilian, by name Taituba, about whom more later, let out a shriek of recognition. He doubled up with his own mirth. He could hardly speak, and when he did he called them *pé de macaco*, monkey foot, a common form of abuse. Instead of clubbing him instantly to death they flung their arms around his shoulders.

The path from the river led up through a banana grove, then past *urucu* bushes (whose pods are crushed to produce bright red make-up), then past manioc, and towards the circle of houses that formed the aldeia. A large open space of dry, brown earth formed the bulk of this circle, and outside each hut was a small fire burning, sending up straight smoke into the windless sky. The initial boisterousness of the group along the path then yielded to the weight of people so obviously very sick. The children were listless, and there were few of them. The women were unkempt, and most of them were sitting and doing nothing. It suddenly seemed a desolate place indeed and the chief, to whom we were introduced by Taituba, was a sad young man with little fire in him. He wearily gave permission for John to have a look at all the sick, and also to collect one day's urine from each fit and adult man.

John Guillebaud's research involved the collection of adult urine. Children, skilful copyists everywhere, were quick to use the plastic bags.

95

Inside the huts it took time to see anything at all. The closely woven thatch kept out most of the sunlight, save where straight shafts of it had discovered holes, but the gap of a doorway was exceptionally small. It took no time to hear the people in each hut, with their coughing and their wheezing, but it was hard to tell how many were making these rasping sounds. Most were lying on beds rather than hammocks, and many were shiny with sweat. (It was easier to see the shiny ones.) Diagnosis was not difficult, according to John, in that everyone, whatever else he or she had, was afflicted with malaria. Their huge spleens, hard and uncomfortable, were only too easy to feel, and it was the start of the rainy season when malaria has its annual peak. The few babies had it; so too the children, the adult and the very old. One woman, so thin in her limbs that she could not walk, seemed to be nothing but spleen beneath her wrinkled skin and tissue breasts. 'It's like injecting a shoe,' said John, as he tried to get a hypodermic into her.

Having used up his entire stock of anti-malarial chloroquine, and having done all he could within these rancid huts, so heavy with sickness, John set about collecting the urine. Such a short time ago all that anyone had ever collected from the Xavante had been an arrow and now, in exchange for fishhooks, nylon line and torch batteries, the men were filling plastic bags for us as we needed them. Every two hours John sounded a gong of iron, and all the Xavante men shuffled up with their wobbling bags of transparent yellow. (Nearly all. Some chose to go fishing instead.) Every two hours, back in the hot confinement of our own hut, John and I poured their contributions into larger containers, one per man.

Our urinal of a dwelling place grew more squalid with each round of this devastating piece of research, but there was an interesting reason behind it. A man who had investigated the Waiana Indians of Surinam had discovered that they excreted 30 to 40 per cent less 17-hydroxycorticosteroid (a hormone whose output is increased under stress) in their 24-hour urines than did a group of normal adults in Glasgow. John Guillebaud wanted to find out whether Brazilian Indians were the same, and he wanted to compare these findings, not with Glaswegians at home, but with the British who were living in the Indian environment. Therefore we all had to suffer the same collecting routine, without the blessing of beads and fishhooks to go with it. (His work produced an unexpected result. There was no significant difference in the levels of this stress hormone between the Indians and the British in Brazil, but there was a difference between the British at home and when they were abroad. In Brazil their output of the hormone was significantly less than back in the hurly-burly of Britain.)

The Kuarup is a festival marking the end of the period for mourning the dead. The men blow sacred flutes and ▷
the haunting noise exorcises all spirits. The young girls, previously in isolation, are released at this time after
months of seclusion. The older women OVERLEAF *have prepared food from fish, manioc and nuts, and wait*
for the ceremony to be concluded before offering it to all those invited to this traditional occasion in the Xingú
headwaters.

When the long Areões day and night had passed, when the last gong had sounded and 6½ gallons of Xavante urine were fairly safely bagged within our room, we had the final and no less warming task of measuring each man's output and bottling 10 c.c. of it as an aliquot for future measurements. Finally, and none too soon, we discarded the remainder, and the bees buzzed frantically at such an effusive libation.

The 22 men who had been such frequent visitors to our hut were the fit ones. Their general gaiety belied the true situation for the majority of people in that aldeia were very ill. The clothes they wore were ragged cast-offs collected, presumably, up the river at Xavantina. There was not a single bow or arrow to be seen in any of the houses. The few crops were being poorly looked after, the four boats were in poor repair, and certainly no one played football between the posts that had been placed by the I.P.S. at either end of their dusty compound. The population, according to their sad protector, was falling because so few children were being born. It was a most weary place, and we eventually took our leave of that man and his five bright-eyed infants. We also said farewell to the 22, and we promised to send them a football although, said John, 'Heaven knows what that'll do to their spleens.' The men thanked us, they gave our boat a great heave into the water, and they even called us pé de macaco, but Taituba, John and I travelled back to Xavantina talking about anything else other than the Indian village we had just seen. Or, more thoughtfully, we kept silent for most of the way.

When the Indian Protection Service was disbanded in 1968, after 58 years of diminishing responsibility, its place was taken by a new organization with new men at the head of it. The *Fundacão Naçional dos Indios* was warmly welcomed as a new hope. Certainly the village at Areões was in far better shape when I, again with Taituba, revisited it some 18 months later. The new governmental representative obviously had both more money and more power. He had an outboard engine. He had stacks of food in a store-house. The medical supplies were more in keeping with the actual needs. Most important of all, after we had again crossed over to the aldeia, the people there were fit. Admittedly it was not the malarial time of year but it was heartening to see podgy children running about and teasing the dogs. It was a pleasant change to duck into the huts without any accompanying nausea. Our gifts were eagerly sought the moment we arrived, the matches, tobacco and fish-line we had brought for them. There was even a padre visiting the village, and worrying on their behalf about some of the nearby land that was no longer theirs to hunt over. More and more developers were crowding the Indians increasingly towards the narrow neck of earth on which their village stood.

We too had an outboard on this second visit, and three young Xavante came back with us to Xavantina after our stay at their aldeia. The river is always liable to be treacherous to the vulnerable blades of a spinning propeller. There are rocks, and there are sandbanks. There are tree trunks brought down at the time of the flood. There are

◁   *The children watched, and waited. Will the ceremony be forgotten when they become men?*

*The new representative (*LEFT*, with two of his children) in charge of the Areões Indians. The Xavante* RIGHT *was an expert guide on the river but vanished when we reached Xavantina.*

also cataracts where the river bubbles noisily, when the engine whines as the boat changes speed and when the fast water threatens to turn one's bow downstream. A Xavante stood in our bow, pointing which way to go and knowing the river precisely as the sun went down to change the water's colour from browny-green to glinting, blinding, streaks of reflection until, when safely set behind the trees, it let the river become black with the warmth of the night. The Xavante laughed. They told each other stories in their epiglottal tongue. They were the kings, for a time, of their kingdom. Only at Xavantina, after our boat had grated on the sandy bank, did they become quiet. Soon they had gone entirely, and we never saw them again.

So much for a couple of hundred Indians, cared for immoderately by the state. They have the remnants of their shattered culture about them, but no more. They have a kind of enclave of their own, but it will not last for long. If there is a policy about them it is obscure, and there seems nothing more positive than a governmental wish that they will somehow become Brazilians. At the present time they are neither Indians nor Brazilians. They are twilight people, existing between two worlds, begging from the twentieth century and retreating into the past. No one is educating them or even telling them about the invasion. They come to Xavantina, and then they go back home. It is just 27 years since white men first shook hands with the Xavante, when their warriors were finally pacified. Not many of them are able to remember that day because the older ones have mainly died. The young know only that they live in a circle of huts by the Areões, and there is nothing much to do or to be done, except fish a bit and beg for hooks when the fish have taken their line.

The Parque Naçional do Xingú is 8,000 square miles of quite a different order. In the nick of time, even though there seems so much land to spare in this region of Brazil, a piece of land nearly 200 miles long and almost 50 miles wide was preserved for the Indians. It is the size of Wales, smaller than Maryland and Vermont, and about a fiftieth of the state of Mato Grosso. It is the only large area in the country exclusively maintained for the Indians, and about 1,700 live in it. They live their own kinds of life, insofar as this is possible, but tribal warfare has happened within the Park and no one would deny that murders happen, whether they are called ritual killings or traditional practices. The Indians are of many tribes, and of several distinct language groups. Physically they look very different from group to group. Their cultures are distinct, and are remaining distinct. Their future is by no means assured but, for the time being, their lives are being lived in a fairly similar fashion to their former existence in and around this area. Their cultures cannot have escaped entirely from the effect of their encirclement by the rest of Brazil, or from the relatively confined space in which they live within their separate encampments, but the difference between their fairly habitual way of life and the emasculated circumstances on the Areões is acute. The new Fundacão Naçional dos Indios is the governmental department in charge of both places, and somehow accepts both systems, but the organizing skill in holding together all the dissident factors at work in the Xingú Park is in the hands of the brothers Orlando and Claudio Villas Boas. They were to experience a series of visits to their park by British doctors, offshoots of the Xavantina/Cachimbo expedition.

It had been the original policy of the two societies in charge of the British expedition that a medical doctor should always be part of the team and that medical research should be undertaken. No one knew quite how dangerous the inner recesses of the Mato Grosso were going to be, both medically and accidentally, and the permanent presence of a qualified man was deemed a sensible precaution. Later it became obvious that the medical men were going to be extremely under-employed. People were being sick insufficiently often and were foregoing accidents so effectively that the greater danger of medically-induced ailments became more of a possibility. At least that was the libellous feeling when camp once had two sick men on its hands, the first suffering from his allergic reaction to a drug prescribed for a lesser ailment the day before, and the other from a painful hole where, until the day before when the doctor had spotted and excised it, a cyst had sat over the years, unwanted but unaching. Until such time as an epidemic should break out, or a rash of accidents, it was thought that medical energies could well be spent on the research programmes planned beforehand in the hope that these could be fulfilled.

Acting as a lure to the west of base camp was the Parque Naçional. Not only was the place regularly in need of medical assistance but the Indians themselves were intriguing exceptions to much of the human race. Isolated from the rest of us they were inevitably different in all kinds of respects, such as in their antibodies, their reactions to disease, their susceptibilities and their strengths. Also, as anthropologists had frequently reported, they made use of various drugs culled from the forest and were able, or so it had been claimed, to promote contraception, even to halt menstruation. Therefore the expedition's medical men were only too ready to visit the Parque. Fortunately, although the place is a sealed area to most people, the Villas Boas brothers were equally ready to welcome the British doctors.

The normal mode of entry into this reserve was to acquire a place on one of the Brazilian Air Force planes making their regular visits to Posto Leonardo, and all other points along that original chain of up-country stepping stones. This involved a lengthy wait, probably at Xavantina, hoping for a plane going in the right direction with space to spare. For days nothing would happen. Suddenly a Dakota would arrive. Its doors would be flung open. People, equipment and messages would be exchanged, hastily. There would be shouted instructions in the wash of the propellers, and soon the plane would take off again. Less than an hour later the doctor, so recently aboard after so long a wait, would be hearing the wince of rubber as the wheels touched down at Posto Leonardo. This time there would be Indians among the waiting knot of people, and one of them would take the visitor to the man customarily in charge of the post, namely Orlando Villas Boas, co-recipient with his brother Claudio of the Royal Geographical Society's gold Founder's medal. If he did not welcome the visitor, suspecting that the arrival would not contribute to the Park in any way, that visitor might as well leap on the next plane out of that place. It would be better still if he could catch the same plane out again.

The most interesting foray into the Xingú area made by any member of the expedition occurred in August 1968. Instead of the waiting and haste of plane-catching a team of three travelled by river to Posto Leonardo, a method also not without its set-backs. Philip Hugh-Jones, the most senior of the medical officers, Kenneth Brecher, a young American anthropologist at Oxford University, and Geoffrey Bridgett, *Times* photographer, travelled down the Suiá Missú river to try and reach their goal. The upper waters of this river valley passed within 20 miles of camp, and there was even a road to it off the main north/south highway.

Various members of the expedition had been along this road to the river to work in this different environment, and the cool clear waters of the Suiá Missú were an attractive alternative to the forest. The riverside trees leant at sharp angles to the river as if to cover over this snaking affront to their authority, and occasionally they toppled too far, but it was an enchanting place and totally welcoming. Admittedly there were sting rays wafting along the bottom, and there were undoubtedly piranhas in the water and small caymans along the banks, but the desire to plunge into the water proved irresistible to everyone who saw it and no one came to any harm. More significantly, from the point of view of access to the Xingú, it was already quite wide and deep enough in the camp area for one to assume that it would provide a satisfactory waterway right to the Park. The air photos bore out this assumption, as the small hair-like thread of the river meandering through the forest did at least remain consistently hair-like. A problem was its phenomenal length due to all those writhings in its course. From the starting place to the Xingú junction at Diauarum was 200 miles. By water the distance was certainly 600 miles, possibly 800. There was then the section, at least another 100 miles, from Diauarum to Posto Leonardo. It was a sizeable journey by any reckoning, however much it might delete the delays of waiting for a weekly Dakota that, by no means, managed to travel every week.

The problem was to take enough fuel for the journey. One 18-foot boat for three people seemed ideal. Unfortunately, when loaded with the requisite 90 gallons of fuel, there was no longer sufficient buoyancy for the three people plus their substantial gear. No one can travel light and empty-handed to the Xingú Park. Gifts, medical supplies and food are all gratefully and necessarily received. Therefore a second boat became necessary, and a second engine and more petrol. The compromise was to take two boats for part of the journey, and then to decant the three men, plus their gear, plus the reduced amount of petrol then necessary, into one boat and for the second boat to return upstream with only its bare essentials. I and Andrelinho (who knew part of the river well) would be the crew of that other boat. Unfortunately we could find no one who had ever heard of anyone travelling all the way down the Suiá Missú, and therefore had little real idea what would be in store for us. How strange it was, or so we thought, to be only a little more than 800 miles from the insane compression of Rio de Janeiro and to be confronted by 800 miles of river, unused and virtually unknown. It was a remarkable state of affairs.

It was an even more wonderful experience. The engines kept us gliding along at some ten knots, and there was always a corner ahead. Around it a group of capybaras would hurtle along the bank and then plunge into the water. A host of ibises, black, white, gray, would leap into the air. Muscovy duck would roar off downstream, looking like some multi-engined flying boat before finally achieving flight. Turtles plopped up and down, more like dabchicks than any reptile, and they even managed to perch, if that is the word, on branches well above their round reflections in the water. There were cormorants looking first with one eye and then, disbelievingly, with the other. Once, upon a particularly beautiful and beach-like sandbank, there was a lizard, five feet long, walking in correct sinusoidal fashion. Also rare were the tapirs, looking more like baby hippos when in the water and early Tertiary horses when out of it. Every now and then were the hanging weaver bird nests and the black and yellow caciques, distractingly flying this way and that, and shrieking as they did so.

Distractions were easy. Concentration upon the navigational uncertainties of the river was harder. The change from simplicity to chaos could be extremely rapid. Having peacefully arranged one's limbs to the satisfaction of every part of them, and having lounged for an hour or more watching those teeming banks glide by, a line of froth around a corner would change all that. It meant rapids, and an equally hasty reaction to their presence. First neutralize the motor, then reverse, then hover awhile looking for

'Admittedly Andrelinho fired his revolver at everything that moved (tapir LEFT, *turtle and cayman), and we and our raucous boat were outrageous insurgents within the peace. . . .'*

an opening, and finally hurtle through it with each end of the boat tending to take an independent course and having to be restrained. Either there was a grating, as boat or engine struck a rock causing everyone to leap out and hold the craft on course, or there was an unexpected silence in all that turbulence, as green rocks loomed like sharks and then vanished, and as the waters once again appeared dark and deep.

Leaping out, following an impact, was no problem. If there were rocks to grate on there was a surface to stand on, although oddly angled and often smooth, but the horrific sounds from the boat's belly made anything preferable, any lessening of weight. To have lost a boat in those remote circumstances was wholly undesirable but it was fairly easy to jump out, to pull the lightened boats off those rocks and then aim them down another waterway. Out in the tranquil mainstream once again the boat drifted silently, gently broadside to the current, and we sorted out the ungainly results of a problem that had so abruptly come our way.

Nights were spent on the *praias*, the sandbanks that have everything to offer. At the top there are trees for hammocks, but there is the soft, dry, squeaky sand as an alternative resting place. For the fire there is ample driftwood, baked into dry brittle bones by the sun. There may even be turtle eggs, if it is the right season (before the rains), with the visible turtle tracks struggling up the hill and then descending from the spot the creatures have concealed with such dogged blatancy. Even at night the *gaivota*, large gull-shaped birds, continue to skim over the water surface, still seeing enough to scoop up fish. To shine a torch on them is often to pick up instead the ruby-red unblinking stare of the caymans, one eye or two according to their position. Up above them is occasionally the high drone of an aircraft, unaware of the emptiness beneath it. Higher still are the satellites, either toppling or steadfast, and uncannily silent as they overtake

'...but it was a kind of ecstasy being there.' *Philip Hugh-Jones,* RIGHT *together with Andrelinho, who chose to travel down the Suiá Missú to do medical research in the Xingú Park.*

the stars all about them. The praias would be a blessing anywhere. As a no-man's-land between the river and the forest they are totally desirable. A night spent on a stretch of river suddenly without these half moons of soft convenience is wretched by comparison.

The emptiness and isolation of this river were extraordinarily impressive. At the junction with the Rio Suiázinho, reached after one-and-a-half day's steady travel, there were five people on the banks, caretakers of a new *fazenda*. Half a day further on there was one empty canoe. For the whole of the next day there was no one and nothing beside all the natural furnishings of that gorgeous place. Later on, and six days after starting out, the main boatload of Philip, Kenneth and Geoffrey were to see their first people for three days. On a praia was a group of men, all heavily armed. These men stood still, and watched. There was no sign of a boat. In fact the only transport system of any kind was quite the most unreal in such desolate circumstances. The man sitting in this wheel-chair was clearly the leader, in that the others were grouped around him, but neither he nor any of the others waved at the intruders. Such well-armed un-friendliness caused the English, equipped with nothing more lethal than a tin-opener, to maintain a hold on the throttle and carry on. The sandbank men were still unmoved and unmoving when the inevitable corner put them out of sight.

Three days beforehand, and after a night on a minute island composed perfectly of sand, laterite and just sufficient trees for our hammocks, we had to separate as planned. The main boat was made heavy with the remaining bulk of the petrol, and I and Andrelinho took as little as we needed. The other three had little freeboard, but it was sufficient and would improve. We two instead sat high in the air, and would be able to speed along twice as fast as their laden craft. A parting is always powerful as two sides turn their backs on each other. A parting in that kind of place, so empty, so wild, is yet more strange. We travelled downstream with them for a while and then, having seen that they were well, returned along our way.

Some day that river will be as polluted as the rest, and the banks will be worn down with people. The place will be of major importance in the welfare of the northern part of Mato Grosso, in the praefecture of Barra do Garças. It will have been included in the modern world. Just for the moment, and on the day that our two boats went their separate ways, it remains as it has ever been. I felt an overwhelming sense of privilege at seeing it, so pristine and pure, and of gliding along on that river's splendid surface. Admittedly Andrelinho fired an ancient ·45 revolver at everything that moved, whether tapir, capybara or monkey in a tree, and we and our raucous boat were outrageous insurgents within the peace, but it was a kind of ecstasy being there, and I sang vigorously for hour after hour. A monstrous headache followed, and Andrelinho was happy to pour scorn upon its possible cause; but when we had landed, and while I was waiting face down for the codeine to have its effect, he caught fish, rubbed salt into their scaly sides, built a wooden framework above the fire, grilled the food and served it up. The feeling of superlative privilege then re-emerged as the headache passed away. It was an Eden. It was a world within a world, a place entirely on its own. I ate the flesh and bones hungrily and then lay flat and supine upon that gorgeous sand.

Meanwhile Philip and the other two were travelling further downstream. After three days, and soon after the wheel-chair encounter, they reached their first Indians, a group of the Suiá. Once again they decided to pass by on the other side and let them be. It would be best to arrive formally before visiting any residents of the Park. Soon the river became such a complexity of backwaters and diversions that they were lost, having no sense of any current and no idea which sheet of water formed the true course of the river. Eventually, by the arbitrary rule of travelling to the right whenever there was a choice, they did indeed meet the vastness of the Xingú, and then the outpost of Diauarum.

Stiff-leggedly they heaved themselves out of their boat before a ragged bunch of Indians but Kenneth, with less heave and greater stiffness, fell headlong into the water. There is nothing like disaster for breaking through linguistic barriers and the group of Suiá, Txukuhamae and Kajabí savoured the incident gratefully. The Kajabí named Merowé, Portuguese-speaking and temporarily in charge of the post, was rather less welcoming and wanted radio confirmation from Orlando at Posto Leonardo that the visitors were acceptable. People do not normally arrive by the Suiá Missú. People normally arrive by air. (Later on the three arrivals were to be disquieted by being told that the Indians along that particular river were extremely liable to kill all those travelling along it. Since the landing strips were the customary method of entry, and

Diauarum, the central post in the Xingú Park, is renowned in the sphere of Indian protection but, when first seen from the air ABOVE *or the river* BELOW, *it appears too small for all its fame.* ▷

since undesirables—such as rubber-tappers, hunters and the like—were both totally unwelcome in the Park and more likely to arrive via the Suiá Missú, it followed that a kind of carte blanche existed along the banks for making certain that no one came too far.)

Diauarum, meaning black jaguar in the Suiá language, is an assortment of well-built huts, several constructed coolingly above ground level, and some fairly ragged dwellings where the Indians live, such as all that are left of the Trumai tribe. There is a runway, half dust, half overgrown, and the tall wires of an efficient radio. There are trees and plants dotted around the compound, such as the loofah, the lime, the Buriti, and various other nut palms, and the dense green mango, giving fruit only once a year but shade for always.

Claudio Villas Boas was away on yet another pacification mission when the three arrived, and the few Indians were in good health. Certainly they had no hesitation in rifling the boat of its valuables during that first night, and all the food, presents and various clothes had gone by the morning. When I arrived with John Thornes and Douglas Botting a year later and by plane, the huts were loud with fearful coughs because the whole Indian community was afflicted with the 'grippe,' a blanket term covering all the virus diseases akin to influenza that have taken such a continental toll of the Amer-Indians. Nevertheless the pilot lost all his spare clothes within a very short while of taking them out of the plane. Diauarum and its inhabitants, so we had been informed, were having to make the adjustment between one world and another. To lose one's possessions instantly, and to listen to all that coughing, was to be reminded forcibly of the point. Both visitors and visited had adjustments to make.

Diauarum is in the centre of the tall rectangle which forms the Park. At the extreme northern end, and still on the Xingú river, are the famous rapids of von Martius. Their original natural barrier to river traffic is now a legal barrier to development from outside. However, as proof of urgency, a ranch is starting up just to the north of these rapids. A further proof is yet another ranch just on the Park's eastern border. The ratification of the Park's boundaries, made official in 1968, occurred none too soon; but, even so, the existence of ranches on the very edge of this Indian enclave makes it rather less remote and less to their liking. A wilderness needs distance between it and developments. It cannot just begin because a line on a map indicates that it has officially begun. Already, due to the existence of those ranches and the certainty of so many more, the 8,000 square miles of the Xingú Park seem to have shrunk. One day, perhaps, there will be a border fence and then the shrinkage will seem even more acute. More and more Indians will probably be brought within the Park, and they will multiply. The sense of confinement, rather than escape from development and developers, will then become increasingly strong. However, it is not yet a cage. It is still a reserve of freedom. It is still a most exciting place.

◁ *The Txukuhamae had been nomadic hunters before being persuaded to live in the Park. Although taught to make large huts, and grow food, the men cling to their old custom of a lip disc.*

Philip Hugh-Jones and the others eventually spoke on the radio with Orlando Villas Boas. He gave them permission to come on south and upstream to Posto Leonardo, and he arranged guides. He also told the Indians he was cross about the thefts, but no one suggested that any of the stolen things should be returned. Anyway the English party, with their guides, left the outpost of Diauarum, that very modest collection of huts and yet world-famous, that mixture of the past and the present where the Indians operate the radio and fix the outboard but succumb so repeatedly to the perpetual virulence of the old world's viruses. Its Txukuhamae, a name meaning the people who have no bows, still wear lip discs, those round sections of wood inserted so disfiguringly into their lower lips, and yet they are keen to beg almost everything from the modern world save for cigarettes. They droolingly explain—and an Indian's Portuguese mixed with saliva is almost an impossibility of comprehension for English ears—that cigarettes burn the projected semi-circle of their lower lip and pipes are preferable.

Diauarum is said, by Claudio Villas Boas, to be 40 years further ahead of Posto Leonardo in its integration. It is therefore small wonder that anthropologists and others welcome an opportunity to study at Posto Leonardo, and in the villages beyond this other outpost, because of all the links with the past embedded there. Diauarum is a half-way stage and therefore, to some, less desirable. Philip, Kenneth, Geoffrey and the guides left it as soon as they could, and Philip's diary recorded their progress.

'After about two hours we reach the Kajabí village, much pleasanter atmosphere than Posto Diauarum. Many paw-paws, pineapples, monkeys, macaws—even a pet otter. We are given a house with an earth floor, chickens, ducks and dogs in it. Filthy dirty. I want to sleep outside but it starts to rain. After food the three of us reluctantly prepare for the night amid the smell of rotten food and animals. But most worrying is the possibility of tritoma bug, the vector of Chaga's disease. I show them my dead specimens of the tritoma which they recognize and name correctly as *barbeiro*. They say they have it in their houses. We sling three hammocks and carefully arrange mosquito nets. Also in the hut are some lovely feather head-dresses and war clubs, the latter to go to America. We don't try to barter, partly because we've had most of our things stolen, but we hope to see better ones later.

'We leave at dawn with some paw-paws—thank goodness. The Xingú is very wide and deep. Most easy to navigate compared with the Suiá Missú. By noon we stop at a lovely sand-bank and swim in clear warm water with fish with bright red tails all around us. Then the guide Cottango shows us how to look for turtle eggs—there are hundreds of them. He collects 2–300 and we set off again. At about 4 p.m. we stop for a meal of rice and turtle eggs. I really don't like them—a very powdery yolk and virtually no white. What a land of plenty this is. Cottango catches 12 large fish in 10 minutes. He also shoots a bird just for fun and laughs.'

Eventually, and on their eleventh river day, they arrive. They turn down a minute tributary of the main river. This offshoot, the Rio Tuaturi, gives no idea of its importance and for an hour they travel up its minute stream, becoming stuck and having to push

◁ *Philip Hugh-Jones drawing the Txukuhamae at Diauarum. The trappings may be different but there is a most distinct expression shared with the Indian on page 115.*

their boat every few minutes. Finally they reach the small hill on which stands the extraordinary Posto Leonardo. Philip's diary records the arrival.

'Orlando welcomes the Indians with us but hardly speaks to us, apparently a typical reaction to strangers he doesn't know. He has a variable temper, but he is often very helpful and his word is law around the Xingú Park. He doesn't like Americans but tolerates visitors who are prepared to help him. He is sympathetic to doctors, scientists, etc.'

Later on, when Philip has had a chance to speak to Orlando, the diary affirms a change of feeling.

'I prepared my best Portuguese speech and approached O. on the subject of visiting the *Waurá*. He couldn't have been more helpful. I really admire him. He runs this place on virtually no money and is responsible for over 1,700 Indians, many of whom commit ritual murder and all of whom could be very difficult to deal with if he didn't keep law and order. I gather he can call in federal troops, but has only once done so.'

Seven doctors from the Xavantina/Cachimbo party and one anthropologist were to visit the Park, to meet one or other Villas Boas, and examine and assist the Indians living in that national park. With the blessing of Claudio or Orlando they all felt extraordinarily grateful, and their various notebooks recorded fragments of their experiences.

'The chief's house was even larger than I thought from the air. It proved to be 100 ft. long, 72 ft. wide and 36 ft. high. It's like a vast cathedral of wood inside, with only the tiny doors letting in light. On the ceiling were models of serpents in basket work.'

'As with us the moon is female and the sun is male. They carry it further, saying the night is female and the day is male. Logically, therefore, all the men urinate in the squatting position at night, and all the women stand whenever they urinate by day.'

'They appeared to need less than the usual doses of anti-bacterial agents. Thus one young man with clinically a fully-fledged right lower lobe pneumonia was fit enough after 36 hours to chase me around very actively in quest of some of the gifts I had brought.'

'I started to wash in the pool, and with soap. As soon as they saw the soap I had 20 men in the pool with me, all using that single bar and cleaning themselves, their hair and their necklaces.'

'My clothes are really awful after living in their huts, especially as everything is red from the urucu dye.'

Medical time in the Park was a combination of work and, for want of a better word indicating a total determination to experience as much as possible, of play. On work:

'I had a variety of conditions to treat. Top of the list was malaria, but mixed anaemias due to infestations, diarrhoeas, upper respiratory tract infections, and various skin conditions were all encountered.'

Although messengers invite various other tribes to attend each Kuarup, all visitors must be prepared to wrestle. ▷
OVERLEAF *A single pair starts the fight, but as each warrior has to wrestle with all the others the ground is soon covered with fighting men.*

' "Uma fleche no ventre"—she's had "an arrow in her belly". What was to be done about this emergency with a dwindling stock of medical supplies and no scalpel? The wound seemed fairly superficial in this 5-year-old, so—surgical principles on penetrating wounds notwithstanding—I did not explore it. The child recovered. Nature is the great healer.'

'Local birth control can be as simple as it is gruesome. After about 28 weeks of pregnancy the woman, lying on a hard surface, grasps the uterus through her abdominal wall and breaks the baby to pieces. Delivery of the stillbirth follows quite rapidly. Maternal death-rate for this procedure is not too high.'

'I see a man with a high fever from a dental abscess and give him antibiotics. Then the *pajé* (medicine man/faith healer) blows smoke into his mouth to decide for himself which spirit is causing the trouble. I consequently feel a bit nervous with such a witchcraft-ridden tribe who have dead bats on the tail-ends of anacondas for decoration.'

On play:

'A man from the Kuikuru arrived at the Kamayurá village where I was working. He presented a length of cotton with 11 knots in it. This was an invitation to a war ritual in 11 days' time and 30 miles away. I decided to accompany the Kamayurá.'

'Each Kuikuru, dressed to represent an animal, approached the dummy human figure in turn and then hurled a stream of oaths and insults at this representation of his enemy and then hurled his spear, usually with deadly accuracy. As one of the visitors I also had the honour of being insulted and my image speared.'

'Singing continued all night.'

'In less than half an hour the tree was felled and after axing a hole along the trunk we were soon eating delicious yellow honey. My companions enjoyed honey, bees and grubs with equal relish. I was more selective.'

'I had a gun and they created exquisite birdcalls to decoy many birds to their doom. These were roasted on an open fire that night.'

'Our guide had deep scratch marks from a fish-tooth comb where blood was made to flow to strengthen him.'

'Every time I look at these woven baskets and my beautifully proportioned Txikão bow I remember that wonderful day in the forest with those men of the forest.'

Claudio and Orlando Villas Boas are indeed brothers, and have many siblings as part of a large family in São Paulo state, but they look very different and are very different. Both are in their fifties, and there are only four-and-a-half years between them, but Orlando is plump-bodied and plump-faced while Claudio has no more fat on him than a 20-year-old. Orlando generally looks after Posto Leonardo, but spends a lot of time on the east coast sorting out the Park's problems with yet another brother. Claudio is mainly at Posto Diauarum, but is usually at the spearhead of any further attempt to bring in and pacify another tribe. He is the more physically energetic of the two, going to see for himself what is happening. Orlando spends more time in his

◁ *Those who have wrestled, now weary, smudged and out of the fight, watch the form of the others.*

hammock and, although he speaks scarcely any of the Indian languages, whether Gé, Tupi, Arawak or Carib (the main groups in the Park), he has a superb intelligence network. Somehow or other he learns everything he wants to know, and then either acts on that information or considers it better to seem ignorant of the whole affair. Claudio, with wiry hair flecked with white, with a slight stoop, and wearing old jeans, an old shirt and dark glasses that correct his sight, is a man who listens attentively and speaks clear and precise Portuguese. Orlando, with straight hair, and probably wearing no more than a pair of shorts, tends to talk rather more, to listen rather less, or else to be completely silent for a very long time. His Portuguese was extremely rapid. To English ears, at least, it was far less comprehensible than Claudio's more pointed delivery.

On one matter they were both equal. If someone was unwelcome he was immediately despatched. One doctor from camp flew in with a Brazilian employee to assist him in his work, there being no assistance of this nature in the Park. The doctor was welcomed; this particular Brazilian went out on the very next plane. Fazendeiros who have flown in from their nearby ranches, and who scatter sweets at the feet of the Indians before inspecting the place as if it were a human zoo, are despatched even faster. Anyone who has, for whatever reason, become *persona non grata* with the Villas Boas might as well forget about the Park. He will never enter it without their blessing.

Claudio's dwelling hut at Diauarum is simplicity itself. It has an earth floor (while guests have a wooden floor built on stilts in a more Pacific fashion) and there are two hammocks slung in the darkness. One bookshelf is neatly full of about 12 feet of books, on philosophy, on medicine, on generalities. Antoine de St. Exupéry seemed to be the principal author, and all the books were in Portuguese. There was one table with a hard bench next to it, and there was an enamel washbasin on a stand. As the final furnishing of the room there was a transceiver radio. With this either he or an Indian spoke to Posto Leonardo at 8 a.m. and 5 p.m. every day. At all times Claudio was at the command of the Indians, particularly with regard to their health. Instead of the bottle tops and old cigarette butts, which form so much of the flotsam of most Brazilian compounds, the open spaces at Diauarum were dotted with medical refuse, with small plastic bottles and empty ampoules, with foil wrappings and one-shot syringes. To help Indians overcome the trauma of contact with civilization (his phrase, and repeatedly used) it was crucial to look primarily after their health. Unless the Indians were kept alive the subsequent problems would not even come to pass. With huts full of Indians coughing from the grippe (and they never seemed to stop by night or by day when I was there) this problem was obviously paramount. Fortunately it was not a dangerous attack of the disease.

However an emergency did present itself and everyone responded. A Suiá had had a canoeing accident involving a paddle—no one was ever quite certain what had happened—and he reached Diauarum two days later. By then he was a very sick man.

At once Claudio spoke on the radio to Posto Leonardo and asked for the English doctor then in residence to come over. Mike Cawley was flown in to Diauarum very rapidly in the Park's own plane, a two-seater whose unshaven pilot seemed a perfect match for it. Mike examined the sick man, thought there had been some kind of rupture, and recommended hospitalization just in case he needed surgery or more than the post at Diauarum could offer.

Again Claudio got on to the radio. The sick man was flown to Posto Leonardo. A Brazilian doctor was flown from Goiás. He had the power to call up a larger plane. The patient was taken and flown to Goiânia. He recovered, and was much later flown back to the Park. Such promptitude, and such expense, for one man is outstanding in central Brazil. Most of the population, whether Brazilian or Indian, could not hope for this kind of treatment. For the Villas Boas brothers such an action not only saves the life of an Indian; it also saves the life of the Park. The trust engendered in the Indians by such prompt vigilance on their behalf must be tremendous. News of such acts must hurtle rapidly around all the aldeias of the Park, and help again to heal those greater wounds left festering from all the injustices of the past.

The Villas Boas brothers believe that the tribes as yet uncontacted will suffer in the age-old fashion when they are finally encircled by the advance of progress. Both sides are suspicious, the pioneering Brazilians and the waiting Indians, and both sides suffer.

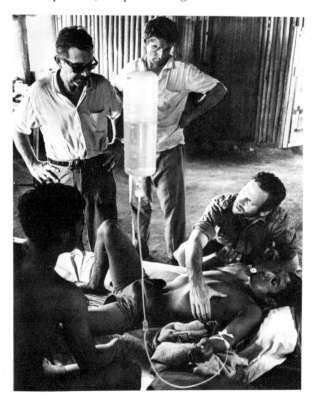

Mike Cawley examined the sick Indian watched by Claudio Villas Boas. Two aeroplanes relayed the sick man to the hospital, and back to the Park when he had recovered.

The Indians

Even if there is no actual slaughter, the trauma both of disease and of contact is a peril only to the Indians. Smallpox or the grippe will attack them as severely as any spattering of bullets from a frightened pioneer. If they survive both kinds of onslaught they will wake up to a situation so hideously different to anything they have known all their lives that they will lose their orientation. As like as not they will die. It is easy to apportion blame for the way in which innumerable tribes have vanished in this fashion but the wretched pioneer, who is so often a wretched being at the end of his tether, is only a pawn of circumstance. Assuming he does not shoot first, and assuming he is free of such virulence as smallpox at the time of contact, even his presence can be medically disastrous for the Indians. Similarly his existence in their citadel can be disastrous to their way of life, to their thread of culture whose laws and customs have bound them together and given them a reason for existence. By leading his way of life, however unobtrusively and unaggressively, he can destroy thousands and be incapable of helping them. If he is belligerent, or antagonistic, or even suspicious of the Indians, the disruption will happen even faster. The story has been repeated so often in the past, so frighteningly often.

It is remarkable that Brazil still possesses many Indian tribes who are virtually as distant from the white man as were, say, the Iroquois when Virginia was colonized. Of course the forest has helped, and the greater reluctance in Brazil to open up the interior, but it is extraordinary that there are still tribes who have not spoken with the invader even 470 years after he landed on those South Atlantic shores. They must all be aware of the invasion, they must have heard stories about it, and watched its planes, but the things that they have heard and seen have not brought them out into the open. The Villas Boas brothers, now provenly adept at contacting new tribes, feel they can offer a fair chance to any such newcomers. They can incorporate them within the Park, inoculate them as soon as it is possible to do so, protect them from unnecessary and unhelpful liaisons, and try to reduce the inevitable shock of such a union.

Even when all goes well with such a programme the problem of subsequent control is far from easy. For years the Waurá, peaceful pot-makers, had been persecuted by the Txikão. When both were living in the Park the Txikão lost much of their principal defensive weapon, namely distrust of others. The Waurá, so this particular story goes, crept out one night and fired their arrows into the Txikão huts at exactly the height where the men slept in their hammocks. (The women sleep at a lower level.) This retribution and other causes severely depleted the Txikão, and there were only 57 of them when they were finally and properly integrated in 1967. A year later there were only 53. As with the dwindling stocks of certain rare forms of animal there must be minimum population numbers for the survival of differing human groups. To sink below a certain level is to be assured of extinction.

At São Marcos mission most of the remaining Xavante Indians were being given a new way of life. ▷

With all its difficulties the Park is undoubtedly a refuge. It is just one four-hundredth part of the area of Brazil, and this small fraction deserves all the help it can get. Admittedly there are only 1,700 Indians living within its gentle control, an even smaller fraction of Brazil's original Indian population, but at least they exist in something akin to their original fashion. At least the Mehinakú, the Txikão, the Suiá, the Txukuhamae, the Waurá, the Kamayurá, the Trumai, the Kuikuru, the Kajabí and the Kalapaló are being given a breathing space. Perhaps more will join them, such as the Kran-Acorore, and others still who have as yet no name and no known whereabouts. The refuge cannot be permanent, as static preservation will be impossible to maintain. Perhaps it only has to seem as if it is permanent for the confusion of change to be less terrifying and less lethal. The place is not a human museum, maintained for the curiosity and amusement of those beyond its bars. It is not an attempt to put back the clock or to capture some Rousseauesque dream of the past. Instead it is a formidable endeavour on behalf of the Indians. It is an achievement all the more remarkable because it is largely the work of that legendary pair, the brothers Villas Boas. Small wonder that they guard their efforts and their charges with such determination.

There are no Xavante in the Park. Therefore a direct comparison between that sad community at the Areões junction, bereft of so much, and the encampment within the Park was impossible. Nevertheless there was all the difference in the world between the poorly clothed beggars on the river and, say, the Kalapaló wrestlers. With a caged Harpy eagle to give them strength, and with thongs tied above their calves and biceps to make them seem stronger, they fought each other with ancient and traditional verve. It is the Park that helps them keep their strength. However, insofar as comparisons are possible, there is a third kind of community. West of Barra do Garças, and about a hundred miles along a road that eventually meanders up to Cuiabá, the state capital, there is São Marcos. It is a missionary establishment, owned and operated by the Salesians, and both self-contained and off that poorly beaten track to Cuiabá. Its importance in the context of this book is that it shelters over half the survivors of the Xavante nation. Over 800 of the 1,500 still alive are at the mission of São Marcos.

A group of us from camp had first met a group of the Marcos Indians along the road to the north of Xavantina. Their unmistakable hairstyle and their broad faces told us at once that they were Xavante, but their behaviour seemed to belie what we saw. Instead of coming to stare and touch and feel and take hopefully, as was the custom with those of their tribe who wandered into Xavantina, they kept about their business. This was mainly eating some meat around a fire, but it was not a Xavante fire. Normally they put four logs in a cross on the ground and push them inwards as they are consumed. This roadside fire was a regular bonfire, blazing, hot and pleasantly disorderly. Over the way

◁ *For physical recreation they hurtled round the compound carrying a chunk of palm tree. For spiritual welfare they knelt each evening before a cross and chanted the Creed in Xavante.*

there was a lorry, and it seemed to be theirs, but once again this fact did not fit in with the normal pattern. Suddenly a middle-aged man appeared, wearing a smock over his shirt and trousers. Plainly this Brazilian was the driver.

In truth he was the driver, but he proved also to be the director of the São Marcos mission. He was Italian, having 'left his country as soon as the fascist war was over', and had been ever since in Mato Grosso. The Indians with him were on an outing, mainly to collect wood for bows, and they knew of a suitable site because they had formerly lived in this area. At this we pricked up our ears, having wondered so frequently where all the survivors had gone. Apparently some 200 had been based rather further from Xavantina than the British camp and had been leading a desultory and disoriented existence when the owners of that land, the men from São Paulo with the title deeds, had arrived to take possession. Once again the old world had encountered the new. The Paulistas had no wish for a bunch of Indians on their property and promptly—the moment an airstrip had been completed—chartered a D.C.4 to remove them. In four consignments all the Xavante, plus such goods and chattels as they wished to take with them, were flown south to the São Marcos mission. There they were delivered into the firm hands of the Salesians.

'Why not go and have a look at *nostri ragazzi*?' said Mario, the director/driver, and then he wrote out a note to Padre Nicolau saying that *questi amici inglesi* would like to see the place.

It was obviously something that had to be done. The Indians of the Serra do Roncador had left the area. They had either coalesced into listless encampments, like the one on the Areões. Or they had been withdrawn into the security of the Xingú Park. Or they had been despatched, for better or for worse, into the hands of the missionaries. The third event was just as germane to the Roncador story, and therefore a group of us from camp travelled bumpily west from Barra do Garças and refuelled—with difficulty—at a broken-down and forgotten town called General Carneiro. Then we had turned off on to the road to Meruré (where the Salesians look after the community of Bororos, a different Indian tribe) and went 30 miles further to try and find those Xavante ragazzi. This was not easy. There were side tracks, but there were no people to ask, and no track appeared preferable to the others. Furthermore, side roads in that kind of area are not necessarily modest affairs leading for a mile or two but can meander on for hours until, like tracking an animal, the visitor eventually comes across the man who had carved that way for himself and had built some kind of a home and farm for his family. The Salesians were certainly not signposting their establishment, but eventually a car came along that road, now rutted almost entirely with our own wheel marks, back and forth, and its driver told us which path of the maze to take.

The cerrado wilderness, made even more familiar by the protracted tedium of that day, emphasized the remarkable sight we were to see. Breasting over one slope, no different from all the others, we suddenly looked down upon a piece of Italy. It was modern Romanesque in that familiar scrubland setting, with occasional lines of Buriti palms fading away in the distance. There were courtyards, and there were all those interweavings of each roof angle with another that the Italians have always loved to build. There were large buildings, topped with squat towers, and not one of us had seen anything like it since arriving in Brazil. Moreover, the runway was of a smart, rectangular appearance. Most of them are like old tennis courts, either with vegetation invading the smooth hard surface, or with smooth hard patches well established among the dusty grass, but this one was both smooth and well defined. A neat windsock showed that there was no wind. Indeed our own breath was taken away by this spectacle, and we drove down into that piazza of a compound with strange feelings of disbelief. Within our cab, apart from the expressions of amazement, it should be said that there were also plenty of assertions that missionaries are bound to do wrong, however great their abnegation, however humble their approach and right their intentions. We liked the look of the place but we all held firm to our prejudices.

By the evening these were far less secure. We had arrived in the middle of a game called, for some peculiar reason, Arabs and Indians. It was a game of almost continuous running by everyone concerned, with each side trying to get a representative through—untouched—to the other side's goal line. The energy involved was prodigious, but no more so than in the football matches that followed. The long Xavante hair flew back as they ran, and the tough Xavante physique was everywhere in excellent condition.

Later on, and for the benefit of their visitors, they arranged a *Corsa del Buriti*. Two sections of Buriti trunk, roughly two feet long and each weighing a couple of hundred pounds, were to be carried by two rival teams along a circular route. In a sense the wood was nothing more than an outsize baton in this most punitive of relay races, but the initial pair of Indians set off with this thing on their shoulders as if it were no impediment whatsoever. Their broad feet thundered over the ground and, as each man tired after 200 yards or so, he quickly rolled it on to the shoulders of another. Instead of waiting at appointed places, as any normal relayist is happy to do, the entire team hurtled round with their temporarily burdened member. Having thrown the Buriti at our feet they then left, whooping and running, for the shower room. We were impressed. We also tried to lift the logs.

Later on that evening they all moved over to the centre of the circle of huts for the evening service. São Marcos was not only an Italianate collection of main buildings, sometimes octagonal and always picturesque, but there was also the traditional circular aldeia of Indian dwellings. Exactly 53 palm-thatched, small-doored bee-hives of the Xavante style were grouped around an open compound. Beside them were all the women and children but in the centre of the area, and around which the men were collecting, was a cross lit up by a few electric light bulbs at strategic points along its shape. It was a vague occasion suddenly made less vague by the chanting, in unison and in Xavante, of the Creed.

'...with their light, brown bodies and their long, lank hair, they seemed like Nazarenes or even early Egyptian labourers.'

Padre Nicolau, Italian-born and aged about 35, then gave an address in Portuguese. Mainly it was an admonishment relating to the three groups of children who had so played with the fires inside their houses that their three houses had promptly been burnt to the ground. Children, said the Father, should be kept in order. Parents should exercise better control. When that was over, everyone then chanted a kind of Ave Maria, recognizable despite its translation into the fiercely epiglottal and halting speech of the Xavante tongue. And with that over a group of the Indians performed one of their traditional dances where the men, grouped in a tight but perfect circle, stuck their elbows out, hunched their shoulders, stamped at the ground, and sang an extraordinarily deep and frightening song.

In the morning, following mass, everyone worked. They welded, they fixed the tractors, made bricks, collected crops, brewed a sugar cake, and proved themselves capable of 101 tasks. The effect on Jonas, the Brazilian *motorista* in charge of our vehicle, was even more interesting to watch. He possessed firmly entrenched opinions about the Indians, about their inability to labour without supervision, their incomprehension of mechanical things, their reluctance to escape from the rural routine of their former ways. He had managed to elevate himself to motorista only recently, and yet here were Indians, not only driving vehicles themselves but removing the cylinder head, welding a connecting rod and performing tasks far above Jonas' own new-found capabilities. This is not to say that Jonas would not have done just as well had he been taught. It is just to emphasize that Jonas' face throughout our guided tour was a beautiful study in bewilderment. Our Xavante guide, detailed to show us all we wished to see, behaved respectfully much like—or so I felt—the head boy taking visitors around a school. He spoke beautiful Portuguese, and quietly answered or diverted all our questions. Do you believe in Christ? Yes. Do you wish to go hunting? We are busy here. Do you wish to visit the big cities of Brazil? We can if we want to. Do you want to be free? There are no gates here.

Watching them at work, with their uniform bright red shorts, their light brown bodies and their long, lank hair, they seemed like Nazarenes or even early Egyptian labourers as they thumped at the clay or dug rhythmically with long-handled spades. Watching them at meal-times was to receive further proof of expended energy and the need for compensation. Large plates overflowing with rice and sauce and piled inches high were effortlessly despatched, and no one was fat. The men ate separately from the women and children who lived entirely in association with the circle of huts. The place teemed with children, another rare sight in the other Indian communities. Of the 800 Xavante at São Marcos, 50 were less than one year old. Each year more babies are born and the population growth rate is proportionately large. The establishment has been planned for 2,000 people, but it will not be long before they reach that figure and that problem. In short, the situation contrasts strikingly with all those other Indians elsewhere whose survival is in doubt and whose breeding is either non-existent or largely vitiated by infant mortality. At Diauarum they were coughing with the grippe. At Areões they were swollen with malaria. At São Marcos they were bursting with life, and piling high their plates again for a further replacement of their extraordinary energy.

In charge of the community were two padres, five brothers (all from Italy or Germany), two sisters and four Brazilians skilled in some of the trades. Everyone was busy learning another language. Padre Nicolau, even if questioned in Italian, would always reply in Portuguese. One Indian would ask another in Portuguese for the time, and the passing German brother would glance at his watch and answer in Xavante. Most of the Indians could read and write in both Xavante and Portuguese, another eye-opener for Jonas who took much time to write even his own name in his own language. They all maintained an efficient electrical supply system whose power originated at a dam they had built on a stream 11 miles away. The supply was far more constant than the wavering uncertainties of Barra do Garças or the more positive uncertainties of Xavantina. There was no resident doctor or dentist at the mission, but one of each makes visits from time to time to check on the situation. Unlike every other farmed land we ever saw in Mato Grosso state a great effort was being made to prevent erosion. All the old sugar cane stems were being laid across any naked soil (a job for the children) to help bind it in preparation for the rainy season. Again Jonas, that wide-eyed reflector, expressed suitable astonishment.

Driving through yet another Arabs v. Indians on the way out, passing a tractor heaped high with Xavante, listening to the cat-calls from the shower room, and taking a last look at that light bulb cross in the ground surrounded by its obstetric circle of huts, we ourselves were silent. Earlier convictions had been replaced by confusion. There was obviously so much to be said for the place and for the other Salesian Xavante community that they described to us. Between them they have 1,100 of the 1,500 surviving members of this tribe, the former sentinels of the Xingú conclave. Areões and a few other villages on the das Mortes have the remainder. The two ways of life are as chalk and cheese, and entirely separate.

Distinct in yet another direction is the Parque Naçional. These three kinds of community are all living in the twilight zone between the aboriginal forest-dwellers, still holding on suspiciously and jealously to their ancient ways, and the fully acclimatized Brazilians who, although plainly of Indian stock, call themselves Brazilians the moment they leave their Indian ways. At least all three, the Park, the mission and the village, are existing in that twilight. For so many of these people there was nothing more than darkness, as west met east, as the Old World met the New, as the trauma proved too much for them.

4 A SQUARE FOR RESEARCH

Each early scientific invader of a new land was frequently on his own or, even if part of a large expedition, the only scientist among its numbers. Therefore, on both occasions, his singular interest had to range widely and the whole of natural history was in his province. Each scientist was expected to be a polymath, and he himself took note of rocks, plants, animals and the indigenous humans with similar fervour. Moreover, with an energy always to be marvelled at, each day's myriad findings were written down most ardently and comprehensively. The day itself may have been a sequence of setbacks, the climate may have been rigorous, the situation uncongenial, and the writer himself playing host to unwelcome diseases, but the daily demand of the diary was always gratified. They were extraordinary men leading extraordinary lives, and some two-thirds of their collection (as with Bates, for example, after his 11-year stint on the Amazon) were new to science. Perhaps this realization helped to keep them going, and sustained them during the long arduous years of their absence from home.

Today's situation is different. Not only is time always in shorter and shorter supply, but no one can embrace all the scientific disciplines any more. Even if he wished to, and even if he were competent in various fields, the current system does not favour such widespread enthusiasm. An ecologist can—and should—take a wide view but even he tends to specialize in certain species or genera either because he is personally fascinated by them or because he feels they can be particularly instructive about the broader themes of his work. In short no one came out to the Mato Grosso camp calling himself a naturalist in the old sense. Each man was more precise about his interests, being primarily concerned with one insect order, for example, and by no means all the subdivisions of that order. Two came out whose dominant interest was with wasps. Another spent most of his time with termites, and yet another spent most of hers with the Acridoid—or short-horned—grasshoppers. Consequently, because not everyone could be an entomologist (unless it had been a very different expedition), even many insect orders in that rich insect world had to be neglected.

Similarly, owing to the prevailing shortage of time, a coverage of even some of the major disciplines proved impossible. There was not always even one entomologist at camp. Each botanist was largely unable to witness both ends of the season, the wet *and* the dry times of the year. Virtually all of the work on fish had to be carried out when the fish were not reproductively active. There was only an ornithologist in residence for eight weeks of the two-year period. No one worked on the ants, the insects who dominate so much of the area. In short, there was too much to do and always too little time to do it in. Also it was difficult for Brazilian scientists to get away from their own commitments. Those who came to camp were gratefully received, as they had so much local knowledge, but they were not able to spend as much time either as they would have liked or as the British contingent would have liked them to spend. The combined stays at camp of all the scientists added up to a quantity of time roughly equal to the period that Bates alone spent in Brazil in those early, less hectic days of the nineteenth century.

However there are similarities between past and present and always will be. The kind of notes written up each evening, whether under the browning thatch of base camp, or at one of the sub-camps, or nowhere in particular, were a mixture of science and speculation and anecdote. So too with Bates. So too with anyone working in an unfamiliar environment. A soil scientist working in a pit four metres deep is primarily interested, of course, in the soil horizons staring at him from every side, but he cannot disregard the rest of life.

'Another glorious day,' wrote David Moffatt; 'pretty standard work routine back in another deep pit. After lunch I suddenly came face to face with an eight-foot snake; magnificent, black on top with bright yellow markings. I tried to chase it into the pit with a stick, but it moved off at incredible speed. It proved to be a *Fer de Lance*. The evening was the usual frantic writing session.'

The soil scientists filled all of us with enormous admiration. They either covered great distances, augering the soil at regular intervals, or they covered no distance whatsoever and spent all day at the bottom of a pit. The insects and the ticks were quick to pounce, much as they do when animals are caught in traps. The trapped animals can be rapidly consumed (and long before any trapper has arrived) but the soil scientists all managed to survive.

'Another good day,' wrote David Moffatt later on. 'Took samples from each profile. Still confused about a lot of the features. In the morning the profile seemed structureless. In the afternoon the face showed definite cracks indicative of the soil being cemented into prisms. Double cleaned everywhere, and became aware of more features. . . . Very hot; so I worked without a shirt. Very dirty; so I walked back covered in red soil from head to foot. Three vultures circled above me, one more than yesterday.'

Turtles were a frequent sight on the Suiá Missú. Insects, OVERLEAF, *were frequent everywhere.* TOP ROW ▷ *(left to right) A bush-cricket of the* Tettigoniidae; *an* Opsiphanes *butterfly; a group of* Bombycine *caterpillars; and a* Stagmatoptera *mantid.* MIDDLE ROW Phanaeus ensifer, *a beetle; an* Automeris *caterpillar; a* Titinacris *locust; another* Tettigoniid *bush-cricket, but better concealed; a well hidden caterpillar, possibly* Sphingidae; *and a* Neuropteran *larva of the* Ascalaphidae. BOTTOM ROW *A stick-like insect of the* Mantidae; *a* Reduviid *bug,* Pothea haglundii; *a* Leucauge *species of spider; and a* Sphingid *moth,* Protambulyx strigilis.

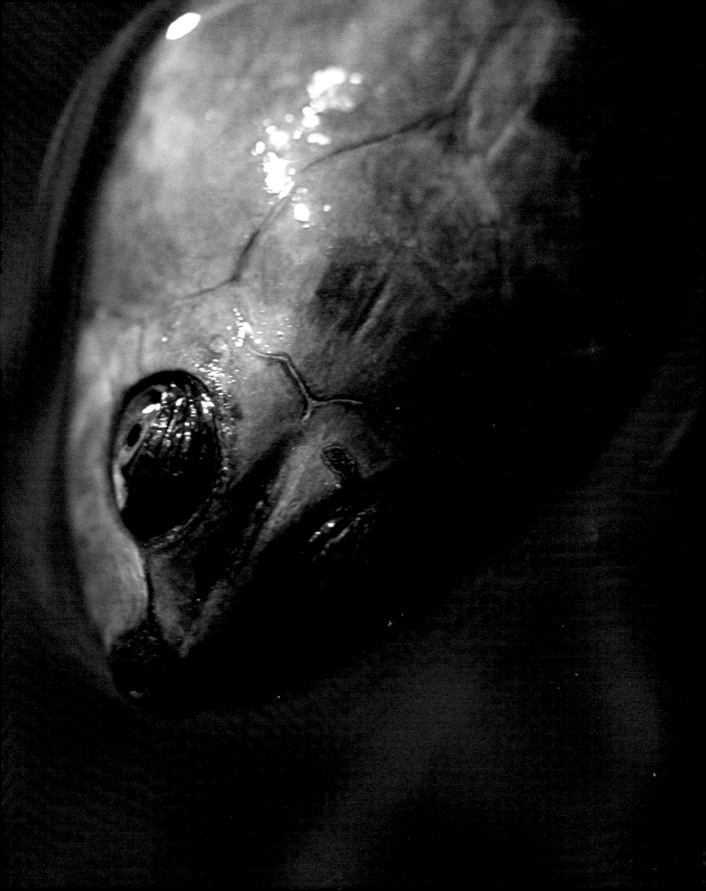

Diaries became similarly streaked with this same red soil. To handle them now is to be reminded instantly of those pits, and of the heat that they contained as well as the soil scientist at the bottom of them.

To an outsider the most conspicuous soil feature of the area was not so much the enormous depth of the weathered material, frequently many yards deep, but the various outcrops of laterite. Hard, angular or rounded lumps of this material capped most of the various hillocks in the region, and formed vicious material to walk over. It also appeared as a layer in many of the soil pits, sometimes thick, sometimes not, sometimes deep and occasionally too deep to reach with a spade. Unfortunately these 'surface cappings and sub-surface layers of concretionary iron pans', glibly called laterite by the rest of us, led to great argument about what the material should really be called. Laterite, apparently, has been too widely used as a descriptive term for too wide a variety of iron-rich materials.

Nevertheless, following the argument, the term was eventually retained at base camp as the substance did accord with the definition (by du Preez) that laterite is 'a vesicular, concretionary, cellular, vermicular, slaglike, pisolitic or concrete-like mass consisting chiefly of ferric iron oxides with or without mechanically entangled quartz and minor quantities of alumina and manganese; it is of varying hardness but it is usually easily shattered when struck a sharp blow with a hammer.' The rest of us, as we stumbled against it, or cut our boots on its angular surfaces, continued to call it laterite, possibly more glibly, but became increasingly intrigued to realise how its layers helped to form the shape of the local landscape. No one knows precisely the conditions necessary for its formation save that iron-rich soils in the wet warmth of the tropics frequently do form laterite, and have done so most noticeably and interestingly in the area being studied.

To look into those deep pits, with soft material so far below the surface, and then to watch the birth of a piece of farm land by the destruction of its trees, is inevitably to wonder about future erosion of this portion of the state of Mato Grosso. The soil scientists reported:

'The low inherent chemical fertility of the predominant dystrophic soils is, itself, a severe limiting factor to agricultural development. Not only is the reserve of nutrients low but it is concentrated in the organic fraction of the soils. Agricultural use generally required the felling and burning of the vegetation which allows but a brief period in which crops can be sustained by the released nutrients. The rapid mineralization of soil humus following clearing will result in a sharp fall in the capacity of the soil to retain nutrient ions, and the leaching of nutrients released by mineralization and from the ash will result in extremely low nutrient levels within one to two years of the burn. Continued crop production would be impossible without the use of fertilizers but their cost in northern Mato Grosso would make their widespread use prohibitive. So, despite the favourable climate and physical attributes of the soils for arable farming, it would seem that cattle ranching is the most likely form of pioneer land

◁ *This* Bothrops *was caught alive and made to pour the haemotoxic venom from its fangs. Snake-bite is generally less dangerous if the animal has recently eaten.*

use for the dystrophic soils and that their more intensive use must await the general development of the region.'

These dystrophic soils, highly weathered and leached (when their minerals are washed down to lower levels), have a very low silt content, a small percentage of organic matter and their weakness in nutrients, such as calcium, magnesium, potassium and phosphorus, is considerable. It would be better for the farmers if they had more of the so-called mesotrophic soils on their land. These look different, in that they are browner, and they feel different. They have more silt in them, and they have been less weathered and leached. However they are yet more crucially distinguished in that they have a high quantity of matter, both organic and inorganic, available for plants. Consequently they have a much higher agricultural potential but, unfortunately, they proved to be much less common in the base camp region. From the air photographs it did seem as if there was a greater quantity of mesotrophic soils to the east of the camp, and so this area could become more important agriculturally, but no land owner invading his new lands seemed to care about the soil. Each one greatly cared about the existing vegetation, always preferring forest to cerrado, but not about the actual potential.

In their report following the conclusion of the expedition the four British soil scientists who had worked in the area ended with a warning:

'Northern Mato Grosso, and the adjacent parts of adjoining states, has survived into the latter part of this century as one of the most extensive areas of tropical wilderness. It is not the purpose of this report to present the case for conservation of such areas, but it would seem that the difficulties within the foreseeable future of intensive agricultural utilization and, especially, of maintaining the precarious balance of fertility on cultivation of the dystrophic soils, are valid additional reasons for the preservation of substantial parts of this undisturbed environment.'

The actual location of base camp was in latitude 12° 49′ south, longitude 51° 46′ west. Its rainfall came predominantly in one season of the year, namely the southern summer. (There were 56 inches of rain in the only complete base camp year.) From November to March (or later) rainfall greatly exceeded evaporation, causing a net addition of water. From May to September rainfall was low but evaporation reached its highest level. Therefore the soil dried out and the level of ground water fell. Sometimes there was quite heavy rain in August, a feature known as the 'small rains' in various other parts of the world but as the 'rain of the flowers' in Brazil, and its sudden arrival was most welcome, not just to those plants that then bloomed so abruptly.

The arrival of this or any other rain made work more difficult for most of those at base camp. There was also the minor handicap of being caught out in a storm, of seeing the cloud, of watching its rain pouring darkly to earth, of hearing its approach over the trees,

◁   *Peter Searle at the top of a soil pit. To spend all day in one of these holes was to provide free meals for every biting fly in the neighbourhood.*

of standing there while the shower did its utmost, and then of trying to walk again with clothes heavy, cold and saturated. It was not noticeably unpleasant, making a curious change in the day, and after a few strides the wetness was almost forgettable; it was only then a matter of casual concern to feel the water table slowly seeping through to the small of one's back, always the last spot to yield its dryness. However, nothing like casual concern affected those at camp who had wearily been measuring land slopes and water levels during the long, dry days of 'winter'. Suddenly their world was convulsed. Streams flowed that had been dormant. Water rose. Rivers changed colour. Everything that had been static happened all at once.

There were some strange findings. It had been expected, for example, that the rain would cause a decrease in the conductivity of the streams. It had been expected to dilute the ions present in the water. This proved not to be the case because the rain, particularly at the start of the wet season, actually had a higher conductivity than the streams, showing that there were more ions in its water. If the rain was heavy, and violent enough to cause run-off over the soil surface, it picked up additional ions and therefore boosted even more the conductivity of those streams. However, water that percolated through the soil to reach the streams lost most of its ions en route and these, presumably, would then become available to plants. As a result, whenever the rain was gentle, the conductivity of the streams was not affected.

In other words, the existing situation is of rainwater well stocked with ions which, due to the small amount of run-off from the well covered land, tend to remain in the soil. Should the future management of this land cause greater run-off, as seems highly likely, the ions will flow downstream before any plant has had the opportunity to make use of them. It is not known how all these ions, particularly of calcium, get into the rainwater but it is probable that the traditional tropical enthusiasm for setting fire to the vegetation is largely responsible. Millions of acres are burned every year, generally deliberately, and the very fine ash carried upwards is likely to form the ionic source. At all events the high ionic content of the subsequent rain is of considerable importance to the area and to the fertility of its soil. Run-off should be prevented, not only to hinder the erosion it will surely help to cause, but to trap as many of those precious ions as possible and stop them reaching the streams.

Needless to say it was also necessary to prevent one's own ions from contaminating the experiment. A single drop of sweat in 100 millilitres of stream water promptly doubled the reading. This fact was made clear to those others at camp who offered to bring back water samples from their particular area of work. This kind of liaison, of urinating for the doctors, of noting plants for the botanists, or of collecting mere water, was one of the great benefits of a camp with such diverse interests. Some forms of mutual aid were more disconcerting than others. Water collected, free from sweat, in simple plastic containers was one thing; to be free from sweat and to collect—or even to observe being collected—the social hymenoptera was quite another. Owain Richards and Bill Hamilton both looked dissimilar and were indeed very different, but both worked primarily on wasps and in this regard, when some bigger or better nest had been discovered, they had extremely marked similarities. They had to collect those wasps, come what may.

Wasps are more abundant and more diverse in South America than any other part of the world, and Brazil has this diversity in full measure. Not a genus is missing from the New World's considerable list but oddly, despite the fact that the American wasps have been so well examined, about 14 per cent of Richards' collection proved to be new species. In fact he decided on his return to do a complete re-classification of the 2–300 species of South American social wasps. Base camp proved to be in a particularly satisfactory area because the Amazon and Guyana fauna could penetrate down to it via the gallery forest whereas the distinct fauna of the drier south-east regions could reach up to it via the cerrado. Therefore a number of species reached their south-eastern or north-western limits not too far from camp. Despite South America's abundance it is thought likely that wasps evolved in south-east Asia and then, like the humans, crossed the Bering Straits at some warmer moment in the history of that crucial continental passageway.

Apart from the new species some of the base-camp wasps proved to have new types of nest architecture, such as a species which makes combs with two lots of cells back-to-back (unique in the Vespidae) and another species in the same genus which makes a set of concentric cylindrical combs (also unique). There were several other more complicated types and therefore many additions to the records of known species whose nests had not been described. All this is important because considerable weight has always been given to nest architecture in the classification of wasps.

South American wasps generally have the castes very little differentiated, much less than in Europe. It is usually necessary to dissect them and to examine the ovarial development in order to distinguish between queens and workers. Owain Richards did about 10,000 dissections at base camp for this purpose and concluded that

'these wasps normally have more than one queen in the nest and little is known about the variation in queen percentage from species to species. We now find that in a small but appreciable fraction of the species there are more marked differences between queen and worker. Structural differences between the castes, even if small, imply that the larvae received different treatment and suggest as a first possibility that some glandular secretion may be added to the food.

'I discovered a fourth kind of gland during work in Mato Grosso. It produces a band of a dark sticky secretion in the queen and not in the worker. In other cases the glands are present in both castes but the secretion is only abundant and coloured in the queen. In several species the gland provides a certain way of distinguishing queens and workers without examining the ovaries. All this is very preliminary; even the use of the word gland might be regarded as a bit of an assumption. The function is quite unknown but as it is normally different in the castes one would obviously expect it either to produce some sort of "queen-substance" or perhaps to be involved in caste-determination.'

Bill Hamilton's dedication to his work was consistently fearless. He would plunge his hand down holes of forbidding appearance in the ground in the hope of discovering their occupants. He was always the first to grab a snake should one slither into camp. He had lost a finger joint from some boyhood experiment and that seemed strictly in keeping with his addiction for discovery. I personally first saw him at work when someone had reported a three-foot nest hanging about a hundred feet up a tree. I went along for the ride, as they say, immensely intrigued how such a delicate problem would be solved.

The particular form of delicacy selected by Bill Hamilton was an axe. The blade bit deep into the tree and black clusters of wasps 'bombed' out of the exit hole, as if parachutists were to leap out clutched together in platoons at a time. A few feet below the nest (but still high above us) these clusters fragmented into individuals once more, and all the wasps flew about roughly on the same horizontal plane as the nest. Meanwhile the axing continued, with the axer surprisingly unmolested and with unbelievable quantities of wasps flying about their hanging pagoda of a home. Their behaviour of searching only the horizontal layer for the cause of the disturbance led those of us on the ground to one elementary and inescapable solution. It was our plight that would be inescapable the moment Bill's axing was over and the whole tree crashed—and buzzed—to the ground. So we fled, while the tree groaned with that twisting cry of pain as a giant falls earthwards, and the axer wearily watched his crashing handiwork. He then moved in to collect samples and examine the nest. Later, with some high-pitched whine still coming from his hair, he joined us happy with the successful conclusion of his endeavours with *Polybia liliacea*. 'Oh yes,' he admitted, 'I have been stung.'

In a report he wrote that:

'According to my view of evolution, the extreme devotion of social insect workers to the welfare of their colony must depend on the very close kinship of all members of the colony, and secondly on the degree to which they are physically channelled into particular social roles by the treatment they receive as larvae. On this view one can understand the single-queen system, in which the colony is simply a single large family, much more easily than one can understand a multi-queen system. The kinship system of a multi-queen species is, indeed, much more like the structure of a human population with colonies corresponding to villages or tribes.

'A great many puzzles remain. Some workers are self-interested to the extent of laying their own eggs instead of helping the queen, presumably more specialized and efficient at this business, to lay more. Other workers are certainly not short of altruism, as anyone meddling with a populous colony soon discovers. Many of the species have workers who sacrifice their lives like honeybees when they sting, leaving the barbed sting with most of their entrails attached. In possessing and daring to use such a sting the workers of these Brazilian species show more devotion to duty than do our monogynic British wasps which, as is well known, favour a hit-and-run tactic. This leads one to wonder how natural selection propagates the genes that induce such suicidal habits. If the workers lay at all, why are they content to lay less than the queens? To what extent *do* they lay? Can it be that unknown habits of inbreeding in these wasps maintain a high general level of relationship within the colony in spite of apparent unrelatedness in the past one or two generations?'

142

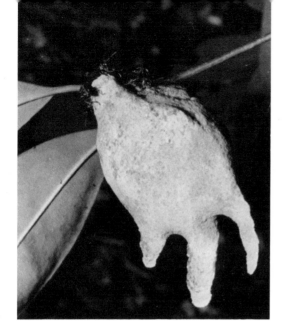

Wasps are more abundant and diverse in South America than elsewhere, their worst enemy being the ant. But the polybia *nest* (LEFT) *is actually protected by nearby ants.* RIGHT, *Bill Hamilton, hymenopterist.*

Wasps pervaded Bill Hamilton's life at base camp just as the life of base camp now relentlessly pervades his report:

'On one occasion Taituba presented me with a spherical clay nest of *Polybia emaciata* which he said had been found deserted. It appeared to be so even on shaking; but when, at Taituba's suggestion, I blew gently at the entrance there was a furious buzzing from within and wasps poured out like chaff from a threshing machine, to the great delight of everyone around.'

'... When I had tried in vain to get my standard sample of five wasps from a nest by throwing sticks at it from a distance, I held up a bit of cotton-wool, wiped previously under my armpit to provide a sweaty mammalian smell, on the end of a long stick and it was immediately blackened by furiously stinging wasps which clung to it even after I had lowered it and shaken it into the net.'

'... In general ants are the most deadly enemies of wasps, and the wasps seem to have no defence against them. A clay nest of the type with the vertical slit entrance, *Polybia singularis*, which I transplanted into the camp area for observation was just recovering its activity and population when it was attacked and completely cleared out by army ants, *Eciton*, in the space of about two hours. The ants dragged out the helpless nymphs and larvae and formed their famous living carpet of bodies to smooth the passage of the booty-carriers on their way to the tree trunk.'

Bill's wife, Christine, was with him at camp. Her devotion was considerable and her stings no less so. Once, after a difficult bout with *Stelopolybia testacea*, which can actually squirt poison if it is frustrated by a veil, the two of them photographed each other. He had a nasty swollen lip, but she had practically disappeared behind the swellings around her eyes. *S. testacea* had been successfully collected but the poison sprayed at her face had left its virulent mark.

The average European, accustomed to assuming that all bees and wasps will sting if given half a chance and will certainly do so if their homes are investigated without due preparation, might initially be amazed to discover in Brazil a large quantity of stingless bees and wasps. At the same time the Brazilians themselves have been recently taken aback at the sudden invasion of their country by a particularly vicious form of honey bee. Probably hives of European bees were brought over to the New World very shortly after the first Europeans had arrived, and these insects were well known for their placid temperament. It was possible even to take the honey from the wild form of this placid bee without being greatly inconvenienced, and the wild bee was itself unable to invade much of the Brazilian hinterland.

Suddenly everything changed. Some African bees were brought over to a São Paulo laboratory to form part of an experiment. They were known to be a vicious bunch, but it was hoped to breed the unpleasantness out of them. Unfortunately a few swarms escaped. By 1965 it was reported that cattle, horses, even people, had been killed by their un-provoked attacks, and that the bees were succeeding in invading the Brazilian interior. No one could casually take the wild honey bee's honey any more, for the Africans inter-bred with the placid colonists and their vehemence became more widespread. At base camp the invading honey bees buzzed around, notably on any laundry left by the streams, and such a sight would have been impossible only a few years beforehand.

One day, hearing tell of a bees' nest suitably located not too far from camp, a group of us went off with the intention of taking its honey. En route we picked up a hitchhiker (we never did discover where he was going to) and he joined in with our intentions. Having surveyed the nest the rest of us started preparing for a fire around it that would have gladdened the heart of any mediaeval witch-burner. The Brazilian scoffed at our preparations. It was only necessary, he said, to cut away at the hole and the honey would be there for the taking. For emphasis he tapped the tree with the back of his hand. For yet greater emphasis a single bee swooped down from nowhere and stung him on the face. He rapidly retreated, while we continued with our pyre and soon had flames and smoke violently on our side.

Unfortunately we boiled some of the honey, and it was not as good as it should have been, but at least we were stung only moderately in our ardent respect for the new form of Brazilian honey bee, now as antagonistic as they come. Perhaps the hitchhiker had not heard of this change of temperament in the place where he had come from, but then we never learnt where that was and we left him as we had found him by the side of the road. This time, however, one side of his face was greatly different from the other.

Of course the Mato Grosso is an entomologist's paradise. Like a big game man in the

Some wasps are nocturnal, such as apoica, *and spend all day clustered together on their nest. By no means were* ▷ *all wasps either so placid or somnolent.* BELOW *Christine and Bill Hamilton after the difficult time they had with* Stelopolybia testacea.

Serengeti or an ornithologist on the Bass Rock he is in a kind of seventh heaven, although a confusing one. As a generalization there are more insect species undescribed in the tropics than described. Probably about 30 per cent of anybody's collection will be new to science. It will be a smaller proportion if he sticks to the more obvious insects, such as the coleoptera, the lepidoptera, and the hymenoptera, because beetles, butterflies, moths, wasps and bees have always attracted interest. It will be a greater proportion if he collects only the less obvious, and one member of the expedition promptly found three new species of Psocoptera by examining palm fronds.

Grasshoppers are large, and might be expected to have received a lot of attention but not according to Maud Richards, Owain's wife, who joined the expedition for a time. In the Old World the main motive for their examination has been economic, due to the depredations of *Schistocerca gregaria*, the notorious African desert locust. This is the only *Schistocerca* species in the Old World but there are a great many in South America. For example, *Schistocerca flavofasciata* was frequently found on the roadside near base camp and did not seem notably gregarious like its famous relative. (However, on the unlikely spot beneath the outstretched arms of Christ on Rio's Corcovado mountain it later showed that it was not too distantly related by being seen to congregate there in large numbers on the hibiscus bushes.)

As these locusts are such effective fliers, and as some of them could be quite capable of flying the Atlantic, the matter for speculation is whether, for example, the South American Plague locust flew to Africa and then ravaged the new-found land, or whether the African Desert locust flew to the New World and then diversified into the variety of species so characteristic of the South American fauna. Another great unknown is why the African locust is such a plague on occasion and why the South American Plague locust is less demanding. It does have outbursts, notably in Argentina, but they are far less violent and damaging.

The rapid growth of tropical vegetation cannot really be contemplated without a sudden awareness that there must be an equally rapid system of decay. It is here that the Isoptera, the termites, play an all-important role. They are crucial destroyers of the plant structure. Trees are being eaten by termites even before reaching maturity, and the invaders enter through a dead root or branch to start work on eating out the centre of the tree. Usually live wood is not touched, and certainly the termites cannot digest everything, but they have bacteria and protozoa within their gut (the young acquire both by eating faeces) and they are quick to make use of wood already partly broken down by fungi. They have nests up trees, in trees, on the ground, below the ground. It was Anthony Mathews who worked on this ubiquitous order and he said, not entirely with pleasure, that it was impossible to dig up a trowel-ful of earth from anywhere without finding termites in it.

◁ *Some nests could only be reached by felling the tree, and nests were sometimes 3 ft. long.*

Dig anywhere in the Mato Grosso, it seemed, and you will find termites. Syntermes grandis, *with its winged forms, its soldiers and its workers, normally lived below ground.*

With such an omnipresent group it follows that there are omnipresent predators. These notably are the ants and spiders. For protection the termites have their soldiers, and the soldiers frequently possess a snout fashioned into a highly effective repeller. It is sometimes possible to see, and frequently to smell, the substance squirted out at the ants and certainly it makes the ants retreat. Those soldiers with an efficient nozzle (correctly called the nasus) often have extremely inefficient jaws but they have speed and can rapidly create an effective barrier with their volatile odour. As there are some 4,000 species of termite all generalizations are likely to be rendered invalid by the exceptions, for there are soldiers with good jaws, and groups without soldiers, and repellents and jaws are far from being their only method of defence. For instance, the workers of some species rupture themselves on one side when attacked and pour out a mass of sticky material. This procedure is, of course, lethal to the ruptured termites but the glue also ensnares the attacking ants.

Sometimes it was possible near camp to watch streams of winged termites pouring out of a hole and all flying off on the same course. Depending on the species this kind of swarming took place at different times of the day, and perhaps two or three times a year from each nest. It was a time of great mortality for the termites because wasps were quick to pounce on those in the air, and the ants and spiders took their toll of those that landed, but it was a way of propagating the species. Any male and female that did survive promptly paired and started a new nest. In general all eggs are fertile and

A termite mound built complete with ventilation shafts by Cornitermes bequaerti, *but now also inhabited by 8 other species. The construction may have started in the stump of a tree.*

all can become queens, but hormones decide which shall remain workers, which soldiers and so on.

A large termite mound on the ground was not only formidably hard but the home of many different species of termite. One species started the mound, and might no longer even be part of the community, as other species moved in when it suited them. Quite apart from differences in the appearance of each species, the pathways they formed, and the type of lining to these channels, were also different. To crack open one of these mounds, itself a formidable undertaking, was to see all these differences and also to watch termite defend itself against termite before the inevitable ants moved in. To watch both ants and termites, and to see both of them at every turn, was to realize that a major expedition could have been mounted whose sole objective in the Mato Grosso went no further than an examination of these two major insect groups. Even then, or so one suspects, their prime conclusion would have been that a yet larger expedition should be mounted to do the same sort of work but to restrict itself just to a few of the more important species. Even by themselves the ants and the termites are just too large a subject for careful scrutiny, and their omnipotence in the Mato Grosso world cannot be overstated.

Whatever kind of work was being done at camp it tended to involve the Brazilian employees living at base camp. These have already been mentioned briefly, but they were a mixed bunch and deserve a fuller account of themselves. They varied from manual labourers who would have been only too happy to get away from the forest, should some suitable employment have presented itself elsewhere, to those for whom the forest was an essential and integral part of their lives. In the main they did well by working for the expedition, and they were also loyal to it. One man, the least likely, one might have thought, did abscond with a certain advance on his wages that had been given to him to help him over a difficult patch (sick family, hospital bills), but the difficulties had plainly been excessive and his loyalty too sorely tried. At most times there were more Brazilians in camp than British and therefore their way of life, their singing in the evening, their guitar-playing, their humour (always best when confronted by misfortune, notably of others) tended to dominate. This, bearing in mind the fact that it was Brazil in which the expedition had encamped itself, was probably not a bad thing. (Jim Ratter, botanist, took more trouble than anyone else to learn the background of these men and his notes form the basis of the following brief biographies; the book would not be complete without them.)

The first man described would undeniably agree that he should be the first to be described, and rightly so for he sauntered along during the expedition's early period in Xavantina and, three days later, explained that he had been seconded by the Central Brazil Foundation both to help the expedition and to help it acquire further employees. His name was Taituba.

Raimundo Aselino de Castro, or Taituba, was born in 1932 in Itaituba (Pará), a small town on the Rio Tapajós. His father was a farmworker and his mother a domestic servant. His father was a Negro; his mother largely Indian. During his childhood, which did not include any schooling, the family collected rubber on the Tapajós. When Taituba was 13 his mother died and he took up a wandering life, living for some time with Indians. Much of his forest knowledge was gained during this period. He also learned the language of the Indian tribe with whom he lived and when with the expedition would speak it to amuse the other Brasilieros.

For about five years in his early twenties he worked for the Brazilian Air Force, first at Campo Jacareacanga, and later at Cachimbo. There he was employed as a hunter, to help keep the base supplied with meat. He then joined the Central Brazil Foundation and was chosen to help the British expedition because of his knowledge of plants and animals and also of the geography of the region. It was Taituba who took Iain Bishop to the site of the base camp. Iain had described the sort of place he wanted—at the junction of cerrado and dry forest—and Taituba remembered as very suitable an old road gang camp of 1966.

His knowledge of plants was by far the greatest amongst the Brasilieros. Paul Richards

Taituba, aged 36, practically illiterate, part Negro through his father, part Indian through his mother, wildly ▷
temperamental, skilful natural historian, excellent company.
OVERLEAF *The coral snake,* Micrurus frontalis, *small, striking, beautiful and venomous.*

said on one occasion that he showed taxonomic judgement which would do great credit to any professor of plant taxonomy. He demonstrated diagnostic characters of the blaze (fibres in bast of woody plants etc.); he could identify *filhotes* (young vegetative plants); he would dig about amongst fallen leaves until he found old fruits or, failing this, would describe their appearance quite accurately. Anyone working with him picked up this knowledge too, and the flow of information operated both ways as he was delighted to be shown the *sporangia* of ferns and various other things he had not understood.

Physically Taituba was small, about 5 ft 3 in., and had a slight curvature of the upper spine. Despite this he was very strong and had plenty of endurance, as shown by his tireless climbing of tall trees. If he liked a task he worked enormously hard; if not he did not. His chief fault was drinking *cachaça* (pinga) in excessive quantities. He often would carry a bottle in his pack and take pulls at it at short intervals. Also when we were in Xavantina he was fond of importuning money for drink and for women. The other Brasilieros respected him for his ability as a 'backwoodsman' and for his knowledge of nature but also considered him rather a clown on occasion. And so he was.

Taituba's domestic life was particularly complex. He had one woman in Xavantina with two sons, of whom he was apparently the father, another in the settlement on the opposite bank of the Rio das Mortes from Xavantina who was a widow with a number of children, the youngest of whom was apparently his. Until May 1968 the widow was in ascendancy and he was intending to marry her but then he started favouring the other bank of the river more frequently. A visit to Aragarças with Taituba tended to be rather an alarming experience as he seemed to know everyone and drank deeply with them. He was almost completely illiterate—his abilities in this direction only extended to writing his own name and a little very simple reading, which he performed like a child by making the sound for each letter and joining them together.

Taituba did an enormous amount for the expedition. He chose most of the other Brazilians who were employed and it was partly due to him that we had such an orderly and honest bunch of men.

Raimundo Reiss de Santos—the doyen of the plant collectors (who had been trained in Belém) was aged 43, with experience of collecting in many parts of Brazil. He was an urbane character, much liked by everyone; in appearance of medium height, plumpish build, handsome, pleasant face, and probably of pure European stock. Very adaptable and could turn his hand to any task, repairing the Jeep, driving, marking out transects, sorting and distributing the specimens, cooking, fishing and hunting. He was much more sophisticated and educated than the Xavantina Brasilieros, but his sophistication was no barrier. A great letter writer, he used to sit up in the Botany hut writing letters home.

◁ *'With more Brazilians in camp than British, their way of life tended to dominate.'* TOP *(left to right): Raimundinho, plant collector; Andrelinho, fisherman; Constancio, cook.* MIDDLE *Antonio I and Leo, labourers.* BOTTOM *Julio and Aurelio, who turned their hand to anything.*

When he arrived back in Belém he found that one of the bites on his leg was not healing. It turned out to be the result of leishmaniasis and was cured by treatment, but left a considerable scar. He always enjoyed a glass of rum, when he could get it, and liked to work with a handy mug of rum and tonic at his side. He would not drink cachaça, which he regarded as gut-rot.

Raimundo Souza (Raimundinho)—he and Raimundo de Santos had worked together for about 20 years, and he was generally known by the diminutive form of his name to distinguish him from his larger namesake. The temperament and abilities of the two were totally different. Raimundinho was small, wiry, and an excellent tree climber of mixed European, Indian and Negro blood. He could not write his own name, nor even the numbers on the newspapers containing the specimens. His strongest points were tree climbing and the arrangement of specimens in the papers—the other collectors regarded him as a specialist in this job. He tended to drink any available alcoholic fluid to excess, but surprisingly was always fit for duty in the morning. Like Taituba he had the fantastic memory of the illiterate and his leisure conversation consisted mainly of joking about his reminiscences.

José Ramos—20 years old and usually irrepressibly gay, not that anyone tried to repress him—was a delightful character, and liked by everyone. Very small, about 5 ft. 1 in., and mainly of Indian blood, with straight black hair and bronze-coloured skin. A very good collector and tree climber. Not only literate but a great writer of scribbled and almost indecipherable letters.

João Bertolda—belonged to the botany team and was employed as a collector but never showed much competence at this. He was born in 1934 in the state of Pará and had also worked with Taituba at Cachimbo. He had a reasonable knowledge of plants, although much inferior to that of Taituba. Business keenly interested him and he saved all his pay, neither smoking nor drinking. His money went on keeping his wife and five children, who lived in Barra do Garças, and on deals involving livestock. The other Brazilians considered him very lazy but the true reason for his lack of energy was discovered while he was with the expedition. A Columbian doctor from the Tropical Diseases Institute at Belém diagnosed that he had a greatly enlarged and weakened heart —the result of either Chagas' disease or syphilis. As a result he was given lighter duties, such as insect collection. He wrote and read well and evidently enjoyed reading. He appreciated the value of education and was very keen that his children should get as much as possible.

Andrelinho (he only had this single name)—came from the state of Maranhão and had wandered about the north and centre of Brazil quite a bit. His mother was dead but as far as he knew his father was still alive. He was a good tree climber and used a different method from the others. They linked their ankles close together using a strap—the old north Brazilian Indian way—but Andrelinho climbed with his legs free. Like most of the frontier Brazilians he lived in something of a neurotic condition over his health. He was also very sensitive to insect pests and used to spend a great portion of his time in the field picking off ticks. Physically he was small but very powerfully built and probably almost entirely of Indian blood—Joaquim called him 'Mundurucú' (an Indian tribe).

Antonio 2—was the most negroid of the expedition Brazilians, but in his eye-shape showed evidence of Indian blood as well. He could neither read nor write. An excellent worker, whether digging soil pits, cutting picadas or later acting as cook at sub-camps. A very good fisherman and hunter; he learned hunting from his father and uncle, with whom he used to go on canoe hunting trips on the Xingú tributaries for the skins of the *ariranha* (giant otter) until, as he said, 'A gente matou todas'—people killed them all. He had not seen much of the world beyond the 'mata' ('I shall never forget,' Jim Ratter has written, 'Antonio's open-mouthed expression of wonder when one evening, by the camp fire at sub-camp two, Taituba was giving a discourse on his visit to Brasília Zoo relating, with particular vigour, data on the genitalia of various species.') He was totally unable to conduct his financial affairs—all his pay went on beer, gin and cigarettes and he was heavily in debt to the *Fundaçao Armazem* in Xavantina. When drunk, which was rather frequent, he was wont to talk cheerfully to people, while hanging tightly on to their shirts and leaning on them heavily as he tried desperately to focus his eyes. He sang very well and played the guitar.

Joaquim Fonseca and *Jezonais Breder*—the two lorry drivers were employees of the University of Brasília and were seconded to the expedition. They were, of course, much more educated and more sophisticated than the Xavantina Brasilieros but fitted in very well with them. Both were absolutely reliable and honest, as shown by the fact that they sometimes had to carry loads of money from Brasília to base camp which represented about three years' pay for them. Neither was married but both became engaged before the end of the expedition.

Jezonais' Portuguese was acknowledged by the Brasilieros to be the best in camp, probably because he came from further south than any of the others. It sounded at first rather strange to our ears but once the ear became attuned he was very easy to understand. He was full of youthful schemes for his future after the end of the expedition. His uncle had wanted him to become a botanical collector, which is well paid, but Jezonais did not like the exams he had to take for this and had not passed them. The idea that appealed to him most was that his father should buy him a VW which he would ply in the streets of Brasília as a taxi.

Constancio was in his mid-twenties, a very hard worker and a good cook. Negroid, with slender build and high-pitched voice, he wore a strange green suit with short pants, and in the cold of the dry season mornings wound a towel about his head for warmth—the whole outfit being most bizarre. He also did the heavier laundry work—trousers, towels, etc.—and proudly distinguished without fail the owners of garments lying in the heap by sniffing them. He had a large family living in the settlement on the opposite bank of the Rio das Mortes from Xavantina and was a good boatman, having sailed with the big cargo canoes on the Rio das Mortes as pilot. He told me he came from a numerous family, some of whom were white and others as black as he was. To fortify himself before a big wash he used to drink a concoction of guarana and condensed milk.

There were others, *Aurelio Ferreira, Leo* (a great digger), *Jonas* (a former rubber-tapper), *Julio* (who became very good with the stereo microscope), *Nilto* (a most basic labourer), and yet others who did not stay the full course. Whereas each of us had strong notions about the friendliness or otherwise of each of them, they plainly had their pre-ferences as well. One easy way to earn their cantankerousness was to disregard the sacred ritual of meal times. Mato Grosso Brazilians eat their mid-day meal early and they must have it. Without it, and if the all-important hour of 11 a.m. is passed by with-out the immediate appearance of food, they would seem to be struck by a sudden death. Eye-balls would roll upwards, and an instant listlessness would overcome them. To the unwary, or to the newcomer, this could be alarming—until he had learnt the cause. A swift transfusion of rice and beans rapidly set everyone on his feet again.

The expedition picked these men up, one way and another, at the start of its time in Brazil. It paid them well, and regularly (which was possibly more important) and then dropped them with regrets when it was all over. In the meantime, and during that period of employment, the scientists were most grateful for the labour and for the com-pany of these men. We never really knew for certain, but I do not think that the Brazilians were greatly displeased with that period of their lives so curiously taken over by the Expedição inglesa.

The British contingent not only had all their different lines of activity to carry out, but were themselves an exceptionally mixed assortment. Chinese are alleged to say, as a reprisal for each Westerner's remarks about their uniformity, that they cannot tell Europeans apart, but then they never visited base camp. The wasp men have already been mentioned, both admittedly uniform in their fearless approach to the subject, but Owain Richards managed to look like a professor at all times, detached and remote, whereas Bill Hamilton appeared as the perpetual student of some Chekhov drama. Bill's attention to the problem was acute when, say, a wasp had indicated the presence of a nearby nest but lesser activities, such as driving a car, demanded less of his attention. It was easiest to assume that someone else must be driving the vehicle, despite the steering wheel and the pedals being rather nearer to Bill's hands and feet than anyone else's.

Owain Richards' brother Paul was also entirely distinctive. Even at a thousand paces he was totally distinguishable from everyone else if only because of the way in which he took his own paces, if that is the word for describing his method of progression over the ground. An anteater with its long claws would better understand his mode of walk for the two of them have a similar shuffle. His whole gait had a frail touch to it, and the story of his acceptance for an expedition to Guyana had a most authentic ring. 'Oh yes,

Angela Bishop with pet capybara in the camp's swimming pool. BELOW *Rhino beetles*, Enema pan. ▷

we will take Richards', the leader had said, 'but I am not certain if we will bring him back.' However he did come back and he has spent much of the rest of his life in savage environments, difficult for men but excellent for plants.

Owain's wife, Maud, was most resentful if anyone should imply for a moment that it was odd for a 60-year-old woman to go and spend a few months in the Mato Grosso pursuing short-horned grasshoppers. She felt her sex was as irrelevant as her age, and that acridoid insects were always fascinating.

Iain and Angela Bishop spent more time at that camp than anyone else. They were the first to move in and the last to leave. Iain was one of those people who manage to retain 3 days' growth of beard for months at a time, to have just half a shirt-tail hanging out for the whole of the time, and somewhere about him, or within an arm's reach, there was always a cigarette burning. Angela would perhaps have been the greatest shock to Percy Harrison Fawcett and all those others who belaboured their way through that forest. She spent most days in her swim-suit not just for the convenience of an afternoon swim but for the suitability of the garment in a hot humid place. When she and Iain prepared for an administrative visit to Brasília they retired to their hut to appear in a little while transformed. Angela merely looked prettier and yet neater. Iain, stripped of that bristle and tucked in everywhere, became someone else.

To some extent everyone had to become uniform to a certain degree merely because of the environment. It was no good wearing flip-flops and short trousers for a walk through the jungle: boots, trousers and long sleeves were generally essential. Even so there was plenty of room for variation even on this enforced similarity, and no one, so far as I can recollect, wore anything at any time that would have gladdened the eye of P. H. Fawcett.

The camp routine was simple. Breakfast was early, with porridge, tea, biscuits and marmalade. People then dispersed to do their work, collecting, dissecting, describing, measuring, observing. Lunch was usually a casual meal, eaten peremptorily by those who happened to be around at the time. Tea occurred if someone felt like making a cup, but dinner was always a more resplendent occasion. It occurred shortly before the last of the light was abruptly going to leave the sky. It occurred when all the savagery of the day's heat had gone, and the hour was a prime time for food, for talk, for sitting back, for taking stock.

We discussed, for example, the style and manner of our particular expedition. Was it, as so many suspected, breaking new ground in being the archetype of all future forays into undeveloped areas? Had the old days of rough and ready adventurers, hacking this way and that, gone for good? Was there any point at all in the wide-ranging survey, the one that inspects miles rather than millimetres, and was even a 20 kilometre square a

◁ *Crowds of butterflies, often several species intermingling, were a particular delight. So was the communal hut in camp, most notably during the long, warm tropical evenings.*

Iain and Angela Bishop lived at the camp for 20 months, being the first to move in and the last to leave. Between them they looked after this Mato Grosso research station.

ludicrous endeavour, too large, too difficult, too varied? Reasonably enough everyone argued from the viewpoint of his or her discipline, with geographers (generally) wanting the big approach, with entomologists (usually) liking the closer inspection and with everyone pooh-poohing anything that smacked of bravado, of foolhardiness, of enterprise for its own sake.

At times it was rewarding that the ages and the disciplines were so intermingled. In most scientific establishments either the ages keep apart from each other, or the differing disciplines keep separate, if only because they are housed in different buildings. A common room, or refectory, does not contain the muddle of people that sat side by side under the thatch of the communal long house. Possibly the various sciences could not help each other greatly, but it was good for each man to hear the problems of another, to become involved in them at least to the tune of arguing about them. Of course everyone had to specialize in that wilderness, but the meal-time conversations helped to break down these artificial barriers, as the ornithologist asked about hymenoptera, or the hydrologist asked about the fish. Fortunately, unlike some more static community, such as those in the Antarctic that are subjected to the same companionship—and the same jokes—for a lengthy period, the membership of base camp was always changing.

On the occasions when the place palled, when someone felt he had had enough of it, the meal could always be a perfunctory business for him, and he could retreat into one of the other buildings. If that was insufficiently far there were always the sub-camps. Almost anyone could think of a valid scientific reason for going to a sub-camp, and virtually everyone spoke of these places with considerable affection afterwards. Initially they were built to save people the labour of walking all the way back along some picada, particularly when someone's first task the following morning would be to walk wearily all the way out again. The sub-camps possessed the Crusoe essentials of life, such as a cleared patch of ground, elementary tables made from poles, and a pathway down to a stream. There were also, of course, suitable trees from which to sling hammocks, admittedly a plentiful commodity in the Mato Grosso, and there was usually a view. This was a factor lacking in the immediate confinement of base camp. Sunsets may have happened there, full of colourful splendour, but they were not witnessed. At the sub-camps, out in the cerrado or with a less all-embracing stand of gallery forest, they were often superb examples of their kind. There was also comparative silence, something rarely heard in that communal site. There was a simplicity, together with a great sense of well-being in those places, and I feel sure that people worked twice as well from them.

At the turning which led off to base camp there had, in the days of building the main road, been an airstrip. By the time the British were arriving the place had been considerably overgrown but a recreational task, always pursued with great verve, was the destruction of that overgrowth with the intention of creating a football field. The more an open space was unfolded the more difficult it became to clear further vegetation, to conform with the arbitrary ruling which dictates that football fields ought to be of a certain size. Eventually this one became fixedly unique, the only square field in play just 30 yards by 30 yards. Beyond it was unkempt wilderness but on it, and using its single pair of goalposts to good effect, the British and the Brazilians gave themselves and the ball a punishing time. The British were a mixed lot; so were the Brazilians; but no Chinaman could be blamed for failing to distinguish anyone at the end of a game. All caked with the same earth, and streaked with sweat, they streamed back into base camp making precisely the same sounds only in different languages.

It was an extraordinarily happy camp. It was not contented, for what human being is for more than moments at a time, but the people there tried to make the most of their environment. They knew their time in that place was short. They knew its time was short. Therefore, by and large, they did their best with it. Moreover they were rarely ill, and this permitted the medical members of the expedition to carry out their own individual plans of research. They had much to contribute.

5 DOCTORS IN THE XINGU

The medical research carried out by members of the Xavantina/Cachimbo expedition was mainly concerned with the Xinguano Indians, the inhabitants of the Xingú National Park who lived amongst the headwater tributaries of that river. The depressing medical history of many areas has followed from one basic dictum: when an isolated Indian community meets up with people who have not led an equally isolated existence, such as Brazilians from the rest of the country, the result is severe for the Indians. The savage outbreak of venereal disease in south-western Europe in 1493 is thought by some (although there is dispute on this point) to have originated with the sailors returning from the New World. The virulence of this epidemic is said, again by some, to have resulted from the Old World's lack of immunity to the new contagion.

What is most certain is that, in this kind of interchange between one world and the other, the Americas have suffered far more than either Europe or Africa, the two old world continents most in contact with the new lands. In the old days little was known, and few cared, about the manner of an Indian's death. Nowadays it is known only too well than an embrace can be as lethal as a bullet, or more so in that one bullet only kills one Indian while the tangible expression of friendship can destroy a community. Whereas in the old days no one could do much to halt the rampant infections that took such a toll, a sadder fact is that so little more can be done even today about these primary contacts between Old and New.

The Kran-Acorore, already mentioned as a tribe in the wilderness, provided an excellent opportunity for medical research. So far as was known they had never had any prolonged association with the invaders, but the Government wanted them to cease their free-living existence for several reasons. For one thing it was believed that Richard Mason had been killed by a group of Kran-Acorore—a camp of theirs was later found only 25 miles from the ambush spot. Secondly one member of the tribe had once sat

Indians in the Xingú Park have a significant new mark on their bodies. It is a vaccination scar.

down on the main runway at Cachimbo, the aerial staging post well to the north of the Xingú Park, and this gentle overture then caused chaos. The man was immediately attacked and reinforcements were rushed in from·elsewhere to counter the alleged threat. One plane-load of soldiers crashed into the jungle, killing many of those on board, and their deaths were attributed in the nation's mind to the savagery of the Kran-Acorore. The Villas Boas brothers believe that the obtrusive, peaceful invasion of the Cachimbo runway was no more than the expression of a desire to make contact, and that the crude rebuff of this gentle feeler sent the Kran-Acorore back into the jungle with a yet greater suspicion of the white man.

The Villas Boas had their own desire to see this new tribe welcomed into the fraternity of their Park, and had no need of any encouragement from the Government. They knew that the tribe would be the greater losers when the inevitable clash came between invaders and invaded. They knew they had little hope of extending some form of protective jurisdiction over the wide-ranging area loosely roamed over by the semi-nomadic Kran-Acorore. They knew too that the uncontacted tribe was a tempting thorn in the flesh of some of the contacted Indians, notably the Txukuhamae, who would go off on raiding parties as retribution for some earlier misadventure in the eternal round of vengeance. The Kran-Acorore were known as killers, in that they never took prisoners of any kind, not even women, not even children. Such determined vigilance may have been one reason for their continuing existence, but it was also one more reason why their extinction was inevitable. They were a primitive people whose axes were of stone and whose principal weapons were clubs and arrows. When fire-power was really put to the test the Indians would lose most assuredly. Forty armed men, as Adrian Cowell said in his brilliant documentary film on this subject, are like a division in the jungle, and the hundred or so Kran-Acorore (or so their numbers are assumed to be) would soon succumb. It was after a nearby group of Txukuhamae had made yet another raid and had captured four children that the Villas Boas brothers decided to make a major foray into the jungle with the hope of bringing these otherwise doomed people into their park.

Philip Hugh-Jones, the medical officer who travelled down the Suiá Missú, asked Orlando if he could join the pacification party which was then in the field. If only he could collect some of the blood of such an isolated fragment of humanity he could then have it analysed. The vital ingredients missing, such as the antibodies providing immunity against so many viral attacks, would be noted and future pacification missions could then arm themselves beforehand with essential boosts to survival. In this way, although it might not help the Kran-Acorore, the future tribes being brought into the fold might not be slaughtered by the first viral infections to come their way.

If it worked, if the appropriate vaccines could be made available, this would be a blessing of a very high order. Of course there would be problems. It must be bad enough for a tribe to have the trauma of new people milling about its encampment without having to yield 10 c.c. or so of blood to the sharp prick of a hypodermic needle. There is also the technical difficulty of keeping that blood, either as whole blood or just as plasma, in good condition so that it is fair for analysis several weeks later, but at least this problem could be overcome. Philip had brought with him from London a small-sized milk churn. Its sinister appearance had caused comment on the airlines. Its weight had caused complaint from all of us. Its protruding metallic form had stuck out from the heap of things on that Suiá Missú boat as it glided past herons, sandbanks, cataracts. However, it was worth any trouble it caused for it would keep all the blood samples at $-70°C$ and therefore in good condition. The solid gas inside it was at this temperature and, as the nitrogen slowly became gaseous, the bottle gradually weighed less and less. In other words it was possible, just by weighing the bottle, to calculate for how many more weeks it would be effective in keeping its contents cold.

The bottle, and the waiting hypodermics, provided the means for getting the blood back to England. The laboratories were ready to perform the analysis, and then to

All isolated communities suffer medically when the barriers are down and they are first exposed to new diseases. The problem is to overcome the virulence of this onslaught. BELOW *Philip Hugh-Jones taking a blood sample.*

manufacture the vaccines. It was up to the Villas Boas brothers, for no one else could do it, to provide the living material. Their expedition had been sent into the interior with an assortment of some 40 Indians to go with them, all wearing clothes to reduce the appearance of belligerence. Unfortunately the four captured children had not helped over the matter of which Indians to take. It had been hoped that they would give some clue as to the language involved, or at least to the language group. Indians who spoke some allied tongue could then have been taken as interpreters. Unfortunately the four children, of whom the eldest was a girl of 5, had not spoken a word in their own tongue since their capture. When they did eventually speak they used the words of their Txukuhamae captors. This gave rise to a thought that the language of both captured and capturer was the same, for it was suspected that the two tribes possessed a similar culture, but it was unlikely. Other tribes, and particularly the isolated ones, had their own distinctive languages. It was therefore considered most probable that the shock of capture had been responsible for the silence. After all, a child only speaks a language because other people, particularly those nearest to the child, speak that language. If they all suddenly disappear the wretched child, even if as much as five years old, will no longer hear that language and will no longer attempt to talk it.

The Villas Boas expedition set off down the Xingú from Diauarum, up the Manitsauá Missú, and then overland. For two months it built a picada, at about a mile a day, and then encountered the river that led them to the Kran-Acorore country. Pebbles were thrown by the invisible inhabitants to attract the attention of the travelling party, but it never received a frontal attack. (Direct assault has never been the method of defence of any Indian from the vicinity, whether Xavante, Txikão, or Txukuhamae.) The party safely reached the Kran-Acorore plantations and there strung up gifts as a peaceful statement of their intentions.

Next day the givers returned to find the pots scattered, the mirrors smashed, the plastic toy aeroplanes quite disregarded but the knives all taken. Most exciting of all was the fact that various long clubs had been left in return. Delighted with this interchange Orlando and Claudio reckoned that it would only be weeks, at worse a few months, before the two parties would actually meet. Further gifts were strung up, such as small axes. To stone-age people, even if they have already been buzzed by aircraft and must know that other people have other products than those they make themselves, the gift of a steel axe must be a kind of manna it is hard for us to visualize. At all events 12 axes were offered and all 12 were taken. The pots, once again, were thrown to the side but the Villas Boas party felt that progress was being made.

The Parque Naçional do Xingú tries to protect the Indian from the inevitable shock of contact with twentieth century man. OVERLEAF *The customary fishing techniques are still carried on by making a dam, stupefying the fish with vegetable poisons, and then waiting for the catch to float and be caught downstream. A difference is that these days there might be a nylon net as part of the dam.* ▷

Unfortunately the rainy season breaking at the end of 1968 marked the end of hopes for a rapid encounter. No more gifts were taken. The Kran-Acorore did not even return to their plantations either to harvest their crops or to pick up their few real possessions— baskets, pots, implements—that they had left there. They retired into their jungle fastness, their doomed enclosure. First Orlando had to fly back from the airstrip they had made, because the Park itself always needed supervision. Then, after months of waiting, Claudio returned along the way he had come, by river, by land, and then by river again.

In any case Philip Hugh-Jones, waiting to join the expedition, had already had to return to London and to his normal work at King's College Hospital. The Kran-Acorore remained uncontacted. No one knows who will get to them first, the trigger-happy prospectors, the landowners, the Villas Boas, or disease. Imagine the excitement and care, if someone should rediscover the dodo on some island near Mauritius, that would be lavished on the species. Yet, west of the Xingú and in many other enclaves in the western half of that country, are a new group of people. Perhaps they will benefit when we catch up with them; perhaps not. At all events disease is still unfortunately bound to take its toll whatever kind of man proves, eventually, to be the first ambassador to their ancient kingdom.

In not every case is the Indian worse off immunologically than the invader. Leish-maniasis is a case in point and provided an excellent subject for research by various members of the expedition. It was examined from every angle. This meant catching the rodents and other animals that provide a natural reservoir of *Leishmania*, catching the flies that transmit it, noting any human infections among the fazendeiros and camp members, and then treating them. Skin-tests were carried out on all available colonizers of the new road to get some idea of the incidence of past and present infections. There was a game, set and match quality to this work in that every aspect was satisfactorily investigated.

Mucocutaneous leishmaniasis, also known as *espundia*, is one of the more unpleasant tropical diseases. The primary lesion can be relatively minor and is the first sign that a particular victim has the disease. Usually, it appears as a persistent, painless pimple which slowly enlarges and eventually ulcerates. Most often there is a single ulcer, more rarely multiple. These sores, unsightly enough in themselves, are a forerunner of what may be worse to come. In some cases the parasite may produce secondary lesions of the nose and palate, often from 5–20 years after the initial lesion has healed and been forgotten. These nose and throat infections can be extremely destructive, eating away at flesh and cartilage until the nose and palate are virtually destroyed. Although the disease is not a direct killer, the patient often dies from a secondary infection and

◁ *There is always a danger from piranha fish, and a single bite makes a nasty wound, but there is a greater hazard in destroying a traditional way of life and livelihood.*

173

pneumonia. The disfigurement is accompanied by a host of secondary effects, not the least of which is the social stigma. Occasionally, because the outward signs have obvious parallels, sufferers from leishmaniasis may be confused with leprosy patients.

Only relatively recently has anyone begun to understand the disease of leishmaniasis in the New World. It was only in the 1960s that forest rodents were shown to be the major hosts. Until this gap in the story was filled no one could understand the full cycle of primary host—vector—secondary host, although the disease itself had long been recognized. The vector that transmits the disease from wild animals to man is a sand-fly but, as with malaria and the mosquito, not every sand-fly (of the genus *Lutzomyia*) is guilty of this role. However, the Societies' expedition was very well placed to investigate the problem. Its camp was surrounded by forest in which the vectors could be expected to live. Its traps collected many rodents which could be expected to form part of the natural mammalian reservoir. Its employees and the other Brazilians up and down the road could show whether the disease was being transmitted to the local people in this particular wilderness, and the nearby Indians could indicate whether they too suffered from the disease or had acquired an immunity to it. Everything, in short, was to hand.

Ralph Lainson and Jeffrey Shaw had already done much of the pioneer work on leishmaniasis, notably in establishing the role of the rodents in this particular zoonotic disease, a disease in which animals play a necessary part. Both worked at the Wellcome Parasitology Unit in Belém and saw, in the Mato Grosso camp, a unique chance to extend their observations from the north to central Brazil. They wanted to examine rodents, sand-flies and people, and they knew precisely what they wanted to find. Iain Bishop, Ruth Jackson and John Woodall helped with the animal trapping. Lynn Aston and Anthony Thorley helped on the human side, and these two went off to the Xingú Park to check on the Indian immunity.

Most of the mammal traps were set either within the dense tangle of the gallery forest or near its border with the dry forest. Baited with banana or maize, the suitable kind of traps were those that kept their catch alive. The 'break-back' types were efficient in killing their captives, but dead animals were a prey to the omnipresent ants and therefore such specimens as were caught in them were frequently useless. Of the 107 mammals satisfactorily caught and suitable for examination, 46 showed skin lesions and 21 of these animals, all of which had been caught in the forest, had lesions positive for leishmaniasis. The lesions were found to be positive by demonstrating the presence of the single-celled parasite within them. All but one of the infected animals were Cricetid rodents, the exception being a small marsupial, *Marmosa murina*. This individual was also exceptional in being the only infected marsupial among the fifteen that were caught. The most frequently infected rodents were of the genus *Oryzomys* and a rat *Nectomys* but infections were also found in a spiny mouse. The tell-tale lesion was almost always a modest and inconspicuous plaque on or near the base of the animal's tail, but sometimes there was more than one lesion and once—with the *Nectomys*—some lesions

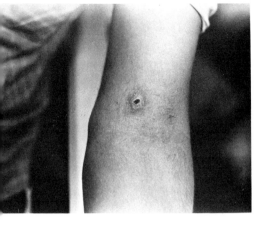

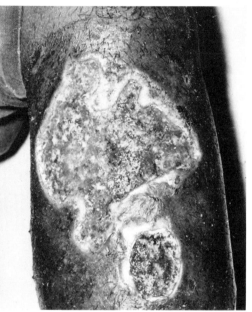

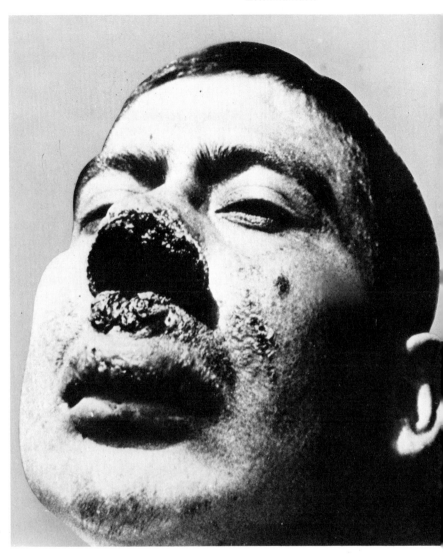

The primary lesion of leishmaniasis is a pimple that slowly enlarges, and it can be followed by severe, secondary lesions of the nose and palate that are extremely destructive.

were on the ear. The Belém scientists had brought some laboratory hamsters with them and into the skin of these the *Leishmania* parasites were inoculated for safe-keeping until such time as the particular strains could be examined back in the Well-come laboratory near the mouth of the Amazon.

To catch the sand-flies both traps and human bait were used. The traps had oil trays surrounding a live animal, and the attracted flies were ensnared in the oil. The human bait, sitting in the forest at night, merely picked the flies off their exposed skin and promptly pickled their attackers in 70 per cent alcohol or brought them back, alive, for dissection. In five weeks, and at various locations, the traps caught 3,280 sand-flies and the men themselves caught many hundreds. Almost all the trapped flies caught with the rodent-baited traps were of one species, *Lutzomyia flaviscutellata*. The females of these small insects then had to be dissected and examined for signs of *Leishmania*. As sand-flies can fly through the mesh of many forms of mosquito-net the finicky nature of this work can readily be imagined, but it was wholly rewarded. In one fly a heavy infection of the parasites was found and these too were inoculated into a hamster in the hope that the strain could eventually be securely isolated. Of all the flies caught by the men off themselves a total of 444 were dissected but no parasites were found. Also only two of these dissections were of *Lutzomyia flaviscutellata* females. Just how many different species bite rodents, and how many bite both man *and* rodents, and how many actually carry the parasite and act as vectors by transmitting it, has all yet to be determined.

It was all too rapidly determined that leishmaniasis could be a hazard to those living in the area. A few of the Brazilians at camp developed the ugly, open, primary lesions, and these men were immediately given the two-week-long course of antimony injections. The disease is usually easy to cure if it is caught early enough and a sufficiency of the correct antimonials is promptly administered. On a nearby and poor fazenda, with a total population of 30 people, five possessed active primary lesions and two had the far nastier secondary nasal involvement. Also two-thirds of this fazenda community indicated, by their positive reactions to skin-test experiments using a small amount of antigen, that they had been infected in the past.

Certainly there was no difficulty in encountering sand-flies in the area of camp, but at least they stayed within the denser, darker forest and at least they were dominantly nocturnal. Therefore to be out in the open at night or within one of the various huts, was to be reasonably safe from their unpleasant bites, quite apart from the yet more unpleasant aftermath. To go into the forest at night, a difficult stumbling procedure not without its own hazards, was to become immediately aware of the presence of sand-flies. After dark no one ever stayed over-long in the particular lavatory that had a forest setting, an excellent spot by day as butterflies flitted in and out of the area and as birds hummed past or stayed to preen themselves, because each nightly foray meant the exposure, however briefly, of a large biting surface. The sand-flies were quick to pounce.

Unfortunately there were other inviting reasons for going into the night-time forest. There were glow-worms to see, and fire-flies, and a beetle with twin head-lamps at the front. Also the termite mounds, dull blocks of earth by day, became Madison Avenue by night. Hundreds of small glow-worms emerged from their holes within these mounds to light up the structure in a most enchanting fashion, and various attempts were made to photograph the sight. Unfortunately, even 12-minute exposures were to prove unsatisfactory and the prevailing memory from these and all other vigils within the darkened forest was of the sand-flies. At night, without a doubt, and making the point in far less than 12 minutes, these attackers came into their own with a vengeance.

With the rodents found and examined, with the flies caught and dissected, and with human cases found and cured, there only remained the matter of the indigenous population, the Indians. Orlando Villas Boas gave permission for Lynn Aston and Anthony Thorley to work in the Xingú Park and help to complete the leishmaniasis story. The plan was to discover whether the Indians ever suffered from the disease, thereby possessing either the relatively mild primary lesions or the fearful secondary damage, and also whether they had developed antibodies specific to the disease. A sub-clinical infection is one which would cause no mark but would result in the formation of the appropriate antibody material, the body's form of defensive reaction tailor-made precisely to the invasion of a particular disease. The lack of scars and the absence of the relevant antibody would, as a further generalization, probably mean the lack of infection. Other doctors visiting the Park, and also more casual observers, had already reported that Indians did not seem to suffer from leishmaniasis as the local Brazilians did. They suffered far more than the Brazilians with so many other diseases, but against this particular infection they appeared to have a better defence.

The two Englishmen wanted to examine the whole population, but they excluded all excitable infants less than two years old. One advantage of the nakedness of most of the Indians meant that the task of looking for primary lesions was greatly simplified, but the similarly casual behaviour of the Indians did not always help the second part of the programme. This necessitated the injection of the antigen one day and then an examination of the same skin area for any sign of reaction two days later. Needless to say, as John Guillebaud had already discovered with his urine work, the calls of fishing or hunting often proved stronger than the desire to obey the strange wishes of a visitor twice in 48 hours. Besides, or so it was occasionally argued in a world where the Brazilian enthusiasm for injections had also intrigued the Indian, the visitors had performed their injection and the subsequent examination was plainly of lesser portent. In all, and in eight Xingú villages, injections of the antigen were made on 500 of the population and 400 of them were available for the essential re-examination 48 hours later. The rest had wandered off.

The technique was often to use one arm as a control. This arm was injected just beneath the skin with the solution minus the antigen, while the other arm received both the antigen and its solution. Any sensitive reaction to the solution itself—always a possibility—could therefore be noted. The point of injection was ringed with indelible marker and a positive reaction—an inflammation of at least three millimetres in diameter—was looked for after that gap of 48 hours.

The results were impressive. No active primary or secondary lesions were observed on any Indian, but 162 (76 per cent) of the men and boys and 88 (47 per cent) of the women and girls reacted positively to the antigen, an average of some two-thirds of the population. Very few of the young children reacted positively but virtually all of the adults judged to be older than 35–40 did so. In other words the men had been infected more than the women, and the adults of both sexes more than the respective children and adolescents. It is presumed that the sex difference exists because of the difference in the two kinds of life. The women spend most of their time in and around the huts and the cleared compound. The children stay largely with the women but the boys spend an increasingly large amount of time accompanying the men on their various expeditions. The forest environment is therefore the major source of infection. It is the place primarily for the men, secondarily for the boys and the women, and least of all for the children. It is also the haunt of the phlebotomine sand-fly.

An exception to the prevailing situation was found to exist, or rather to have existed, among the Waurá. In the early 1960s a sudden outbreak occurred among this pleasant, pot-making Indian community living in the security of the park. Fortunately the infection was cleared up with antimonial drugs, but there was greater curiosity why it had arisen, bearing the Indians' traditional immunity in mind. When the British team were at the Waurá village, with its 97 inhabitants, the leishmaniasis attack was both vividly remembered and had left its mark. Of the 71 Waurá examined in 1968 by the British sixteen of them had old inactive scars of leishmanial infection. Of the eleven who were male seven were then aged 5–10, implying that the infection had been more common among the very young, but since 1964 the tribe had been as free from the disease as before.

The most significant fact in this story is that, some few months before the infection began, the tribe had been moved to a new camp site from its previous home four hours' canoe journey up the Rio Batovi. This suggests that they had moved into an area either with more infection among the flies or that the infection was of an antigenically different strain. In any case, to move for a mere four hours along a twisting river, and then to succumb to a particular infection, is to give yet another proof of the medical problems involved in the care of isolated communities. It is small wonder that the isolated Indians often die so readily when they meet people who have brought new diseases with them from another continent very many hundreds of paddle-hours distant.

New World cutaneous leishmaniasis has an ancient history. The Mayas and Incas probably knew of the disease, for they depicted similar lesions most accurately on some of their pottery. The Brazilians have also known about it for a very long time, despite its confusion with leprosy, and it is rightly feared. Various mining and logging companies have forbidden their employees, on pain of dismissal, from ever entering the forest at night lest they should be infected. Other Brazilians, such as the squatters near camp carving out an existence for themselves along the new road, could not be so wisely cautious for they lived virtually within the forest. Consequently the disease became part of their lives as much as malaria, as much as the forest itself. Local *fazendeiros*, commuting back and forth to their other ranches in the east, could catch it. However, they could have it cured, having both the means and the opportunity to suffer the 14 injec-

The pharmacy is often the busiest store in town, or seemingly the only store in town. Self-medication is an inevitable response to a lack of doctors in such difficult areas.

tions spread over two weeks. Others along the road were generally less fortunate, and the camp's medical log records the visits of those who came to be cured by the British expedition. The most memorable was a small girl who wandered in and out of the various huts in a listless manner, always ready for someone to stop work and talk to her.

The medical unpleasantness of being a poor man in a remote area must have greatly hindered the opening up of Central Brazil. Admittedly hypochondria is widespread in the country, but it is replaced by a more genuine and entirely reasonable fear when money is absent, when doctors are non-existent and when diseases are easily caught. John Gunther wrote, when the population was smaller but the story was as true as it is today, that 79 million out of 80 million Brazilians are doctors. In the Mato Grosso the people might wish to be doctors with equal fervour, or probably more so as the diseases are more prevalent, but problems of distance and money are far more acute. The smallest towns each have a busy *drogaria*, and often it is far and away the most active establishment; but that is of little use when your fazenda of two huts, one horse and ten cows is 300 miles away from that attractive battery of medications.

The expedition doctors were frequently alarmed by the extent of local self-medication. Either a man was desperately in need of, for example, antimonials for leishmaniasis or chloroquine for malaria, or he was pouring medicine into himself guided by the principle that the more the merrier. The system of polypharmacy, said one man, was plainly an attempt to compensate for diagnostic short-comings, probably of the patient by the patient. Therefore fever, or even the suspicion of fever, was routinely and collectively treated with an antimalarial, an antibiotic and an antipyretic, and often a steroid was added for good measure. Such a sledge-hammer technique could make the vital drugs less effective when the real need for them arose. One 'tonic' contained mainly B-group vitamins but possessed chloramphenicol as well, a drug of enormous consequence at the proper time. Not all of Brazil's 79 million doctors know what they are about, but the drug shops make a fair trade whether the medication is valid or otherwise. Another generalization is that the hypodermic is warmly thought of as the most important discovery of medical science: pills, tablets, tonics, ointments, salves, lotions and potions are good, but injections are always better.

Doctors in the Xingú

An example of all this occurred one day when David Philcox, botanist, returned to camp having been told of a man down the road with a burned stomach that 'looked horrible'. John Guillebaud visited the man, confirmed the horrible part of the story, but realized that the abdominal area was burning and painful rather than burned. With difficulty he diagnosed *Herpes zoster*, but he understood his diagnostic difficulty when he subsequently learned of the self-medication being applied for shingles. The man's grandmother's advice had been cow-dung and milk over the aggravated area. The man's own extras, given frequently and intravenously, were streptomycin (which he apparently took for most complaints) and chloramphenicol (which he believed to be some kind of masterstroke). The shingles was responding to this joint treatment only with the pain of fire. John dismissed all the earlier medication and recommended both a bath and some simple analgesic but he had every doubt, as he left the place, that such unexciting advice would be taken. Presumably any doctor actually intending to practise in the area should work first in the local druggist's in order to discover what, apart from the disease, might be complicating the issue. Hypochondriasis is one thing and folk medicine is another, but polypharmacy making use of some extremely modern and potent drugs can be a yet more crucial factor and needs to be taken into account.

What also needs to be understood, and could have enormous consequences, is the kind of pharmacy that has been employed in the region long, long before the arrival of chloramphenicol and the like. The knowledge collected as part of their culture by the various Indian tribes is as mortal as the Indians themselves. Many of today's vital drugs, such as cocaine, digitalis and ergot, had their origins back in a herbal past and much information must have been lost as various communities were emancipated into the world at large. Sir William Osler wrote that 'the desire to take medicine is perhaps the greatest feature which distinguishes man from animals' and Amer-Indian man is no exception to this general rule. Anthropologists and others have continuously brought back stories not just of medication but of highly successful medication.

Unfortunately such research is complicated. Firstly the Indians have to produce a sample of a particular concoction. They have to say what plant or tree they got it from, then produce a portion of it for identification, and finally describe what they do with it to make the potion. After all a substance can be dramatically changed even by such an elementary process as boiling and squeezing, as with the removal of prussic acid from the untreated manioc (and one wonders how on earth that vital process was discovered). The value or effectiveness of the substance then has to be described or, better still, demonstrated, preferably on more than one patient.

Clouding all such experimentation would be the eternal presence of the medicine man. Not only does he—probably—implicitly believe in his powers but his community, yet more certainly, believes in him and the spirits at his command. Therefore it is necessary

Lip discs make men prefer pipes to cigarettes. Txukuhamae women have no discs but follow suit. ▷

to find out whether the medicine is effective because he says it is, and they believe it is, or whether it has inherent properties that would be equally efficacious in the clinical environment of the double-blind trial where neither doctor nor patients know—until later—which patients have received the drug. Finally, when some bark of a tree has been treated in a particular manner, and then administered in a particular manner to someone suffering from a definite complaint, and when that substance has been proved valuable in alleviating that complaint, there still remains the problem of identifying and isolating its vital ingredient. Ergot had a history well over a century ago of being used in pregnancy to stop undue bleeding after a woman had been delivered of her child. Its fame in this connection had probably reached back even earlier in history, and long before the medical profession started to make use of it, but it was not until 1906 that ergotoxine—itself still a mixture—was isolated and another thirty years before ergometrine was finally extracted to be such a vital obstetric tool in modern medicine. Hearing an Indian tell of a medicine is one thing; extracting the crucial chemical is quite another.

Nevertheless it is vital to talk to the Indian and to hear his story before it is too late either because he himself no longer knows the facts, or will not give them, or is no longer around to give them. Bob Mills spent less than a couple of months in the Park, but totally filled his time taking blood samples, hunting with the Indians, testing revolvers with Claudio, treating the sick, visiting as many of the villages as he could and, somewhere along this hectic line, collecting information about local medicaments, their origins and their uses. The list below is a selection of those substances he brought back to England which are now being analysed. Some were only for the pajés, the medicine men/spirit healers, and some were for their patients, but within this list there may be one or more holding a vital key to some all-important drug of the future.

Mémat   (Txikão tribe)
Drunk as a beverage. No specific medicinal use. (Leaves of plant)

Kuhítse   (Kuikuru)
Red resin, dissolved in water and used as aphrodisiac. (? efficacy)

Tolotutu or Nõntutu   (Kuikuru—but widely used by Xinguano tribes and known under a variety of names)
There is little doubt that this works as an oral contraceptive, at least as judged from the general confidence expressed by several tribes. It appears to inhibit ovulation just as long as the unappetizing brew is being regularly inbibed. (Bark from a small tree)

◁   Ryania mansoana, *alias* Mata collado *(the silent killer), is lethal if the fumes are inhaled when it is burnt. But much Indian knowledge of plants is likely to die out with them.*

183

Puyalú   (Yawalapiti)
Beverage drunk by initiates in seclusion 'to make them strong'. (Small shrub)

Kalalatiri   (Yawalapiti)
Toxic beverage which is drunk and immediately vomited, otherwise convulsions, coma and death result. Drunk by pajés to demonstrate their powers over death. It is one of the aspects of a healing ritual for the healer to be near to death and so commune with the spirits responsible for disease. (Whole trunk of small tree). (Toxins drunk by pajés in the past have caused quite considerable mortality. Attempts to curtail this by the Villas Boas have been unsuccessful.)

Kumairuqú   (Yawalapiti)
An ointment for babies applied to head and face. (Prophylactic). (Small plant)

Makukawá-Inuhri   (Yawalapiti)
Used as eyedrops for extra lucid vision. (Small whole plant.) (Other eyedrops are used by the Txikão to cleanse the eyes after a death has occurred. The use of these is much dreaded as the application is an irritant and produces severe conjunctivitis.)

Katepũ-Eglũ   (Txikão)
Used as beverage, but mainly as tattooing juice. Applied to the skin and pricked in with needles of the 'dogfish'—*peixo-cachorra*. The sap oxidizes to a navy-blue colour, and remains so under the skin. (Sap of the Jatobá tree)

Inát   (Txikão)
Widely-used fish poison. Most effective. Modest concentrations preferred. The fish then swim slowly near the surface and are easily shot with bow and arrow. If heavily poisoned fish are eaten, stupor results. (Timbó plant)

Upuyá   (Txikão)
Efficacious beverage against diarrhoea. (Plant leaf.) (I personally used it to good effect against Hookworm diarrhoea.)

Noto   (Txikão)
Another very effective remedial in diarrhoea. (Small creeper)

Airi   (Yawalapiti)
Cigar smoked by the pajé during all healing rituals. Very strong and containing more than tobacco. Seems to be outer leaf (? narcotic), binding tobacco, and also strands of another plant. (?)

Urucu   (used by all tribes except those with a northern origin)
Apart from its more obvious decorative qualities and fine scent, it is the most effective insect repellent I know. (Urucu plant)

When Bob Mills returned eventually to the English house at Xavantina, that transit establishment used by all the expedition members in their trips up and down the line, a group of us were to meet him on our way north. A major blessing of Xavantina was the excellence of the Rio das Mortes, both to look at and to bathe in. One day, as the rest of us swam or sat in the shallows of that water, we were all enormously impressed by the fearful sight of Bob Mills. Somehow the effulgence of his beard made him seem even thinner, but it was his scars, his sores and general suppuration that most intrigued us. Every mosquito/pium/tick bite seemed to have gone septic, and cautiously each one of us moved upstream of him.

He also seemed weak, and not unreasonably, for later on I was to read his diary and begin to understand how any doctor visiting such an area, even for a period no longer than eight weeks, is liable to transfer some of the complaints of others to his own body. Oddly—on reflection—he did not mention any of the external signs, having picked up even more internally than we realized that day as the rest of us finished the swim and made doubly certain it was our towels we were using to rub ourselves. His diary abruptly changes from a record of Indian complaints to laconic comments upon his own.

June 17 and 18
Kurikuru baby bleeding to death from umbilical cord stump. No room to tie the cord. It is the custom in these tribes to cut the cord flush with the abdominal wall. The baby had not fed since birth and I put it on a drip. It survived and returned in two weeks to Kurikuru.

July 6
Arrived Matipu, and left for Kalapaló village with Kalakumãn. Travelled naked and found it very relaxing. Used urucu to ward off flies. Usual problems at Kalapaló—'Têm muito doença aqui'. Started to deal with 'much sickness'.

July 10
Examined Marica—70-year-old Kamayurá elder. A very interesting old man, who had been a prisoner of the Suiá in his youth. He made me some arrows used for warfare in the old days. He had a squamous cell carcinoma of the penis. (Confirmed by histology in São Paulo and London.) First recorded case of cancer in the Parque.

July 16
Research and talk with Orlando and Claudio. Sutured a leg tendon on a cockerel belonging to the Yawalapiti. Made reasonable recovery—for a cockerel.

July 22
Returned to Posto Leonardo, and was sorting and staining the Waurá blood when a group of Txikão arrived carrying a young girl, saying that she was very ill. This was interesting, because they must have been very worried about her to bring her to P.L. Sick persons were normally left in their hammocks for quite a while before anything so drastic was done. Her name was Kolé, she was 11–12 years old, and allegedly somewhat retarded. I asked 'Ono-gómó?'—'What is your name?' She replied very quietly, 'Kolé' and that was the last word she ever spoke. I examined her and took blood specimens, which showed large quantities of meningococcal organisms, and not primarily malarial parasites, as I had expected.

By this time she was unrousable. Intra-venous and intra-muscular antibiotics were given as well as antimalarials and supportive measures. Her pulse was very fast (140/min) and blood pressure low (75–80 systolic), and she had a mild pyrexia. Lumbar puncture was performed, a purulent sample was obtained and antibiotics were introduced at the same time. Stained smears of the CSF showed large concentrations of meningococci. No sulphona-mides were available, and these are the most effective drugs in this disease, due to their high potency against meningococci, and high concentration in the CSF. No penicillin G was available either. Other penicillins and chloramphenicol had to be used, as well as tetra-cycline and antimalarials. About 4 p.m. she developed respiratory difficulties, and it was necessary to do a tracheostomy.

At this stage Claudio came in with the sister and brother-in-law of the girl. The Indians were weeping and Claudio was particularly upset, as the Txikão are very dear to his heart and there are only 53 left. He fears that if too many deaths occur they will want to leave the Parque. I stress the necessity of having sulphonamides as drug of first choice. He radios São Paulo to put some on the next FAB plane. Three Txikão pajés request to see the girl. All agree that she would not survive, and in fact consider her dead and want the body for burial while technically still alive. I refuse! By this time all the Txikão bar a few were outside repeatedly chanting and wailing 'You-dirty-Txikão-you'—this would apparently be their reaction to dangerous, communicable disease, coupled with wanting to bury the sufferer before death, and get the source of infection out of the way.

The object of the tracheostomy was explained to them and the pajés seemed very interested. I performed the operation about 6 p.m., using basic equipment and a sterilized piece of rubber tube from the place. Respiration was much less laboured following a large quantity of mucus and blood through the tube. A steam kettle and sterile maintenance procedure was set up on a rota system. Catheter passed. Intra-ven. inf. set up.

July 23
Respiratory state improved, but cerebral state worse. Bladder washed out. Passing very little urine. All Txikão very depressed, and can't understand why I will not let them have the body for burial.

July 24
Hoping to get the next plane back to Xavantina. FAB willing. Most of the day spent between listening for reports of the plane leaving Rio, attending to Kolé, and packing for a rapid exit. Can hold very little hope of Kolé recovering consciousness. Virtually anuric, and respiration becoming worse; clinically has pulmonary oedema.

July 25
1 a.m. Kolé died and was rapidly buried with very little ceremony inside the hut, wrapped in a blanket inside her hammock. Hole about 6 feet deep was dug by two men *inside* the long house, thus differing from other tribes. Ritual cleansing of everybody, their possessions and their food started from now on. Chanting to continue for ten days according to tradition.

The Snowy Egret Leucophoyx thula. OVERLEAF TOP *(left to right)*: *Rufous-tailed Jacamar* Galbula ruficauda; *Pileated Finch* Coryphospingus pileatus; *Red-headed Manakin* Pipra rubrocapilla; *Stripe-necked Tody-tyrant* Idioptilon striaticolle. CENTRE *(left to right)*: *Swallow-Tanager* Tersina viridis; *Buff-throated Woodcreeper* Xiphorhynchus guttatus; *Rusty-margined Flycatcher* Myiozetetes cayanensis; *Pygmy Kingfisher* Chloroceryle aenea. BOTTOM *(left to right)*: *Rufous-collared Sparrow* Zonotrichia capensis; *Blue Dacnis* Dacnis cayana; *Flame-crowned Manakin* Heterocercus linteatus; *White-eared Puffbird* Nystalus chacuru.

July 26

Up extra early waiting for the plane as there is nothing to hold me at the Posto now. Saw Pabru (Txikão chief) instilling eyedrops into eyes of all tribe members, to purify the eyes, presumably after seeing the disease.

July 27

Up all night with generalized body pains, rigors and diarrhoea. What a time to get it! Blood positive for Plasmodium (falciparum)—but I had been taking weekly Darachlor, which contains Daraprim and Pyrimethamine. It seems that a twice-weekly dose is necessary in this area to maintain adequate blood levels. Paludrine was not available when I left base camp. Treated self, felt very unwell for some days.

Heard plane had left Cachimbo, said hurried farewells to all at Posto, promised to send *Shooter's Bible* to Claudio. No hitches getting on to plane.

July 28

Resting up in Casa Inglesa, and diarrhoea slightly better. Stools later positive for Hookworm (*Necator americanus*), and this turned out to be very resistant to treatment (Alcopar).

July 29–August 2

Usual existence in Xavantina.

August 2

Some expedition members arrived, and joined them on trip up to camp.

One infection which Bob Mills did not have, and which was rightly feared by all of us, was Chagas' disease. Various insects have been suspected of being its vector, notably the tritoma or assassin bug, and in particular *Rhodnius prolixus*, but the method is always the same. Instead of injecting the parasite along with its saliva, which is the method exploited by the mosquitoes and many others, this vector deposits the parasites along with its faeces. Apparently the act of engorging itself with blood stimulates the process of defaecation. As the bug is about half an inch long the faeces are therefore deposited quite a way from the point at which the proboscis has punctured the skin, and the victim is safe unless he assists the parasite to gain access. This he does, as like as not, in being irritated by the bite, by scratching it and therefore by helpfully spreading the faeces over the punctured area.

It has been suggested that Charles Darwin picked up Chagas' disease during his time in Latin America. It was this, allegedly, more than hypochondria or any other complaint that caused his health to be so poor, even though he lived to a determined old age. Most victims of the disease are nothing like so fortunate and it is responsible for a large number of deaths.

No one ever found a suspected vector at the expedition's camp although one or two of the employees were sometimes suspected of having the disease, but to a minor degree.

◁ *Birds, like this tanager, were caught, measured, then released. Mammals, like the maned wolf, were more intractable.*

Indians in the Park said they were aware of the insect and its unpleasant bite, and therefore the expedition was in potential danger from this disease. Its greatest hazard, so far as many were concerned who expect such things as parasitic illnesses to be directly curable, is that there is no known remedy or treatment for Chagas' disease. It was fortunate that no one contracted it, not even the heavily bitten, well-scarred and festering Bob Mills. It was also good that the red dust, which always covered everything on the back of the lorry, soon turned him a decent pink overall like the rest of us.

All the medical members of the expedition, whether they were pushing research further ahead as with the problem of leishmaniasis, or pursuing the normal mixture of activities expected of a medical round in a rural setting, helped by their work to emphasize the overwhelming lack of general practice in the area. The camp's *Casa médica* must have been the best equipped surgery for hundreds of miles on either side. Even Aragarças hospital, suddenly in need of morphine to help in the amputation of a nurse's leg following a road accident, had to send a vehicle to base camp for this essential drug, thus involving a round trip of 500 difficult miles. It was excellent that so many of the local inhabitants dropped in to have themselves cured not just because they left fitter than they had arrived but because our helpfulness on this score made them all so helpful on countless other scores. Needless to say they were never charged but they often brought gifts for the camp larder, such as eggs and fruit, both of which had a value higher than rubies when supplies had been short for a lengthy period and the qualities of rice, beans and pale tinned meat were beginning to flag even as topics for ribald conversation.

To invade the Mato Grosso, whether as settler, employee or semi-itinerant squatter, had its complications. These were inevitably exacerbated by the medical hazards of this tropical environment, rich in disease and a long expensive way from professional care. To live for a time in the Mato Grosso, even with a well-equipped dispensary to hand, was also not without its difficulties. Even two of the medical members of the expedition were to suffer later on from the unpleasant rigours of malaria. Tick and other bites could readily become septic, and the ticks could choose the very worst of masculine places to implant themselves. Once a man fell and some sharp sedge grass cut at his good eye with potentially fraught possibilities. Once another man let a screwdriver fall and thereby chopped off two joints from his fingers; it had fallen on to the starter motor, connected electrical leads, started the engine, and the whirring fan blades then cut his fingers. Accidents can of course happen anywhere, and they need not be of great consequence if near-immediate assistance and the right medical aids are to hand. For a man on his own, with only his family to hand, plus a few cows and a couple of huts, they must be just as great a fear as the general concern over disease. 'What is your greatest need?' we had once asked some isolated men. 'Good health' they had said.

6 MAMMALS, BIRDS, FISH AND PLANTS

The large animals of Africa have fascinated so many visitors to that continent for so long, and have been so well documented and photographed, that anyone visiting South America for the first time is likely to look in vain for similarly large herds. On failing to see them he is then liable to wonder why South America should be so different, why it has no large herbivores (filling the role of the elephant), why it has no major groups (such as all those African grazers), and why a man can walk all day in some undeveloped zone without seeing or even hearing a single mammal. To walk in many parts of Africa even today is to offer opportunities to buffalo, lion, rhinoceros or crocodile. To walk in the forests of South America is perhaps to see the footprints of a jaguar, but to be far more likely to fall foul of vicious vegetation than any predator.

It is probably more reasonable to wonder why Africa has such an abundance of plains game, and therefore an attendant abundance of meat-eaters, than to expect that every other continent should be in step with this prime example. There used to exist large numbers of, for example, guanaco on the pampas of South America but its forests have never housed great numbers of large and readily visible animals. (Nor indeed have the forests of the Congo.) The continent does have a narrow strip linking it to North America, but it is virtually isolated. Also its major rivers must act, and must have acted, as further geographical barriers, and the great abundance of these large rivers must have limited the spread and diversification of all those species unable to cross them.

Moreover, these days, South America has an exceptionally poor record of animal conservation. Wherever there is development, there is a speedy removal of all saleable fur, skins, claws, and the like. Once at São Félix a party from camp encountered a jaguar hunter. He catered for tourists who wished to add at least one jaguar to their global bag and who had to have an animal more or less guaranteed for them. The hunter used to be certain of finding one not too far from the Araguaia river and also not too far from the location of the British base camp, but in the past few years the Araguaia has lost virtually all its jaguars, and the American trophy collectors are now being taken to the Xingú river, near where it crosses latitude 6°S. Soon the process of calling up jaguars, by pulling a waxy thread inside a gourd and thereby making a snarl of a noise that creates an irresistible curiosity in the animal, will no longer be successful even at that distant spot.

The major groups of South American mammals tend to contain small forms and they are therefore less conspicuous, particularly in that Mato Grosso setting either of cerrado or of forest. There are 46 genera of rodents, mainly small but including the largest rodent of them all, the capybara: *Hydrochoerus*. (It has been said that capybaras have difficulty in defaecating out of water. The tame capybara kept at camp for almost a year had no difficulty whatsoever, and the stream was about the only place kept free from his excrement.) There are 52 genera of bats, eight of marsupials and eleven of edentates. These last two are relic fauna, remains of far more extensive groups. The marsupials have dominated in Australasia, whereas the placentals are the mammal group to have dominated everywhere else, but in South America the marsupials exist side by side with placentals, although to a lesser extent. In Brazil there is in fact only one marsupial family, the Didelphidae, and this contains 12 genera.

The Mato Grosso expedition had experience of a good many types of mammal in that it saw, caught or even kept quite a few of them. Fleetingly it saw deer (Capridae), before they shot off into the forest. It saw tapir (Tapiridae), but only in the vicinity of rivers. It caught a maned wolf (Canidae), and this beautiful long-legged animal lived briefly before being mercifully shot. It saw various forms of large cat (Felidae) that had been caught by the road gangs both as extra meat and for their skins. It occasionally saw primates, such as capuchin monkeys, particularly if there was a Brazilian around who was good at calling them up. It saw the distinctively pointed tracks of the agouti in almost every muddy spot, but only very rarely did it see the animal making them. Occasionally, a tayra, *Eira barbara*, a large form of marten, climbed quickly up a tree to have a look and then, not liking what it saw, would noisily disappear.

Among the edentates several armadillos, anteaters and sloths lived for a while in camp. The sloths (three-toed: *Bradypus tridactylus*) climbed straight up into the wooden framework of the roof or else moved remarkably swiftly over the ground. The armadillos proved their extreme ability at burrowing, even when as many hands as possible were hanging restrainingly on to their tails. Just once we saw the very rare giant otter, *Pteroneura brasiliensis*, as it scrambled up a bank with its family. And so it should scramble for this largest of the world's otters has been violently hunted and is already extinct in many areas.

The camp trapping programme, with a variety of live and snap traps, collected 676 mammals, representing about 33 genera and some 36–40 species. (These last figures will undoubtedly change as the skins are examined more closely in laboratories with all the comparative material more conveniently to hand.) Throughout the year in which

A captured sloth, Bradypus tridactylus, *lived for a while among the beams of the long hut.* ▷

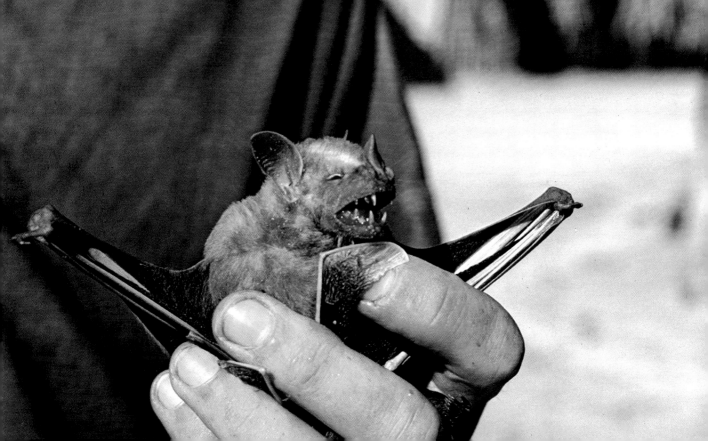

trapping was regularly carried out the capture rate was not noticeably high, with about one per cent of those traps being successful.

There were two other more pointed indications that the traps were not collecting all that they might have done. Firstly, the actual and peculiar habitat of base camp itself, with its huts and food stores, produced over 40 rodents. The majority of these were Oryzomine species which were never caught elsewhere. Secondly, the soil pits, mere holes in the ground dug by the soil scientists for quite another purpose, vied with the traps in their ability to catch animals. In all some 30 mammals were found to have fallen into the pits, and of these a total of eight belonged to three genera that were never trapped, *Cavia*, *Scapteromys* and *Lutreolina*. If traps are not catching an animal it is only too easy to say that the animal must be rare or non-existent in the area. The soil pits, by effortlessly ensnaring quite a different variety of creatures, helped to give the lie to any such erroneous thinking.

One member of the expedition, Ruth Jackson, was exceptionally diligent in trying to keep animals alive that had been taken from the traps—or the pits. Marsupials were far harder to keep than the rodents, but two species of *Marmosa* did at least eat. The other marsupials always failed to do so, but these two were given an incredibly complex diet including cooked rice, egg, milk, raw meat, banana, paw paw (*mamão*), houseflies, flying ants, termites, and moths. On this assorted ration one of them stayed alive for three months, having been caught when extremely young. For the rodents a simpler diet of raw maize, or rice, egg and milk was sufficient. Two—both *Proechimys*—even gave birth in captivity, although one ate its young after a few days. The fact that so many rodents survived so well on such a basic diet does not mean that they disdained other food. From time to time they were given, and ate, insects such as honey bees and cicadas, and countless fruits such as those from Buriti palm, lianas, and various species of Rubiaceae and Myrtaceae.

For a time, and during Ron Pine's presence at base camp, all the emphasis was on bats. He caught them mainly with mist nets, strong enough so that the bats could not easily bite through them and suspended so that the animals would readily fly into them. They proved to be much more diverse than, for example, the rodents. Out of the 120 caught in the nets or shot there were 26 species from 18 genera. The most commonly represented species were *Artibius* and *Molossus*, but there were some surprises. For example, there were no specimens of *Desmodus*, a vampire normally very common in collections from Brazil. Conversely eleven specimens of two species were caught that had only previously been recorded from Trinidad and Panama.

According to the Brazilian statistics there are about 20,000 snake-bites every year on human beings in that country and about 5,000 prove to be fatal. It is easy to suspect

◁ *Monkey sightings were usually rare and fleeting affairs among the tree tops. Bats were also never numerous, even though there was a large variety of genera and species in the area.*

Keeping animals alive at the base camp was forever a problem. As always it was easiest if the animals were caught young and when most adaptable to new conditions.

these figures, particularly when they are viewed from the Mato Grosso where statistics of all kinds are treated casually, but undoubtedly a lot of people do most genuinely die from snake-bite. Fortunately no one in camp was ever bitten, even though one man was struck at—the strike hit his boot—and others wondered why they had not been when they suddenly saw the snake. Of the 200 species of Brazilian snakes only 16 can be dangerous and they all belong to the Crotalidae, save for the infamous Coral snake which is a Colubrid. The best known biters are the Jararaca (a *Bothrops*), discovered at base camp almost the very day that the expedition moved in, the Jararacuçu (another *Bothrops*), the Cascavel (a *Crotalus*), and the Coral (a *Micrurus*).

Many more Coral snakes were thought to be seen, and backed away from, than was actually the case, owing to their striking resemblance to the false Corals. These other snakes have no fangs, a broader head, larger eyes and a longer tail which is not held upright when the snake is moving, but such considerations tended to be disregarded when a snake with all the bright and variegated colouring of the true coral, and of the same size, was in the vicinity. In either case the Brazilians killed the animal. They even killed snakes that ate other snakes, so deep was their habit of killing anything and snakes in particular.

This enthusiasm for killing was not necessarily logical or relevant, in that the animal victim was either harmful or good to eat, but it was virtually universal. If a giant anteater, rare, beautiful and totally harmless, happened to cross the road—as it did on occasion—the vehicle would skid to a halt with an equally rare alacrity, and its Brazilian contingent would pour out in pursuit. Normally this animal shuffles about on its big claws with a meandering simplicity, but it can move faster and particularly when

Among the successful inmates were an anteater FAR LEFT, *a tapir (with Ruth Jackson) and an armadillo* RIGHT, *all three of which were uncommon sights in the difficult environment of the Mato Grosso.*

pursued by a whooping crowd of people collecting weapons as they run. Eventually, a mile or more from the road, they would catch up with it, club at it and continue the clubbing long after it is dead. Still whooping they then return to carry on with the journey so intemperately interrupted by the giant anteater.

Hilary Fry, ornithologist, spent eight weeks at base camp. His arrival and his presence were greatly welcomed, because the profusion of birds had caused other scientists to spend long hours either arguing over their nomenclature or thumbing through the books. An idea of the profusion, and of Hilary Fry's energy, emerges from his report for he netted 940 birds of 161 species and recorded 102 more species by observation alone. (Any British ornithologist who has, after a life-time of bird-watching in the British Isles, observed this total of 263 species has done extraordinarily well. The species-rich avian world of the Mato Grosso is more rewarding—and more exhausting.) He was still recording birds new to his list almost every day even at the end of his stay and therefore he concluded that he could have listed a total of 400 species had he worked in the vicinity of base camp for a full year. For a comparison he had worked for such a period in an area of comparable size and location in Africa and had only amassed 266 species, including 26 migrants from the temperate zone. Brazil's endemic avifauna is indeed rich.

The greatest number of bird species occurring exclusively in one habitat zone was 60—in the cerrado. The gallery forest contained only 33 species not found anywhere else, the dry forest only 25, the cerradão only five, and the campo only five. Strangely the thickets bordering either side of the Suiá Missú river contained ten species not seen anywhere else, thus suggesting a most distinctive extra habitat.

199

Lizards, so common in many warm countries, were infrequently seen near base camp and caught only very rarely. ABOVE Tupinambis teguixin, *killed during capture.*

There was not always a ready explanation why one species should choose a particular habitat, or even two habitats, without invading a third. Fry wrote that:

'I would venture to suggest the most potent single factor [in choice of habitat] is in fact psychological, that an individual bird remains within the bounds of a particular habitat because it feels ill-at-ease out of it . . . A similar view was expressed by Moreau: "We may regard the invocation of subjective factors as a suspicious expedient to be used as sparingly as possible; as a last resort of ignorance; as a confession of despair; but so much appears to be explicable by no factors other than the subjective that we are forced to postulate their existence."'

Along the rivers and the streams inside the gallery forests all five of South America's kingfishers were either seen or netted. Apart from the large *Ceryle torquatus*, the other four all belong to the *Chloroceryle* family. These four do have minor habitat differences but their co-existence in the same general area is probably dependent upon the fact that they prey upon different kinds of fish. *C. aenea* weighs about 13 grams (i.e. half-an-ounce), *C. americana* weighs about twice as much, *C. inda* weighs four times as much, and *C. amazona* almost eight times as much. Their beak sizes are in the proportions 1 to 1·5 to 2 to 2·5 respectively, and presumably the fish caught are also in the same respective sizes.

Having spent a good deal of time in Africa, and having spent much of that time studying its bee-eaters, Hilary Fry found himself studying quite a different and unrelated

Still alive, but no more commonly observed, South America's famous Boa constrictor. *This specimen was over 5 feet long but would grow at least twice, perhaps three times, this size.*

group of birds in Brazil, the jacamars, that had marked similarities to the African bee-eaters. Convergence between unrelated groups, particularly when they are separated by an ocean, is always intriguing and the parallel similarities between these two kinds of birds existed to a marked degree. So he compared them both, the Piciformes: Galbulidae of the New World and the Coraciiformes: Meropidae of the Old, and he wrote about them:

'Both comprise small bright-plumaged birds, with long pointed beaks and very short legs. The sexes are similar in plumage, which is chiefly green, with a tendency to buff underparts and to contrast between throat and chest. They hunt for flying insects from elevated vantage points, chiefly in forest (jacamars) and savannah (bee-eaters). Neither family has much ecological variation; there are sixteen species of jacamar in five genera, and 24 species of bee-eaters in three genera.

'The degree of convergence, as shown by the representative jacamar *Galbula ruficauda* and bee-eater *Merops bulocki*, is probably the result of their diets being practically identical, for what a bird eats and the way it obtains its food exert a profound effect not only on beak morphology but on many other characters of plumage, behaviour and breeding biology.

'The food of the two families is virtually identical, and the question arises to what extent other resemblances are consequent or are coincidental. The matter is largely speculative. Their long pointed inflexible beaks are adapted to capturing flying insects which sting. Bee-eaters devenom their prey by means of an innate pattern of behaviour, but no analogous behaviour in jacamars has yet been observed. In common with other birds preying on dispersed flying insects (such as swifts, swallows), jacamars and bee-eaters nest in holes,

Hilary Fry, here taking a Red-eyed Vireo from a mist net, caught 940 birds of 161 species by this fashion and recorded another 102 species, all within 8 weeks.

although why they should excavate earth tunnels with terminal egg-chambers rather than utilize cavities in trees or rocks is not apparent. Possibly the habit has evolved because of a scarcity of natural cavities, a predilection for waterside situations (where prey is abundant?) providing suitable cliffs, and a beak fitted for excavation. Clutch size, incubation and fledging periods are the same, probably a result of the availability and quality of food at various times during breeding, which is about the beginning of the local wet season.'

For the main part all the collectors, whether of fish, mammal, plant or bird, were almost always extending the range of those species among their collections that were not new to science. Naturally enough, most of Brazil's fauna and flora had been collected from its more developed areas and there had never before been such intensive collection from the base camp area. As this was on the convenient border-line between forest and cerrado, a frontier that must have oscillated back and forth from time immemorial following climatic and other changes, the extensions to the range of a particular species tended to be of two main kinds. Either an equatorial or forest form had not been encountered so far south before, or a more southerly species had not been collected beforehand from such a northerly or westerly situation.

Rosemary McConnell worked on fish. As she had previously worked in Guyana she too was eternally interested in the differences between the two places and what parallels could be drawn from the range and behaviour of the specimens she observed. Working in Brazil appeared to be more arduous but the Mato Grosso had more than sufficient compensations.

'I did a lot of fishing at night as experience in Guyana had taught me that was the most productive way to get fish with the limited gear I had with me. Among these South American fishes certain groups (cichlids and most characoids) are active by day and hide away motionless by night, often along the river bank, while others (the many types of catfish and the electric gymnotoids) are nocturnal. By night with a good torch one can bail out the sleeping fishes with a dip net and also take the active nocturnal fishes more easily as these have then emerged from crevices where they hide by day. Their gleaming eyes, red, orange or silvery yellow, catch the torchlight and give their presence away. The many freshwater prawns also have bright gleaming eyes, and the innumerable spiders, some of which used to run on the water surface at night while others lined the river bank with eyes glinting like diamonds, were extremely abundant. Also nightjar eyes were like candles in the torchlight and easily reflected in the dark water.

'I was delighted to find that base camp was right on a complex of streams with pools in them. So I was able to pop in and out, catching and watching fishes at all times of day and night. It was surprising what large fishes appeared in these small streams at night, gymnotids 15 in. long *(Sternopygus* and *Gymnotus)*, long thin fishes, bodies held rigid, sliding backwards and forwards with equal ease (for they use the electric field around the body to sense their environment). We rigged up the tape recorder to pick up their electric signals, which are of a specific frequency, and proved that we had three species in the river near the camp. At night the armoured catfish *Callichthys* (some six inches long) searched among the leaves carpeting the pools for Ephemeropteran nymphs and other food items, always searching like a terrier after a rat. *Callichthys* proved to be a remarkably tough fish that used to climb out of bowls in the lab, live out of water a long time, wriggle across the ground with tail flexures and pelvic fins and even survive a long period in the deep freeze compartment of the fridge. The cichlid *Aequidens* in these stream headwaters were also very tough, withstanding lower oxygen concentrations than most of the other species were able to do. Many of these species have accessory respiratory devices that cope with the low oxygen content of these leaf-decomposing streams and are therefore able to withstand the acid conditions of the headwaters. Several of the nocturnal fishes, and some others such as piranha, made noises, squeaking when caught.

'. . . Of course one was wet through from chest downwards every day and almost every night. I always worked in clothes, a habit developed in Guyana where piranha were bad. Therefore one kept cool while soil scientists were finding it very hot. Sitting on muddy river banks to examine the catch in sopping wet trousers gets clothes into an indescribable state, and wet material splits easily. (My luggage had been reduced to an absolute minimum to allow for the fishing gear.) Sweat bees used to swarm to the damp fish as I was measuring them, mixed with a few stinging feral 'Europa' bees. Biting flies were also very bad near the streams, particularly small midges, with some simulium and mosquitoes.

'One snag about the fish work was the amount of gear one had to carry to catch the fish and preserve them before they went bad, as they do so fast in the tropics. One traipsed through the bush looking like the White Knight. Many of the Brasilieros were very skilful fishermen and enjoyed it very much, but most of them were very noisy in the bush compared with the Amer-Indians I had worked with in Guyana. It was hard work physically as we had to improvize and even set gill nets by swimming (in the absence of any boat) and with circumspection, as I was only too well aware what electric eels and piranha can do. However, the water was clear in many places and one could watch the fish (with polaroid glasses) and assess what was there before disturbing them by trying to catch them.'

In all she collected between 50 and 100 species in her two months in the area. It will be a long time before a more precise total can be achieved, but almost half of the species collected are already believed to be new to science. Certain groups of fishes, notably the characids, will have to go to various experts for more specialized study. She had expected —from her Guyana experience—that she might encounter some 200–300 species, and was particularly surprised to find only about a dozen from the base camp area itself, with its permanent streams in the middle of those arms of gallery forest. However, as compensation, some 50 species were caught from the Rio das Mortes at Xavantina and about 20–30 from the Suiá Missú. Plainly the base camp streams, however permanent, provided a rigorous habitat, due mainly to that lack of oxygen. The commonest cichlid in these streams, *Aequidens*, the characid *Hoploerythrinus* and the armoured catfish *Callichthys* were all tough enough to live out of water for several hours.

No fishes were breeding when she was in Brazil at the end of the rainy season (March–May). The gonads indicated that most species must spawn early in the rains, and the dry season represents a 'physiological winter' when the fishes feed poorly and grow only a little. Therefore the end of the rains was a good time to study the comparative ecology of closely related species and how much they overlap in their food habits. For example, different species of the characid genus *Creatochanes* were often caught together and were therefore, presumably, competing for the same kind of food at the season of maximum population pressure. A curious feature of the tropics is not so much the abundance of species as the co-existence of similar and related species in the same niche at the same time. Are there in fact more niches than would appear to be the case? Or more food? Or greater tolerance between species in a manner that would be unlikely in higher latitudes?

Fishermen of England, accustomed to whole days without reward, would be amazed at the South American abundance and its willingness to be caught. For example, one particular lake was encountered by Rosemary McConnell and three accompanying Brazilians from camp, a lake which had probably never been fished before save— possibly—by the Indians in the past. Within three hours, and with the bait taken almost the moment the hook was thrown in, the catch comprised 41 *Aequidens*, 14 *Hoploerythrinus*, 1 *Hoplias*, 6 *Leporinus*, 3 *Crenicichla*, 2 *Acestrorhynchus* and 1 *Moenkhausia*. Some

TOP ROW *left hand page (left to right)*: Andropogon bicornis *(Gramineae)*; Lafoensia pacari *(Lythraceae)*; Lycopodium eichleri *(Lycopodiaceae)*. MIDDLE ROW: Tibouchina aegopogon *(Melastomataceae)*; Paepalanthus speciosus *(Eriocaulaceae)*. BOTTOM ROW: Cespedesia brasiliana *(Ochnaceae)*; *species unknown (Loasaceae)*. TOP ROW *right hand page*: *left and right* Calliandra longipes *(Mimosoideae)*; *centre* Sarcoglottis *sp (Orchidaceae)*. MIDDLE ROW: Catasetum macrocarpum *(Orchidaceae)*; Caryocar brasiliense *(Caryocaraceae)*. BOTTOM ROW: Xylopia aromatica *(Annonaceae)*; Sterculia striata *(Sterculiaceae)*.

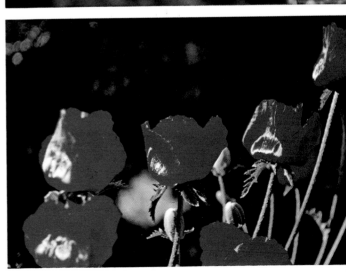

pacu (*Metynnis* or *Myleus*) were seen but not caught and the catch totalled a commendable eleven pounds.

Every new member of the expedition was regaled, particularly when he wandered down to that well-worn spot to bathe in the Rio das Mortes, with tales of the fish that burrowed energetically into any available orifice. Human sphincters contracted as the story was told, for the barbs on these invaders allegedly made their extraction either difficult or impossible. Invasion was bad enough; the thought of permanence added an extra lustre to the story. Rosemary McConnell did catch *candiru*—the Portuguese name —down by the riverside, the relevant fish of the family trichomycteriids (those attracted by urine) of the genus *Vandelia*, but she caught them in a net. They are indeed bottom-dwellers, normally parasitic on the gills of other fishes, and they do have spines on the side of their head, and therefore people were quite correct in standing bolt upright the moment they heard the story rather than continue sitting in that gentle, cooling, refreshing and previously relaxing water of the Rio das Mortes. Perhaps such alacrity paid dividends. Certainly no one suffered physically from the attentions of the candiru, however severe the mental apprehension.

Plant collections were being made throughout the period of the expedition's residence in the Mato Grosso, and there were four separate and major collections. David Philcox amassed 2,000 numbers, Ray Harley 1,500 numbers, Jim Ratter and David Gifford a further 2,000 numbers and George Argent and Paul Richards yet another 1,000 numbers. It should immediately be pointed out that a number is only what it says, and not necessarily a different species. It may look like a new species, and therefore deserve a new number, but it may well turn out to be the same as some earlier number, collected when the plant appeared dissimilar. In short, bearing in mind the likelihood of duplication, and the fact that four different teams were at work, although mainly in different areas and at different seasons, the 6,500 numbers will not represent 6,500 different species. Other smaller collections, some by visiting scientists from Brazil, brought the total up to a formidable collection of 8,000 numbers.

David Philcox reports that:

'From the approximate total of 8,000 collections made, to date about 1,000 have been critically studied and names applied and, of these, certain plants seem to be new to science.

'Before the start of this work it was realized that any collections made from the area would be of value and interest to botanists the world over. Mato Grosso as an area had of course been collected from earlier, but the territory covered by this recent visit was hitherto untouched by botanists, a fact which has been made more obvious since taxonomic studies and naming have been started.

'Another point of even greater interest which is becoming clear is that for the first time we

◁ TOP ROW (*left to right*): *Possibly Connaraceae; Aspidosperma sp. (Apocynaceae);* Helicteres macropetala *(Sterculiaceae).* MIDDLE ROW: Delonix regia *(Caesalpinoideae), originally from Madagascar;* Astrocaryum *(Palmae).* BOTTOM ROW: Spiranthera odoratissima *(Rutaceae);* Kielmeyera *sp. (Theaceae).*

are now able to record a great southwards trend in the distribution of a number of plants previously not recorded from localities further south than the Amazon basin.

Because other institutions wanted specimens, and because Brazil wanted specimens of the British collection to be left behind in Brazil, the botanists collected ten examples of each number. Consequently the collecting, numbering, pressing and drying of ten examples each of 8,000 numbers was an even more formidable undertaking than might at first be supposed. By comparison a botanist in Britain would be unlikely to get 8,000 numbers since only about 1,500 species have ever been collected from the British Isles and only some 1,300 species from any one area, such as an English county.

Will any of these new plants from Brazil have any commercial use? Perhaps, or perhaps not, but the list of useful plants already to have emerged from the New World of the Americas is lengthy. The potato and tobacco (highly useful to some) came back early, but these are only two of a considerable assortment. This includes pineapple, groundnuts, Brazil nuts (these did not, alas, grow in the area of base camp), cashew nuts, quinine, cocaine, rubber, tomatoes, paw paw (*mamão*), cocoa, cassava (manioc), curare (a mixture from several plants), arrowroot, Indian corn (or maize, a major mystery because no wild species has been found anything like it), custard apple, resin guaiacum (medical uses), cascara sagrada, ipecacuanha, and vanilla. Conversely, Brazil's main crop—coffee—came to Brazil from Arabia but originated in Africa.

Most of the botanical discoveries will have to wait until all those numbers, and all those species contained within them, have been properly identified. This may take ten years, perhaps even longer. Other findings, particularly those actually encountered in the field, will take less long to be presented to a wider audience. For example, Ray Harley was fascinated to watch some pollination that was achieved by an elaborate explosive mechanism.

'*Eriope crassipes* is a not uncommon plant of the South and Central Brazilian savannah (known as cerrado), extending its range into Bolivia and possibly Venezuela. It is an erect, sparsely branched herb with spindly stems arising from a stout, woody, digitately lobed root-stock. The flowers, which measure only 6–8 mm. from the base of the corolla to the tip of the upper lip, bear four stamens which, in common with the other members of the Ocimoideae, are deflexed onto the concave lower lip of the corolla. The flower buds, which are suffused with a khaki yellow colour, have a characteristic inflated appearance prior to opening. Opening occurs gradually, but rapidly enough to be easily observed, and the corolla then assumes the untriggered position.

'The pollinating agent is a very small bee, scarcely 6 mm. long. The bee, no doubt in search of nectar, alights on the lower lip. Immediately the lower lip flips back with great rapidity. As it does so, the stamens, on which the tension has suddenly been released, flick up to deposit a mass of pollen on the underside of the bee's abdomen. The pollen, which is of a clear yellow colour, is usually in sufficient quantity to be readily detectable on the bee, even when it is in

◁ *Whether anaconda or constrictor no one could say, as the head had gone, but this large snake had undoubtedly been far larger than any living snake seen during the expedition.*

flight. In most of the examples observed the sudden movement of the lip and stamens was sufficient to disturb the bee which often returned almost at once to visit another flower. Immediately after being triggered, the flower fairly rapidly loses much of its brown coloration to become a lavender blue.

'The stigma during this procedure appears to be unreceptive and remains short and often concealed in the long staminal hairs. After being released, however, the stamens, which initially assume an ascending position begin to deflex until the stigma is no longer concealed by the hairs. It seems likely that in this position the stamens act as an alighting platform for visiting bees and thus allow pollen to be transferred to the stigma. Finally the anthers become completely deflexed, by which time the stigma has elongated considerably, and within a matter of hours the corolla falls.

'Under the conditions prevailing at the time, the flowers normally open between 8 a.m. and 11 a.m., and are triggered off fairly rapidly after opening. In no case actually observed did an untriggered flower remain in this condition, from time of opening, for longer than 60 minutes and usually the time was much shorter. This would explain why very few flowers are recorded in the untriggered position.'

Unfortunately, from the point of view of knowing whether the tropical predilection for burning the countryside so frequently and so determinedly is beneficial to that countryside, no one at base camp had the opportunity to study this phenomenon deeply, but David Philcox points out that herbaceous plants are the principal losers in the struggle for survival. Trees and shrubs have a thick corky bark which is virtually fire-resistant, and so only lose their vegetative parts, but the herbs have to depend on a sturdy root system to store all food and materials necessary for re-growth whenever the aerial part of the plant is lost. It is therefore not surprising that very few annuals were encountered, and the total of annual herb species collected was extremely low when compared with collections from temperate areas.

To stand in the middle of a fire advancing through the cerrado is initially to wonder that anything can survive such a fierce wave of flame. The carpet of leaves and dead material permits the fire to crawl along the ground and, whenever it reaches a dry clump of grass or some other readily combustible commodity, it snarls noisily and burns yet more furiously for the moment. Remarkably the ground and the tree-trunks feel quite cool almost the moment the fire has passed them by. Work in South Africa and elsewhere on that continent has shown that burning grassland temperatures are high but short-lived. Soil temperature at the surface rises, according to wind and the kind of grass, by between $100°C$ and $850°C$ but returns to ambient temperature within a few minutes. Soil temperature 2 cms. below the surface rises, by $14°C$ at most, but sometimes only by $3-4°C$.

Tropical burning has certainly caused concern in many other areas of the world, even though Brazilians in the Mato Grosso appear most casual about its hazards and insist

The three-toed sloth can seem misplaced when hanging from a bough, but it can either walk or appear yet more ▷
hideously deranged when placed upon the ground.

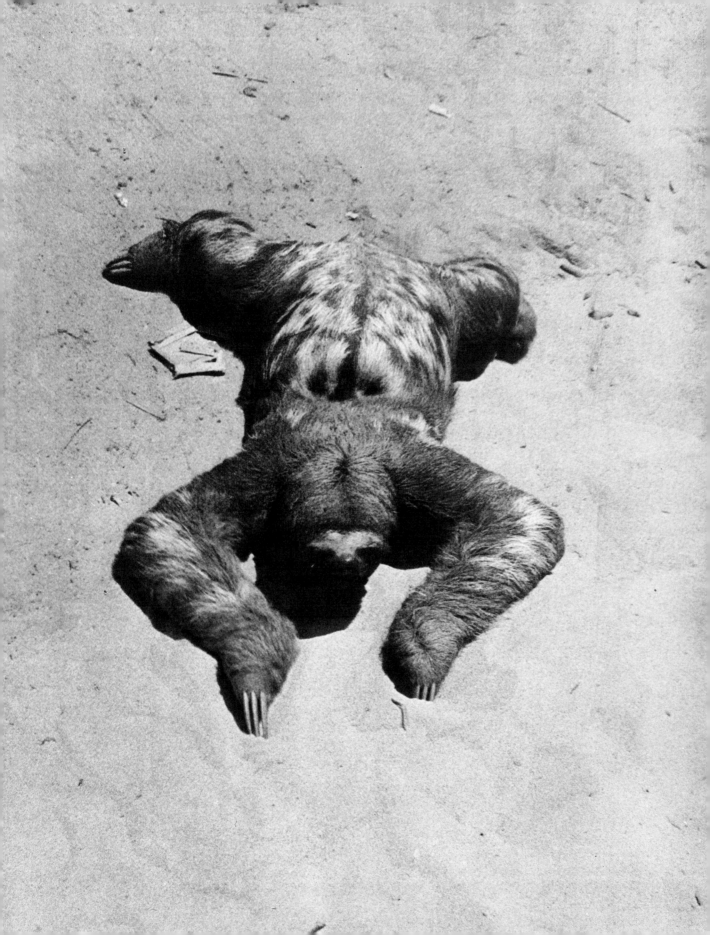

upon its benefits. For example, Duncan M. Porter has written about the same problem elsewhere in Latin America:

'For centuries, agriculture [in Panama] has depended on the slash-and-burn technique, widely used throughout the tropics. Farming and grazing populations throughout the world employ this method, to the detriment of their whole environment. Trees and shrubs are hacked down, allowed to dry, and burned. The resulting ash supplies nutrients for the growth of crops. This release is especially noticeable in the tropics, where the living vegetation ties up most nutrients, and therefore soils are poor. After the natural vegetation is burned, crops are planted in the newly fertile soil. In a few years the fertility of the soil is again depleted, and the farmer moves on further into the forest to repeat the cycle.

'. . . Not only do the fires destroy the vegetation cover, but they do untold damage to the underlying soil as well. Leaf litter and humus are destroyed, and the soils become virtually sterile. Tropical soils are notoriously impoverished, notwithstanding the luxuriant forests that may be growing on them.

Eric Brown, geographer, having had a look at the major fazendas being hacked out of the jungle so near to base camp, was also extremely concerned about the future of the area. 'The know-how,' he said, 'that exists around the world in international agencies and development programmes is not being used in this particular environment, and this to me is tragic.' From the untouched world of base camp, where the scientists moved about with a good understanding of the Garden of Eden in which they were trespassing, along to the big fazendas just down the road was such a short step. The Eden is becoming the fazenda, almost overnight.

David Gifford making field notes, Julio pressing plants, and both in a piece of cerrado to the north-east of the 20-kilometre square.

7 RICH MAN, POOR MAN

God created the world, they say, but the Dutch made Holland. Indeed quite a sizeable fraction of that country today is below sea level, but the total area of Holland is only 13,000 square miles and the fraction of land created by the Dutch is a couple of thousand square miles. It is therefore hard for Europeans to absorb the extent of the land bonanza that Brazil keeps on opening up both with little effort and within her own frontiers. The state of Mato Grosso is almost 400,000 square miles, and the states of Pará and Amazonas are yet greater. Each one is therefore at least some 30 times larger than the whole of Holland, let alone her precious hard-won reclamations from the sea. The enormous size of Brazil's internal empire needs to be absorbed before it can be understood.

The single road from Xavantina to São Félix, exactly 324 miles long, opened up an area far larger than Holland or indeed Britain. It was more like a road from England to the Continent across the North Sea which, by some skilful Dutch contrivance, had suddenly become dry land. Furthermore the road was not the first that the Brazilians had made through virgin country, leaving them with a useful causeway and mile upon mile of brand new land. One way and another the Brazilians had been carving out new areas for themselves ever since the country had begun. Like some rich inheritor, they had always been able to consume capital when the income was inadequate. Only Russians and Canadians must know what it is like to have such a rich carpet of forest as their permanent hinterland, but neither Russia nor Canada possesses the lavish tropical stands of the Brazilian backwoods.

One might therefore expect that the Brazilians have acquired a most positive policy for opening up their precious reserves. After all they have done it before and the supply is not unlimited. They know that land cannot be exploited forever and has to be developed. They know, just as well as any inheritor, that capital is exhaustible but income can be manipulated to proceed forever. Their country needs food, particularly for the north-easterners who suffer such a marginal existence, and the extra lands can supply that want. Their people are multiplying at over three per cent a year, and there is room enough for them in the empty places. Therefore, in an old country with a near-perpetual panacea of new land able to solve so many of its requirements, one might expect the tightest regulations, the greatest determination to use this finest of gifts in the best possible manner.

Instead there is next to nothing of the kind. 'If you want to find out what is going on in Brazil' said an English Foreign Office man in Rio, 'just stay here in Rio.' Unfortunately Rio appears largely uninterested in such obsequies as the right or wrong way to destroy a forest. What has that got to do with the price of apartment blocks? Most of Rio has no idea what is going on in most of the Mato Grosso for the basic reason that most of Rio does not care. If you want to find out what is going on in the new land there is only one thing to do. Go there.

The invasion of this ancient place, and the manner of it, would astonish almost everyone. It would certainly astound the Russians, who are reaching into the resources of Siberia with such planned deliberation. It would also amaze all those earlier American governments that were responsible for such an even distribution of the new lands, as genuine homesteaders arrayed themselves on the border and then set out to claim their 640 acres, their one square mile. The Dutch have organized their new places and know precisely who will farm all the brand new fields long before the polder land has been pumped dry. The new Aswan dam, by its control of irrigation water, caused another two million acres of desert to become valuable and all those new acres were clearly allocated.

Only a third of this planet Earth is land and only a fraction (12 per cent) of this land is suitable for cultivation. Consequently there is a great premium on it. Only a portion of that small fraction is within the tropics, where a rich rainfall can often do much even with a poor soil, and where rain plus warmth plus a really good soil can produce a growth-rate among crops that cannot be equalled elsewhere in the world. The Mato Grosso is tropical. Its rainfall is considerable, at least for half the year, and the soil is variable, sometimes poor, sometimes good. Consequently, to make the point yet again, one would expect a most delicate handling of this most precious possession as more and more of it falls into the hands of the conquerors and there is less and less of it to come.

The actual situation is quite different. In much of the new land one's first finding, as like as not, is the shack of a *porceiro*. Such people are squatters and have either no rights or every right to the land, according to your point of view. Certainly they own no title deeds; in fact they own very little of anything. They probably came either from a more southern part of Mato Grosso state or from North East Brazil, filtering in by way of Goiás, and almost certainly they came because they had been pushed off someone else's land. With an expanding country like Brazil, remorselessly swelling within itself to occupy more of its own volume, it has always been possible for the porceiro to move on, to leave the rantings of one owner and to settle down a good deal farther on where some

Without rights, without money, and with little idea of the future, the squatters moved in. ▷

other owner's presence has not yet made itself felt. The road north from Xavantina, particularly where it cuts through the more southerly section of cerrado, was just such an area as soon as it had been completed. Whether by horse, or by foot, or by lorry (with horse, people and possessions all upright on the back) this quiet invasion happened surreptitiously and steadily. The road looked much the same on each long journey back and forth from camp but, if the huts and shacks on either side were actually noted and counted on these bumpy lurching trips, there were more and more of them each time. They were each entirely unique, but almost identical in their similarity.

Firstly they all have names. If there is one named Agua Boa there are a score because the finding of good water is obviously more important than scratching around for another name. Secondly, within these thatched dark houses, there are always many more people than could ever have seemed possible from the outside. One's eyes gradually accustom themselves to the inhabitants, to the children around the door, then to one's host or hostess offering a seat, then to all the other children in the shadows and finally to the old man in the bed. The floor is earth. The walls are either of earth or of vertical sticks, or a wattle and daub mixture of the two.

Walking permanently through the house, stumbling over the threshold to get in and stumbling again to get out, are the smaller pigs. Inevitably stretching their audacity too far they are inevitably hit/kicked/shooed by someone, and they always hurry off with the same affronted squeak. Chickens, ducks and turkeys would also tread, stumble and stride through the room, and they too expressed similar noises of haughty panic when they had adventured too much. On the beams above there was always a calendar. There was also saddlery of sorts, hard dry leather that felt like wood. There were implements, axes and spades, and lesser things with a hand-made touch to them. Everyone seemed to possess a kind of cheese grater, made by hammering nail points through a sheet of tin, but I never saw one that was either in use or without an un-harmed coating of rust. Sometimes there were orchids, cut from their epiphytic position on the forest trees and then lashed instead on to the beams of the home. Always, however poor the place, there was coffee. The beans do not grow—as yet—in the northern Mato Grosso, and therefore they have to be bought, but how they were bought was always a matter for discussion.

'Do you sell anything from here?'

'No, nada.'

'Do you have money?'

'No. Não têm.'

'How did you buy the coffee?'

'We bought it.'

Nevertheless, however unproductive the discussion, the small thick china cups were

Mary Mason, geographer, set herself the task of finding out who was living along the new road, where they had come from, what they were doing and what they planned to do.

ideal refreshment. It always came from the same kind of fireplace, an earthen thing with a groove along the top in which the wood was placed. On top of this fiery groove was a piece of cast-iron possessing both holes and lids to fill those holes. The enamel coffee pot, itself quite tall and green or brown, stood on the hot iron before being made to pour its strong sweet syrup of coffee into everyone's cup. One would have given next to no money for most of the possessions in all of those rooms, but would happily have bartered a considerable sum for a steady supply of the deep, black liquid. Particularly when the air was hot. And the room was breathless. And there were sick children, perhaps shuffling their fat bodies and thin legs over the floor, or shuffling nowhere and staring vacantly.

Outside there were more animals, more pigs in the shade, more chickens having no difficulty in scratching a living. There were macaws and parrots, either gorgeous in their livery or plucked bare in great patches of pimply nakedness. There were small wooden wigwams where the chickens spent the night. Sometimes, bubbling on their own from the smallest of fires, were flat tureens of winking brew that would eventually become a kind of soap. Unmindful of the smell or the heat, stood a horse or two beneath a tree, so weary in their stance. (There is a famous photograph of Fawcett at a spot he named Dead Horse camp, where his living animals hung their heads in the same doleful manner.)

For crops there was manioc, with its delicate patterning of leaves. There was sugar cane, tall and topped with feathery whiteness, and bananas whose broad leaves are torn so easily by the wind. However vague the collection of crops, which usually sprouted from among the ruins of the trees cut down to make the open space, it was usually dignified by its creators and called a *roça*, the word for a clearing which can become a plantation.

Mary Mason, a geographer of University College, London, was the principal investigator, having determined to make a thesis about the development of this road. Armed with a large notebook and with considerable curiosity she would step through the pigs and the chickens, discover the head of the household, apologize for her intrusion, and then start on her questions with all the diligence of, say, a tax assessor. Is this your wife? Are the children all yours? How much produce do you sell a year? Where (and this one was always doomed) did you get the money to buy this excellent coffee?

They never threw her out on her ear. Indeed they never even objected, or hesitated, or had fear at exposing their means of livelihood. Congratulations, therefore, to her ability for the task was not an easy one. They even answered her unswervingly when they assumed, or confessed afterwards, that they had taken her for a representative of the land's legitimate owner. The status of women in most of the Mato Grosso is traditional, and unadventurous, and therefore her sex made the interviewees doubly amazed, but they answered dutifully and her notebook bulged.

'466 kms. Café do Povo. Squatters. Been here 4 years. Born Cuiabá. Raised in Barra do G. Came here via R. das Mortes and canoe. Has large roça of five hectares. Sells some surplus in São Félix. Wife is Paulista. A daughter-in-law is Japanese. Has 2 partners who share profits. . . . She makes her own bread, delicious. . . . Also produces own cotton which family weaves into hammock lengths. . . . The *vaqueiro* (cow-boy) earns 1 : 4, i.e. one calf for every 4 produced. . . . 472 kms Rio Xavantiana. . . . 476 kms. Squatter just arrived. Born Piaui. Came to M.G. via Maranhão and São Félix. Been in S.F. for 3 years with roça. Widow has ?son to help her, but she extremely sad. . . . Faz. Valparaiso. 'Owner' 14 yrs in Goiás, 5 yrs in M. Grosso, 5 yrs in another place, then 2 here. Always moved on by real owner. 4 hectare roça. 30 head of cattle grazing in cerrado. Sells one when necessary, perhaps for 140 n.cruzeiros. 13 children; 6 grown up. All men have spurs but no shoes. . . . 'Owner' has built rice threshing machine powered by water; beautiful simplicity. . . . Woman has 3 sons at school in Xavantina. She sends food to them. Money for all this? . . . House scrupulously clean. Even a cloth with places for toothbrushes to be hung up. How can the floor look so clean? . . . Crops manioc, maize, bananas, paw paw (wonderful. Got given two). Fat mother has 17 children; cheerfully explains não tem jeito (like old woman who lived in a shoe). . . . Everyone sick; no one would speak to me. . . . Hut proved to be empty. . . . Two crosses by side of road.'

In theory the two strips on either side of a new road are safe for squatters, for those who want to make something of the place but cannot afford any kind of down payment, as it is federal property, designed for later road widening. But the squatter's roça usually extends well away from the road, and here he has no rights. But there are all kinds of deals between owning the land and being thrown off it. The owner, once he has realized which land it is that he does own, may be happy at finding some people conveniently at hand. He can, for example, employ them to put a picada around his new-found possession. Or he can promote them to *moradores*, the caretakers who take care that nothing untoward happens to the land while the owner is making up his mind what to do with it. Failing that, and sometimes better than that, the squatter can become a share-cropper (a *parceiro*, no longer just a porceiro) keeping 50 per cent of the produce for himself, sometimes 90 per cent. Better still, as with Geraldão whose half-way house became that convenient coffee stop for members of the expedition, he can be given a portion of land for some kind of services rendered.

It is not a bad thing, if you happen to own a thousand square miles of land, to have as corner stones a few men happily indebted for ever because of a present of a couple of hundred acres. Such good neighbours can rarely be bought for such a price elsewhere. Nevertheless, be all that as it may, the amount of planning involved in all this by high authority is virtually negligible. Private enterprise, and a little determined pushing in the right quarters, coupled with the power of money, all have greater effect than any wise and careful edicts. Or perhaps the governmental intention is that the strong shall flourish, and so become stronger. To him that hath shall be given. Or, to rephrase the point and as the radio says repeatedly in its own fashion, 'the best thing about capitalism is its capitalists'.

Whereas the meek are not inheriting the earth, even that narrow band of it on either side of the road theoretically set aside for squatters, there is much to be said for their lot over that of others. At least these porceiros can just move in, build a small house for little effort, let their flock graze in the neighbouring wilderness, and then sell a cow or two when they have need of money. Subsistence living can seem fairly desperate to an outsider, when an egg is eaten because the chicken has laid it, when the family grows fat or thin according to the leanness of the year. It is desperate, with its lack of security and of hope, but the employee on a deserted estate can fare even less well. Their hopelessness is of quite a different order.

Some 30 miles north of Xavantina there was a turning to the east. It even had a signpost although no sign. The road was bad, unbelievably so, and not made any better for us by the recent passage of a group of cattle from some nearby fazenda. Such herds leave a trail of tabanids in their wake, the monstrous blood-suckers who make even the

The practice of creating new vegetation by burning the old is a tropical custom. It is now being applied to the ▷
mighty forest of the Mato Grosso, and leaves it resembling OVERLEAF *the carnage of an Armageddon. But it makes the place more suitable for the all-important cow.*

thick-hided cattle jump when they are bitten. At the end of this dismal track and some 25 miles from the main road there was a group of houses. Until then there had been nothing.

It had been our intention to pass the night at this place. Fazendas frequently experienced this imposition when the lateness of the hour and our willingness to stop both coincided happily, but the warmth of each night and the slinging of several hammocks always made the imposition extremely slight and undemanding. It merely meant that any early-riser of a vaqueiro, walking sleepily along a well-worn route, would suddenly encounter some figure fully stretched between the chicken hut and the paw-paw tree. The snug cocoon of a hammock then became a most conspicuous resting place. Its occupant woke up to realize this fact and the day abruptly began. Equally quickly, just by untying a couple of knots, the night could be put away, and no fazendeiro, morador or porceiro ever did complain at such a transitory tenancy of their suitable attachment points. Indeed they always made us most welcome, and we therefore had every intention of slinging ourselves somewhere within the remote precincts lying at the end of that 25-mile cul-de-sac. Within much less than 25 minutes we were far less sure of our intent.

It is often amazing within the insect-rich tropics that so few houseflies and allied species actually gather when the situation seems so right for them. Given half a chance, and some suitable decaying matter within the world's temperate zone, the place is soon alive with their buzzing. Take even an abattoir in the tropics and, according to the observations of many, it is strangely neglected. Therefore it was particularly striking to encounter dozens of flies in the first house we encountered at the end of that road. There was food on the table and there were flies on it. There were children nearby, and there were flies on them. Very quickly there were flies on us and, however exceptional, they were resented no less vehemently. The dogs were totally untouchable. It is hard exuding the customary European affection for dogs in up-country Brazil, as one never knows in what condition a hand will return if it is offered for a stroke or a pat, but these particular dogs were far, far worse and in a scabious class of their own. They festered and panted, and had difficulty in raising their eyelids, let alone their ears. The chickens, too, seemed more plucked than ever but it was the desperate condition of the people that was, of course, most disturbing. It was just that the backdrop of agile flies and wretched animals drew attention to their plight.

The owner had started up this fazenda in high spirits and with good capital. He and his money had built that road. He had constructed the houses, and cleared some land. He had brought in cattle and intended bringing in more. Then, having established people to look after the place for him, either he or his backers lost interest. Either way the effect of this change was a slow stranglehold on the people at the end of the road.

◁ *This machine—and its stoker—seemed to contradict the energy laws, by pumping water, sharpening saws, severing planks, and quietly creating more sawdust than its furnace consumed.*

Their paypackets did not come. Fresh work and new ideas did not materialize to act as stimulants. In fact nothing happened, and certainly the owner did not appear to check on the situation.

There were still cattle and various crops to harvest, but these were the property of the absent fazendeiro. An employee already substantially in debt with the local armazem for his grocery needs, and presumably in debt with his relations insofar as they were able to help him, can lose courage and be unwilling to take more from a landlord, however righteous such an act may be. These people were not taking; they were waiting. They did not have the fundamental effrontery of the squatter who knows from the outset that he has no rights, and therefore sends his cattle to graze in the nearby land with as much abandon as he takes water from the well. The employees did not possess such independence. In the absence of their employer they merely sank, first as creditors, then as those who could raise no more. The flies flew in and settled on the food, on the children. We did not spend the night, but crudely moved on elsewhere.

Much later, and as a contrast, we were to spend two nights at the clearing known as Fazenda Dr. Paulo. It was on the same north–south road; it had been started at about the same time as the fly-ridden patch of neglect, and was also financed from the east, but it bore little comparison. For one thing it was a going concern, and not an aborted enterprise. For another it was up in the forest region and there was a general belief, not without reason, that a better ranch could be made out of former forest than the former scrubland of cerrado. It undoubtedly cost more to develop a forest because the cattle can graze in the cerrado from the very first day, but it was thought to be worth all that labour of destruction to have a piece of forest land. When the northern part of Mato Grosso state was sold off by the Government, and gently administered by the praefecture of Barra do Garças, there was not even an air map of the territory. Perreira might know that he had bought Area 354, and that it measured 30 by 35 miles, but he would not know as they wrote his name in the rectangle whether the area was forest, cerrado or campo any more than he would know its kind of soil or if a river passed through it. He would only know for sure that he had paid some £8,000 for his plot of the wilderness. He might not even care and would sell it to another, at a higher price, who would be similarly ignorant of the crucial variables of the piece of land he had acquired. More re-selling would happen, and the price would forever improve, as rumours spread along the rich eastern beaches of a governmental plan to drive a road through that potentially valuable part of the territory.

When the roadwork began the whole affair had suddenly taken on a less theoretical appearance, and it became important to know if this new road would actually pass by, near or even through Area 354. It might even be necessary to try to divert the road from its intended route if it seemed to give too wide a berth to one's property. (The workers cutting the road's advance picada reported that they had suddenly been told to retreat for ten miles, and start cutting again in a slightly different direction. The reason given was not an engineering one: it was said to be 'política'.) At all events the road either did or did not end up conveniently situated from each plot-owner's point of view. By then the plot-owner could either sell to a man who actually wanted to develop the place or he could develop it himself. A piece of paper—a title deed—had suddenly become a tangible and accessible piece of reality.

Dr. Paulo, trained as a lawyer, had already built himself a place in the state of São Paulo. He called it a *cidade*, but it was an estate more than a city, possessing houses for the workers and plenty of work for them to do. Now he wanted to do the same again, but on a far larger scale in Mato Grosso and right from scratch. To this end he found a bank and a relative to support him. Money was thereby assured. He also despatched an old English steam engine, manufactured by Marshall & Sons of Gainsborough, to travel overland to the new ranch. It could thrive on sawdust and was ready to build its second cidade. Power was therefore assured. Dr. Paulo then took on a few key men, notably an Italian/Brazilian whose parents had emigrated from a poor village south of Naples when the boy was six. He would be manager and, with the use of a powerful transmitter, he would keep in touch with São Paulo twice every working day. Other employees would be found nearer the area, and transported to the new estate. Some 50 men would be necessary as a beginning and later on it would be about 100. It need not take a large labour force to tame a piece of forest the size of Yorkshire or Hawaii and then to make a ranch out of it. It need not even be a full-time occupation for the owner, however interested he may be in the project.

Once a month Dr. Paulo flew up to Fazenda Dr. Paulo. The airstrip, parallel to the road and a few yards from it, was one of the first priorities. Another was to cut down a sizeable portion of forest. Imagine being confronted, as you step from a plane, by a wall of forest and having plans buzzing in your head for an avenue of workers' houses, a communal feeding area, a tractor yard, a sawmill with its steam engine, a manager's house, your own house, a permanent pool, store sheds. The first thing you reach for is an axe. Or rather you turn to the lorry load of caboclos who have arrived with you, having been hired 300 miles to the south at a wage of £15 a month with £6 a month deducted for food and board: you tell them to get going with the axes.

Later, and in the dry month of August, you tell them to put a match to all the carnage lying about them. This is really quite a dangerous business, and everyone must know that the time for firing has come. The tree tops and the dead and dying material brought down with each tree are turned to tinder during those dry season months, and a great hazard is that the whole lot will catch fire before its time. The typical caboclo is normally a casual man with such unwanted possessions as the end of a cigarette. Not so when he is standing in a knocked-down forest. He does not even drop the cigarette to tread on it. He finds instead a piece of moss in a damp portion of a tree and he stubs out his cigarette on that with great deliberation.

In short, setting fire to the carnage is easy. Europeans who have spent time huffing and puffing at carefully arranged assortments of twigs would be perpetually envious of the Brazilian ability to put a match virtually anywhere with success. The length of the match's flame is suddenly transformed into a fast and scarcely visible area of heat as a bush is rapidly consumed, and very soon whole trees are alight as the fire expands with incredible noise. The man with the match retreats into the standing forest because the fire cannot invade its precincts with the same avarice. It may jump a few crowns, if they are dry enough, and it may even trickle briefly along the forest floor, but it will not have the frightening enthusiasm of that fire consuming the accumulated shambles created by the axe men. In fact the very draught feeding those flames will lead away from the forest as the air first gives its oxygen to the fire and then flies upwards in a twisting, licking column of smoke. Flaming leaves and great lumps of blackness are carried upwards to a considerable height and there mingle in the hazy obscurity with the hawks and vultures circling over the conflagration down below.

The men watching the first atomic explosion in the Alamogordo desert each suffered the same dread thought—that the thing would go on expanding for ever, consuming everything. Watching a fire of material spread out over an area of several square miles is also frightening as the combustion goes on and on reaching for its peak. The flames go higher and higher, and faster, and the wall of standing forest resisting the destruction is increasingly hidden by all that heat. It seems to have disappeared, along with everything else, and to have risen upward into the blackened blue of the sky. Eventually, as in that barren zone of New Mexico, the zenith is reached. The thing begins to lose its power, to wither, to die away. With a piece of the Mato Grosso forest this takes time. The single furnace becomes a group of smaller fires, each raging away in their own fashion, and then an array of columns of smoke, some slow and white, some still fast and scarcely visible. Out of the carnage, amazingly, the main tree trunks survive, a lattice-work of boles lying in every direction. There are fires around them, beneath them, even inside a few of them, but they are still there to lie about as distinct and obstructive reminders of the forest that has gone.

Dr. Paulo and his men, having retreated, then advance again to attempt to clear and clean a main working area. With tractors they pull up the roots of those former trees. They build themselves huts, and they hurry because the rainy season is on its way. They bulldoze some pathways, plant a little manioc for themselves and plan further destruction for the following year.

In the meantime the blackened ground starts springing to life. So many of its nutrients, previously locked within the timber formerly standing there, have now been liberated that there is great richness to the soil. There is also plenty of moisture, because some fifty inches of rain fall between November and April, and there is always warmth in the

The quaint, poor-flying hoatzin lives close to rivers but defies classification. Some say it is a kind of pheasant, ▷
some a pigeon, and some that it resembles Archeopteryx, *the fossil bird.*

air. By the time another dry season has arrived, and a further group of axe men have been hired, the black boles lying on every side have been hidden by fresh green growth. This will dry out as the season progresses, and will then provide excellent material with which to set fire again to the same piece of land. So, once more, the flames will leap into the sky, the birds will circle, the fire will expand and die down, and the black trunks of the forest trees will still emerge from the wreckage, but less positively than before.

At the third season, when the green growth has once again turned dry in the heat, and when the tree trunks have been dragged together to aid yet again in the destruction of each other, the third firing of the jungle will almost complete the task. There will be stumps, and a few long black boles, and there will be the remains of trees left standing, now entirely dead, but the primary work is over. The place may look like Passchendaele, but to Dr. Paulo and the others it is now *derrubado* or cleared land. To Dr. Paulo, rather more than to the others, it is now worth about 200 times as much as before when he, his relatives and the bank bought this piece of forest by a road.

As soon as Fazenda Dr. Paulo started to rise, phoenix-like, from the combustion on every side, it was time to start the steam engine. It was of the kind that used to power steam rollers, save that this one had no wheels, but it purred sweetly with all the rhythmic pulse of those splendid machines. From its drive shaft there was one belt, slapping against itself as it turned innumerable other shafts and other belts, and all these other sources of the same power drove band saws, vertical saws, grindstones, and water pumps. The water was necessary for the steam engine, now with a 100 ft. chimney rising out of it. The grindstones were to sharpen the saws. The saws created planks and sawdust. The planks were used to create the main construction members of this splendidly efficient arrangement, and the sawdust and trimmings provided the sole fuel for the steam engine. It was a most excellent system, apparently defying the strict laws of energy by consuming less sawdust than it produced, and by creating many more planks than were necessary for its own construction. Even more important, at least to those of us on the expedition who had had experience of the failure of sophisticated devices in primitive areas, was its simplicity. The engine was simple, and a tried and tested device. The belts could be replaced, switched or lengthened without difficulty. The wooden framework could be modified readily, with bits tacked on, others sawn off, and all the planners of the Tanganyikan groundnut scheme could have learnt a lot by watching that engine, and seeing what could be done with a few men, even fewer basic tools and one elementary power source puffing at the base of its 100 ft. smoke stack.

Three years after driving to his fazenda, and stepping out of his truck for the first time at the correct distance north of Xavantina, and then telling the axe men to go ahead, Dr. Paulo's place had been transformed. In the battlefield ruins of the annual conflagrations

◁   *The wattled jacana is another misfit, being perhaps an aberrant rail rather than a form of wader. To float down the Xingú at any hour was to be eternally surprised by strange bird life.*

Both forest and Indian yield to the invader. Even large trees only take a minute or two.

he had planted *capim colonião*, a tall grass that grew in clusters. This had the effect of keeping the rest of the vegetation at bay and it also provided food for the zebu cattle brought in as soon as there was enough of it for them to eat. The cows stumbled over the tree stumps, and picked their way past half-burnt hulks of trees, but the tall, wiry grass was good for them and they thrived.

Other sections of the former forest, insufficiently advanced for the grass and the cattle, had by then suffered either their first or second burning, and they showed all the appropriate scars of this half-way stage. The last contingent of axe men, again only hired for the four driest months from May to August, were given a further section to destroy and were therefore busy with the felling of it. Every evening the men doing all this work plunged into the blackness of a pool that had been created from a minor stream. They soaped their multi-racial skins, dark-brown and light-brown, at that excellent hour of the Brazilian day when the sun is about to touch the trees, and the colour of everything is brighter, gayer and infinitely more rewarding than it had ever been since dawn had ended. Shadows then are long, and the rich brown of the earth has a warmth and a savour to it that is captivating. It is also fleeting; the long blackness of the tropical night so quickly takes its place.

234

The men in the pool, receiving five new cruzeiros a day (10s.) and having two new cruzeiros immediately taken away from them for their keep, were therefore left with three new cruzeiros. At local prices this would buy them slightly more than one bottle of beer or three packets of cigarettes. In the towns, both over 150 miles away at either end of the road, the beer would be cheaper but the cigarettes about the same. They worked hard to get this modest money. They worked with perhaps 400 sweat bees on them, or with their shirts black with other insects and sodden with sweat from 7 a.m. to 6 p.m. They could wield their axes with precision and with strength. Squash an insect, place it suitably on the trunk of a tree, suggest that an axe should carve it in two, and then watch as the axe bit deep into the very spot where the creature had been. With the skill of woodmen everywhere they could also lay down a tree precisely in the right direction. When the hooter hooted, to produce an incongruous noise in the middle of that forest, they walked back along the tree trunks of their destruction, leaping from one to another, and keeping above the shambles crushed on every side.

Should the men fall, or should they have any other kind of industrial accident, their pay was instantly stopped. A group of us from camp met one man hobbling about on a bright red foot. Apparently others had let go of a heavy weight, and he had been left holding it briefly before it caught him below the ankle. The accident had happened six weeks beforehand and he had therefore been living on credit ever since. The foot was healing well, and he would be back at work within a month, but neither he nor his workmates expressed either anger or bitterness at the stoppage of his pay.

As there was no doctor for hundreds of miles the Fazenda Dr. Paulo was quick to appreciate the value of a modern camp just down the road, lavishly equipped medically and often with a resident doctor. The worst case was a man who had 'fallen on an axe' but lesser ailments frequently arrived from this and all the other fazendas within fair reach of the acampamento inglês. The Brazilian medical community is either too hard pressed in the greatest centres of population or else unwilling to serve in primitive areas. At all events it is rare to find a doctor eking out a slender living in a remote area where sickness is the dominant handicap and where the huge distances can turn minor and untreated complications into disasters.

Dr. Paulo himself, although back in São Paulo for most of the time and never more than ten days at a stretch with his up-country fazenda, emphasized the critical importance of health by being himself afflicted with leishmaniasis. It had given him an unsightly and suppurating lesion on his forehead, an ulcer about half-an-inch in diameter. Fortunately a doctor in São Paulo had correctly diagnosed the cause, and had given him the series of injections which effect a cure. Scar tissue then did its best to conceal the damage after the parasites had been removed from his bloodstream, but his workers were less fortunate. Some of them came to the British camp for the same course of injections but others probably doctored themselves or did nothing and were therefore due to suffer the second stage of this disease when, in leprous fashion, it starts to consume

flesh and bone. Good health and good luck are both primary needs. A man already in debt, receiving a small wage, incapable of paying his way to the nearest doctor, and yet more incapable of paying for the medical attention, is not just inconvenienced by bad health. It can so easily be the death of him.

Of course the fazenda is costing a lot of money to develop, at least as judged by the pockets of most of those involved. On the other hand, as judged by large-scale projects current in many other parts of the world, it is being developed at an extraordinarily moderate price. A labour force of about 100 is being maintained, including food, for about 150 new cruzeiros per month per man, or a total of some £18,000 a year. The houses are all built on the spot, partly by that solitary steam engine, and partly with axes and hammers. The vehicles include two tractors, one Chevrolet pick-up, a bull-dozer, and a few jeeps. There is a small generator for electric light, and just a few commodities have to be brought in by road. In short, a total of about £100,000 in the first three years would be sufficient to pay for all the needs.

For this sum Dr. Paulo and his financial colleagues transformed a large proportion of their 300,000 acre estate from jungle into valuable investment. By the end of the third year there were 1,500 cattle grazing among the stumps, 5,000 acres had been cleared, two roads and an airstrip had been built and many communal buildings were in good shape. The cleared land had risen in value at least a couple of hundred times above its original peppercorn purchase price.

Dr. Paulo is about as far removed from the conventional picture of a rich man as could be. There is, for a start, that leishmaniasis scar and beneath it a face that has obviously led a rigorous life. His clothes are ancient, and he himself must be about 50. Apart from the fact that he is white, which immediately distinguishes him from most of his darker employees, there is nothing to show that he is not one of his labour force. When he and a group of them, plus his manager and a foreman, are all within the entrails of some piece of machinery, the hierarchy is extremely confused. He is poles apart in his appearance from the dapper, T-shirted pilot with the dark glasses who flies him up from São Paulo every month. Dr. Paulo is not the man from town trying to look the part of a backwoodsman. He is far more of a backwoodsman who would look totally out of place in a town.

Nevertheless, appearances apart, he is the man with the money, with the financial confidence of relations, and with a bank behind him. He is the man who will make it pay, who will develop that piece of forest on the Xavantina-São Félix road, starting 305 kms north of Xavantina, ending 345 kms north of it, and extending for 30 kms to the west of that road. At the moment he has created destruction, with 1,500 cattle picking their way through it. He already knows where the hotel and the filling station will go,

◁ *Once a month Dr Paulo flew up from the east, attended to the needs of the fazenda being hacked out of the Mato Grosso, and thereby carved a profit for himself and his backers.*

the main street avenue, and the permanent buildings. It will be the second cidade of his—and that engine's—labours. It will be the Fazenda Dr. Paulo, and it will be worth millions in any currency.

Not all fazendas have the arterial support of a main road running straight past them. Some have to make do with a feeder road leading to that main highway and they have to make the road themselves. Such self-sufficiency seems initially impressive when one is told that the road in question is perhaps 50 miles long and involves several bridges. Nevertheless, in the eyes of the people who are about to chop down hundreds of square miles of forest, the construction of a small link road to that area is no great handicap.

Essentially there were two kinds of road that could be built through the forest. (A road through the cerrado was a relatively simple matter.) The first was no more than a narrow band, a strip of road about ten yards wide that wove its way around the biggest trees. The forest canopy stretched over such a track, and no travel along it could be fast, but its creation meant the destruction of only about four acres per mile. To men cutting down many thousands of acres this is a small price to pay for access. The cost is not much greater if the road is 40 yards wide, with a smooth central section and a large border on either side to take all the debris. 40 yards for 50 miles means only 900 acres, another small price if it also means rapid travel to the hundreds of thousands of acres at the other end.

The suddenness with which the Xavantina road struck north from Xavantina, after so long a deliberation, and the suddenness with which its work was halted meant that the plans of others frequently backfired with similar abruptness. In 1967 the road had been making rapid travel northwards and everyone generally assumed that it would bend westwards to reach the Cachoeira von Martius in next to no time. Various fazendas were started up in anticipation of the brand-new road, and various fazendas then found themselves embarrassingly ahead of the situation. No place was further ahead, and therefore more remote from the road-head, than the fazenda built just to the north of the actual cachoeira. It had been realized that the road must cross the Xingú either on these convenient rapids, which provided rocky footholds for any bridge, or on the Cachoeira das Pedras, a similar spot just six miles downstream and to the north. At both sets of waterfall there were satisfactory ridges through the foothills, notably on the western side, that would be useful to the engineers. In other words the road was bound to come marching through the area in time and the man who happened to own this portion of land woke up to the fact.

Unfortunately he woke up with too great a start. He amassed a team of 36 men and despatched them to the area. This in itself was no easy task. Most of them embarked at Garapú on the Rio Sete de Setembro. Then, in the rainy season, they sailed downstream to meet the Culuene and finally the Xingú. The first part of the journey would have been impossible in the drier months, and the second part would have been equally impossible without the authority of the Villas Boas brothers because the river route lay straight through their Indian reservation. At all events it was a long journey. The rapids not only marked the northern end of the Park's jursidiction but the spot at which every-one had to disembark, off-load the cargo, man-handle the boats over the rocky tur-bulence, and then load everything again for the journey's final leg. A mere six miles further on, and sheltered from the broad main stream of the Xingú, lay a convenient disembarkation point. Here they landed once again, this time in a patch of water hyacinth, cut their way on to the bank, and were impressed by the magnitude of the task that lay ahead of them. That night they slung their hammocks just next to the boats. Later that night they shot their first jaguar.

In the morning they cut their way inland. The first mile of land was still partially flooded after the rains, and this riverside area was plainly unsatisfactory as a location for an airfield and all the other primary requirements of an up-country fazenda; but, after that mile, the land began to dry out. There they began on the greater destruction, cutting down the trees, burning them, removing the roots in the 800 yards of airstrip, flattening the earth, and creating their own living places from the available material. One hut was thatched with Buriti palm in the conventional fashion. The other made use of banana-type leaves, the broad and fragile shapes that are easier to acquire but less easy to make waterproof.

After a few months came an additional 42 men, again by river, and also with the intention of cutting down trees for the biggest bonfire of them all. Both contingents of men slept mainly in the woods, preferring the extreme simplicity of a rough camp down by a small river that flowed into the Xingú rather than any hut. By day they attacked more of the area, 25 miles from north to south and 38 miles from east to west, that was known as the Fazenda Cachoeira von Martius from the moment that the first group had cut their way into this virgin land.

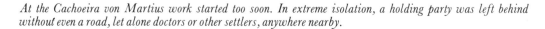

At the Cachoeira von Martius work started too soon. In extreme isolation, a holding party was left behind without even a road, let alone doctors or other settlers, anywhere nearby.

Rich man, poor man

No one knows which party first realized that the roadmaking had stopped, whether the owners of this new fazenda who lived back in São Paulo or the men they were employing. Anyway there was suddenly no longer any need for urgent destruction. The road-head was still 200 miles short of the rapids. The possibility of getting cattle either to or from the fazenda was out of the question, and no one knew when the roadwork would begin again. In short there was no longer any point to the fazenda, and no more than there had ever been since Brazil had been colonized.

However that was no reason for letting all that good destructive work go to waste. A tropical forest is quick to make amends and would quickly cover up such an exposed affront to its autocracy. To let it be and to do nothing would be to encounter just as severe a problem when the road did eventually reach the area, and there would then be the need for just as many men to tame that airstrip and those few square miles all over again. Therefore a holding party was essential. They would cut and burn as much as was necessary to check the forest and keep it tamed. They would also maintain the runway in a state that would not mean the immediate destruction of any aircraft landing on it. They would also inhabit the place so that any passers-by did not take it over. This was an unlikely happening, but one worth preventing.

So the main working party sailed away, and a holding party of 15 people stayed behind. This was the manager and his wife, the gang-leader, his wife and two children, and the gang of nine employees. By that time there were also two macaws, three dogs, three cats and a small black monkey with a prehensile tail who defaecated from his position in the beams whenever strangers passed beneath. Three of us from the base camp arrived at this lonely spot by air about a year after the holding party had been on its own.

We flew from the relative urbanity of Dr. Paulo's fazenda, travelling slightly north of west, and in the morning. From 8.50 to 10.20 the scene below, and on either side and ahead of us, was of the same expanse of forest. I read the excellent 'Survival Handbook' on board, with its instructions about edible palms, and how much water could be found in Bromeliads, and which birds could be caught and how, but there was one glaring omission. It gave no instructions whatsoever for landing on that uneven canopy down below. The plane would be swiftly swallowed up, as if in quicksands, whether its passengers survived or not. Even assuming survival they would then have difficulty in making their existence known to any aerial rescuers. They could light a fire, and punily attempt to compete with the smoke stacks rising high on every horizon from all the other fires that burn almost perpetually in Brazil. They could try to enlarge that modest swathe cut by the plane's final plunge through the trees, but it would be hard to compete

Fortunately the monkey's aim from the rafters was not perfect, but the pium BELOW *were far more relentless;* ▷
even the camera does not precisely halt them in their flight around the author's head.

OVERLEAF *From their village of Pororí, the Indians waved at us to indicate an airstrip right next to them.*

240

with all the chaos caused naturally when the larger trees fall on their own account and bring so much down with them. Therefore it was emphatically just as well to learn how to eat and drink in that environment and how to escape from it on one's own and without help from elsewhere. The chances of aid by others were extremely slim and self-sufficiency was the keynote of the area. It always had been and always would be, until such time as the place is no more.

After 90 minutes of flight the Xingú appeared ahead. We were impressed. Unlike the twisting thread of the Suiá Missú, with small sandbanks and little lakes, this new river was far more magnificent. Its sandbanks were enormous, its ox-bows gargantuan. Its greater width held every shade of green, from the brown-green of the shallows to the black-green of its depths. When the sun glinted back from its surface it did so with a blinding, dancing brilliance. We above, now comforted by the security inherent in a river, and with the handbook back beneath the seat, were entranced. A Kajabí village appeared ahead. We circled lower and lower, watching our shadow flick over the trees before it travelled jerkily over their circle of huts and finally shot out over the sheen of that powerful river. The Indians waved bows, and indicated the airstrip built right next to them. What a muddle of technology! They used arrows to live by and yet had an air-strip. They lived in their thatched simplicity and knew the rest of the world only by its aircraft which, first as a hum on the horizon and then as a roaring thing, might touch down beside them. They probably had need for torches, bullets and fishhooks, and welcomed the planes for they brought more of these things, but they expressed no real curiosity about the outside environment, and who made these things they wanted, and how. The village was the northernmost one in the Villas Boas Park; hence the airstrip, the familiarity with planes, and the welcome.

We flew on, reserving our gifts for the fazenda and keeping our minds upon this entirely different objective. Within a very short time there were the von Martius falls, a black and white barrier to the smooth green of the Xingú whose abrupt turbulence swiftly petered out downstream. There was no one at the falls and no sign that anyone had ever been to this famous spot, but we circled and took pictures and tried to imagine what it would look like when a bridge strode across it and people lived on either side. For the moment it looked serene, and the herons over·the water had a timeless, un-hurried beat to their flying. There was not a hint that this was a crucial frontier between old and new, that the Park was to the south and a fazenda to the north.

We first caught sight of the fazenda very soon after heading north from the rapids, and saw its straight lines of destruction standing out by the side of that river's permanent curves. The airstrip looked much the same as with the Indians, but there were only two huts by the side of it and no one came out of them to wave or to point welcomingly at the runway. We circled and landed quickly on its soft, brown soil. By the time we had taxied

◁   *From north-east Brazil, according to his hat, this young man was one of those left behind at von Martius.*

to the huts a man had appeared. His head was haloed with midges, and he hit at them absent-mindedly.

'Tem pium?' we said into the silence left by the engine.

'Tem' he said, and left it at that.

The three of us and our pilot could talk of nothing else as we each collected our own haloes of biting midges and walked towards the manager's house. The wilderness was bad enough. To be a biting wilderness made it dramatically less attractive. Inside the house was darkness, an absence of pium, and welcome cups of coffee. We explained, with as much politeness as the situation so obviously demanded, that we had come to stay for a few days, that we wanted to use their canoes to look at the area, and that we would inevitably be overflowing with questions throughout our stay.

'E possível?' we asked.

'Sim' he said, and once more left it at that.

Inside we sipped our coffee gratefully and wondered why anyone ever ventured outside. Eventually the pilot decided it was time for him to go. The macaws shrieked. The monkey defaecated. And the pium came from nowhere, or indeed everywhere, as we walked to the plane. The pilot climbed aboard, shut the windows, and slapped both at his face and at the windscreen of his cockpit. He was still slapping as the plane roared by on its take-off run, but perhaps it was a wave as well. With decent haste the three of us then strode determinedly back to the house, thwarting the monkey's aim as we ducked into the darkened doorway.

Later, with collars buttoned, shirt-sleeves rolled down, and with faces well smeared with anything of a repellent nature, we did emerge. We walked along the runway and we watched the men work. We got to know them all and they took us to the rapids, an upstream journey made increasingly severe as we reached the faster waters just beneath our goal. After we had landed, the beautiful tranquillity of the scene was utterly destroyed by those wretched pium, but the others caught fish and then smoked them over a fire. We took pictures and our band of men struck poses suitable for the occasion, with all their revolvers, bandoliers, gun belts and knives brought well into view. They could indeed have been a bunch of bandeirantes, exploring Brazil only a century ago. They certainly looked the part, and felt a little of that former bravado, but they were only a bunch of men left high and dry by a premature decision made back in the east. They banged off their guns occasionally, but only at rocks to make a ricochet, or at tin cans to make them sink. Eventually we paddled back, and found more time for talk in the gentler downstream run.

'What if you are sick?' we ask.

'We go with the outboard for three days downstream, and then radio for a doctor.'

It was unnecessary to follow the simplicity of this answer by telling them what they certainly knew, that the outboard did not work and that doctors were not always able to respond to such unknown appeals from unknown places.

The manager and his wife, the gang leader and his wife, and two children, the gang of nine employees, two macaws, three dogs, three cats and a small black monkey, living in the wilderness at the Cachoeira fazenda. 'A plane will surely come. We have never been for more than four months without one.'

'What do you think of your government?'

'It has nothing to do with us. Politics are for the people living in towns, not in the Mato.'

'Would you like to live in Rio?'

'Yes, of course, but what could we do there? We are men of the Mato.'

'Would you like to stay here?'

'No.'

'Supposing you were given some land here. Would you then stay?'

'Of course, but first I would go back to Maranhão to collect all my brothers.'

'Are you lonely?'

'No, there are always people here.'

'Do you feel isolated?'

'No, a plane will always come. We have never been more than four months without a plane.'

'Do you like the Indians who visit you?'

'No, because they come and take things and leave us bows and arrows. What do we want with bows and arrows? The Indians get angry when we refuse them. They threaten to kill us. Everyone says it's natural if an Indian kills a white man. But if we were to kill an Indian that would be the end of us.'

No one man disagreed with anyone else. They had no harsh words for the rich young man who owned the land and who paid them. They knew little about their country and far less about South America as a whole, all agreeing that Mexico was the capital of

Argentina. They understood far more about the English football team and spoke of Nobby Stiles as if they knew him personally. The importance of this game in Brazil cannot be over-emphasized. A country among the world's leaders of football is inevitably among the greatest countries in the world, or so this argument runs, and Brazil's football is pre-eminent. The subject, once broached, is difficult to change and it kept us going for the rest of the journey. As a topic it only paused briefly while our canoe ploughed its nose into the tangle of water hyacinth lodged by the mooring place. We then tried to explain, not without linguistic difficulty, how this floating plant, *Eichhornia crassipes*, had found its way—allegedly via the addiction of ambassadorial wives for its beauty and speed of growth—into the rivers of Africa, and had all but clogged them. We spoke of the Congo, the Nile and Kariba, but the message misfired.

'Contraband. They took it as contraband. Why does everyone rob Brazil?'

Fortunately, that very evening and in the colossal Maracana stadium in Rio, Nobby Stiles and the others did not rob Brazil of victory. Pele and the other Brazilian gods saw to it that the final score was a satisfactory 2–1 against the English visitors. Thereafter the radio droned on with its everlasting commercials and told us to exchange that dirty old refrigerator for a bright bright, new new one, and told us how blinds would let new light into our lives. Blinds! We did not even have windows, let alone all the other luxurious nick-nacks of civilization. However, no one seemed to mind. No one even listened. They ate their rice and beans, this time garnished with piranha, and chewed with remembered relish over the game broadcast from Rio. What goals! What brilliance! What a match! It would have been severe for the three of us from England had England won that day.

The plane was due to collect us on a Saturday. This had been arranged a couple of weeks beforehand when the most available air taxi in the area had chanced to drop in at Dr. Paulo's for refuelling. Iain had hurried over to arrange the details, but the pilot could only think of slopping in the petrol as fast as possible because he had to get somewhere else before nightfall.

'Can you bring two people back from Cachoeira von Martius?'

'Yup. When?'

'On the Saturday after next?'

'Yup.'

And with that he flung down the empty can, pulled out the handkerchief he had been using as a filter, screwed on the cap, threw away the box he had been standing on, rushed to the cabin to adjust switches and throttle, rushed round to the front to swing the propeller, then back again to the cabin to climb in, and with a roar he was off down the runway and soon out of sight and sound. We blinked at each other in the dust, and wondered if the appointment, made with such frantic casualness, would ever come to pass.

Douglas Botting and I, the last two due to leave the Cachoeira fazenda, were to look at each other more than once when that Saturday came and wonder increasingly if the pilot even remembered talking to anyone, let alone fixing a time and a place. We reckoned that, if he was coming, he would come by noon in order to leave good time for the return journey. The Mato Grosso was a difficult place to fly over in the daylight; the situation worsened rapidly as the sun sank quickly in the sky. When noon had come and gone, and when rice and beans had come and were casually regurgitating, we re-calculated hopefully that 3 p.m. was the very last hour at which he could arrive to take us to Dr. Paulo's and then return to his home base. When 3 p.m. came and also went it was occasion for the two of us, now with our beans silent and still, to retire into our hammocks and let the desolation of that place sink deep into our systems.

The manager was being paid £25 a month. Everyone else was being paid less. Most of the men did not have their families with them and they would be stuck with their own company for the two-year stint. The Indians visited them, but were not welcomed and nor, for that matter, were they particularly welcoming. Other people, such as us, did come and did change the routine but our very freedom, both with cash and with time, cannot have been disregarded. To visit the fazenda for a few days was to be fairly certain of not succumbing to any ailment in that time. To be there for two years, however satisfactory one's teeth, appendix or general condition before arriving, is to be convinced that something serious will occur. Even hypochondria, a malady with a devastating power, is likely to fester increasingly in such a place. It is difficult enough wondering whether to call in the doctor under ordinary urban circumstances. It must be horrific deciding whether to paddle off downstream for many days, call for one on the radio and then either receive his attention and his bill or, in spite of all efforts, receive nothing at all. Just how much malaria and leishmaniasis and how bad a snake bite does one have to possess before embarking on that doubtful journey?

The manager was our host. It was in a store room attached to his house that we had slung our hammocks. It was to this room that we had retreated when the plane had not come and when the sky had remained its unbroken and silent blue. He came in to ask for yet another pill as the ulcerous edge to an extracted tooth hole was still giving him trouble. Unfortunately we had no more, as he already knew, and he sipped water instead from the jar resting on its three-legged stand in the corner. He reckoned it had been a disaster to leave the north-east in the hope of finding a better life in the west because he had found only loneliness and greater hardships. He might end up with some money in his pocket, and he might therefore have some capital with which to start a new existence near his home, but it had been pointless to imagine that the areas being opened up were not also being closed to his kind right from the outset.

He had come west, hopefully, and with his new, young wife. Any door that he had seen, any piece of land waiting to be developed, any venture he would have liked, had been denied to him. He took £25 a month because it was better pay than most, although the conditions made him earn it, and he stood a chance of taking something back. Along with this cash he would also take a total dislike of the place, an enmity that would encourage few others to chance their arm. We felt it would all be so straightforward before we went there. Parts of Brazil were crowded and the lands were inadequate to keep them, and parts of Brazil were empty and the lands quite new, but for one to make use of the other proved to be nothing like so simple in the raw actuality.

The manager sipped his water and left. Douglas and I slumped further back into our hammocks. We stared into the darkness of that room and wondered at the pium outside, at the misery of this particular piece of pioneering, at the Indians who no longer belonged and who troubled the invaders who also did not belong. I think we spoke a bit but Douglas can be splendidly deaf when he has something on his mind. He can also be inarticulate in such circumstances, but deafness is the principal expedient. It was therefore extremely alarming when he sat up, insofar as a hammock permits this, exclaiming that he had heard something. Had tabanids frequented huts I would have assumed, judging by the suddenness of his action, that he had received their penetrating attentions; but they do not live in huts and he was positive that he had heard something. In fact he was positive that he had heard a plane. More than that, he said it was single-engined and rushed out of the room.

The pilot landed in his traditional flurry. He leapt from the cockpit, found a box, stood on it, unscrewed a cap, poured in petrol and flung words at us about there being little time. We tried to untie our hammocks, to roll them up with a decently reluctant speed. We tried not to show excessive delight that the plane had materialized, and we were indeed sorry to say farewell to our host and the various members of the gang who happened to be around at the time. We poured food, money, cigarettes, even a knife, into their hands and then walked with a confident step to the Cessna just in time to see the last of the petrol go in, the box thrown away, the pilot beckon us to our seats. There must have been pium out there but we did not notice them. The view of overgrown destruction was no less awful but it suddenly looked well. It looked better still through that well-scratched perspex. The manager stood to watch us go, a minute figure in the immensity of someone else's land.

We banked round over the Xingú, took one last look at the fazenda, such as it was, and then at the falls, such as they were. Then, taking a long look at the forest ahead of us, we settled down on an easterly course. I glanced at where a gyro compass might have been, an easy instrument for checking our course, but the space was occupied with a small picture of the Virgin Mary. The last of the pium were walking over her features and over everything else quite as casually as they had walked over us for all the preceding days, but it was nice watching them stiffen as the plane slowly climbed into the cooler atmosphere.

250

8 THE END OF THE FOREST

To enter anyone's dwelling along that Xavantina–São Félix road meant being given refreshment, and predominantly coffee. To look into that cup, and then either at the wooden or earthen floor beyond it, was to savour much of the atmosphere of the place. Where could the cup be put down? On the firm earth and out of the way of the blundering pigs, on a table, on a box, or was there nowhere to put it save in one's own cupped hands? The feet of the man being interviewed, which were usually somewhere in the background beyond the cup as one stared deeply into it, could be either bare or yet more poorly-clad in ancient and useless shoes.

It was therefore totally astounding one day, when still along that road and in a dwelling by its side, to find oneself staring equally deeply into a tall, cool glass, all clinking with the ice-cubes packed from top to bottom. The drink itself was grape juice. The table on which to rest the glass stood squarely on all four legs and on the terracotta tiles beneath it. Instead of using boxes or the ground all of us sat on neat, clean, new, aluminium deckchairs and the feet of the man being interviewed were well hidden within shiny, black, leather boots reaching up to his calves. There were antlers nailed in baronial fashion to the wall behind his head. There was an elegant wife, all set to fly to Bananal for the weekend, smiling beneath her large tinted sunglasses and her brightly tinted hair. There was nothing similar in this establishment to any of the places we had been visiting for this was the Fazenda Suiá Missú.

Anywhere with a substantial number of employees has a *gerente*, or administrator. They too proved to be as varied as the cups they provided, and the one in charge of Suiá Missú looked the part as the boss of the largest, most advanced and most forthright of all the current development projects along that Xavantina road. He was stocky, his hair was thinning, he listened before he spoke, and he drove everywhere in an open jeep. At his home, which had a roofed terrace running around it and a white, open-bricked wall around the garden, he lived in a style unimaginable for most of that area and most of its people. It was a colonial style of house, with cool rooms opening on to each other, and each with soft furnishings in suitable excess. It was also quiet with servants appearing, djinn-like, from nowhere in particular but whenever wanted. There was mosquito mesh over the windows, but no mosquitoes, and there were bushes and shrubs in the garden, equally untouched by insects. That solitary figure who had watched our plane depart from Cachoeira von Martius had been a gerente. We remembered him as we stared deeply into our icy grape juice, and felt astounded by the novel circumstances. Yet both spots had been carved from the forest such a short time before, and before their respective gerentes had come to live in them.

The owner of Suiá Missú was Dr. Erminio Ometto. His family possesses 13 sugar factories and these supply the bustling populous state of São Paulo with 35 per cent of its sugar. The father of Dr. Ometto, an Italian immigrant, had arrived in Brazil with nothing. This immigrant's first acquaintance with sugar had been when he planted 100 acres with the crop, and the family's fortunes had flourished increasingly ever since. Some of its money and its energy had been diverted to the Mato Grosso in 1962 when it bought a piece of land 260 miles north of Xavantina and about 70 miles south-west of São Félix. It so happened that this land proved to be directly alongside the new road which would be linking the two towns. The size of the land was 300,000 *alqueires* and the cost was about 1·25 new cruzeiros an alqueire.

Such measures, both of area and money, need elaboration. The trouble with the alqueire as a unit of measurement is that its definition varies from state to state. In Mato Grosso it was often assumed to be five hectares. In São Paulo and on Dr. Ometto's fazenda it was said to be 2·2 hectares. The trouble with money in an economy of enthusiastic inflation is that prices alter dramatically from year to year. The cruzeiro had been the principal unit of the monetary system, but inflation had demoted its value considerably. In 1967 its position was enhanced when they removed three noughts put there by inflation. (It was not the first time Brazil had adopted this manoeuvre.) Overnight 1,000 old cruzeiros officially became one new cruzeiro (or *conto*) and it is still difficult disentangling the two kinds, particularly as many of the old notes are still in circulation or overprinted. Therefore it is even more difficult, bearing both the shifting alqueire and financial instability in mind, to find out how much anyone paid per acre. Nevertheless the purchase price of Fazenda Suiá Missú was extremely small by most standards, being about a few pence an acre. To pay that kind of money for a desert proven to have no resources of any kind whatsoever is perhaps reasonable. To pay it for land already supporting tropical forest is remarkable.

Work began on the Fazenda Suiá Missú—so named on account of the river well to the west of its territory—in 1964. There had been a party of Xavante Indians already on the site but these were the ones who were air-lifted away to the São Marcos mission as soon as it was possible to do so. There were no other Indians in the vicinity and work

Tinted glasses and tinted hair on the gerente's veranda. Dark faces and sweaty shirts among those cutting down the secondary growth caused by the felling of the trees. ▷

could therefore proceed without further impediment from them. The easiest point of access at that time was from São Félix—itself a recent development on the west side of the Rio Araguaia—and the final part of the journey was on foot. Because no one had been living in those parts, all labour had to be imported from elsewhere. As with the Dr. Paulo fazenda further south towards Xavantina, and as with every piece of farmland being created out of the forest, the first task is to start cutting it down.

The gerente reckoned that it took a man 47 days to cut down one alqueire. That means that a single axe with a good operator, who is being paid according to the destruction he can cause, can be made to cut down about five acres in that time. From April to August, the driest months, 250 extra men are customarily taken on by the fazenda, mainly as forest clearers. Their combined efforts in each winter season therefore lead to the felling of a further 3,000–4,000 acres and then, when the match has been struck, to the bonfire burning furiously over that portion of the land. Because some of the forest was less thick than other parts, and because some of the fazenda was campo and some cerrado, both of which require less effort to be tamed, the gerente was able to report at the end of the first five years that 30,000 acres had been opened up. The intention was to open up another 500,000 in Phase 1 of the operation, but even destruction on that scale, being carried out with commendably effective haste, would still leave 850,000 acres of forest standing within the confines of this single fazenda. It takes time even for a Paulista to realize his assets in the Mato Grosso.

At the end of five years much of the cleared land had been planted with grass, the Colonial, Jarague and Napier types that do so well in the scorched earth at the foot of a burnt forest. No part of the estate was without its straggly reminders that a forest had formerly stood there, the bare poles of trees still standing where once they had flourished. They stood gaunt above all the tall clusters of grass and, however well the grass grew, it could not hide those stumps and lumps of trees never totally consumed by the annual fires. Of course the airstrip had been totally cleared, and the living areas, and the corrals, and the roadways, but the rest of the land now fit for cattle to graze still showed all the signs of the recent conflict.

By the time those first 30,000 acres had been cleared there were 15,000 cattle grazing off them, a tribute both to the nutrition of the planted grass and to the energy involved in the accumulation of such a herd, but some of the cattle were also grazing off a few of the untouched portions of cerrado. Large numbers of the animals had been made to walk to the fazenda from the east but there was also an extensive breeding programme and the lesser herds of yearling cattle showed up the rate at which this was being achieved. The walkers were driven to the Araguaia during the dry season, packed thickly into a ferry boat (on the argument that shifting cargo is dangerous, and shifting

◁ *The rain falls most heavily in the early part of each new year. At present the forest mops it up, but too much open land may lead to hideous erosion in the future.*

is impossible if the packing is tight enough) and disembarked a few miles south of São Félix. During the wet summer months so many miles of the land on either side of the Araguaia are flooded that such a transport arrangement is impossible. Midwinter is a good time and, during a final visit, some of us from base camp watched preparations being made for a herd of 4,000 due to swell the cattle population of 15,000 into a yet more impressive total of 19,000.

Once the cattle are over the river it is again the job of the Suiá Missu vaqueiros to drive the herd. There was no direct road from river to fazenda and, even if there had been such a way or the men and cows had gone via the road leading south from São Félix, the passage of such a migration would not have gone well with the hooting, frustrated activities of conventional traffic. Instead the huge herd was made to travel through the cerrado and the animals battered their way past its varied vegetation, its spiny palms, its burnt-cork bark. Any cow further than, say, 40 yards away in this sparse but dense kind of growth would probably be impossible to see, and therefore the cattlemen had a job on their hands, but they handled it excellently. Their mounts were either small horses or large mules, and the mules seemed marginally more adept at picking a sure-footed way through the tangle. The cattle tended to stay in a herd without the efforts of the mule-men on their flanks but, even so, it was remarkable that none were lost and that any strays were rapidly found again.

The cattle were all of the droop-eared type, with heavy folds of skin beneath their necks and—to European eyes at least—with a less handsome look than the average European cow. Basically they were zebu cattle and were said by the local people to be of the *nellore* type, but the original purity of the breed had probably been lost in the confusion of interbreeding long ago. Nevertheless the result was hardy and appeared to be remarkably unsusceptible to disease. The animals often had long scars on them or open wounds, or even ears totally missing, but those appeared to be the basic hazards of living in a savage environment. Even when wounded the beasts still looked well. The gerente did have a veterinary guide-book, and he did spend time trying to discover *carbúnculo simpático* within its pages (and it took us time to realize he was talking about anthrax), but there was certainly no veterinary surgeon on the estate and no plans to have one. Such a luxury, or even a doctor for the employees, or a good many of the benefits of an advanced community, would militate financially against the experiment.

The gerente spoke of all such things as if they were the thin end of a wedge that had to be kept firmly in its place. He said that the cattle were being inoculated, for some prophylaxis had already proved itself most necessary, but a large-scale epidemic of some disease was a risk that had to be taken. A veterinary surgeon might have been able to prevent it, but such experts were expensive. Very sick people could be flown out if necessary, and a dispensary existed to administer to the more basic complaints. Perhaps a vet and a doctor would prove necessary, but such extra luxuries would only be admitted when proved vital. So too with fertilizers. Perhaps they will become necessary,

The mixed stocks of zebu cattle, stumbling over the stumps of burnt out trees, do well in all the chaos.

said the gerente, in 25 years' time and when the soils have been violently depleted, but the idea of using them in the early, difficult and unrewarding days was quite out of the question. For the time being, no, nothing, nada.

The gerente's terrace, his shrubs and the place where he parked his jeep all had the touch of a decent antiquity to them. Beyond them the fazenda's own plane was parked beneath a windsock which, in the customary fashion of central Brazil, would only rarely lift itself from its limp and windless position. It too, and all the houses within sight, the sawmill and the slaughterhouse with its perpetual attendance of black vultures—the whole scene had an ancient look. Yet, only five years before, the trees had been everywhere and there must have been termites and ticks where the terrace tiles now took their place. On the horizon there were still trees, a thin streak between the sky and the land, and beyond that abrupt frontier was the ancient world. We asked if there was any intention to keep any of it or whether the axe would sink deeper and deeper. Surprisingly the answer was that 30 per cent would remain, a total of 400,000 acres standing as it stood. You see, he explained, it is necessary for the flora and fauna, for the climate and, most of all, for our philosophy. If necessary we will even plant more trees.

Conflicting with such optimism is the fact that it has not been the custom to be so conservationist in the rest of Brazil, and pressures will surely build up to chop down or

257

prune that 30 per cent. Similarly the moister areas, those which will return the best short-term reward, lie on either side of the drainage zones. To take away their forest is to increase the chances of rampant erosion, of gullying and of destroying the new-found land. After all a good many mistakes on this score have been made all over the world, and to fly over developed Brazil is to see some excellent examples, but human nature is weak at anticipating even predictable trouble. It prefers making amends for the disaster once it has occurred, by damming the flood waters, checking the annual loss of soil, and restoring the habitat hopefully before it is too late. There were no plans at the Suiá Missú to check such destruction, save for keeping that uncertain 30 per cent. Some loss of soil will be inevitable. Some destruction is certain. A kind of disaster is probable. Only when it really happens will all the varying parameters be widely known.

The current stability will surely change when Fazenda Suiá Missú, Fazenda Dr. Paulo and all the other pioneering estates have spawned countless more. The soil, plus the great depth of soil-like material more accurately known as weathered rock that lies beneath it, will both be dramatically affected. At the fazendas the normal leafy, springy covering to the land has already become a fine dusty tilth which puffs away as you walk on it. For much of the area it is possible to dig a hole—and the British soil scientists frequently did so—several yards deep without encountering changes noticeable to those who are not soil scientists. Some of the Brazilian squatters have built wells and these have been dug through 30–40 ft. of soil-like material before the water has prevented all further digging, although a further depth of this soft material was more than likely. It will prove highly susceptible to erosion, if erosion is given half a chance.

John Thornes, the geographer who worked on the waters of the Suiá Missú, was amazed by the constancy of that river and what this implied about the land on either side. From its source to its union with the Rio Xingú many hundreds of miles distant its transport both of dissolved ions and of suspended matter was outstandingly uniform. Normally a river shows up, by the varying levels of its solvents, the varying forms of land development on either side. If there is erosion there will probably be a greater quantity of both dissolved and suspended matter in the water. The Suiá Missú, so clear and so clean, is carrying hardly anything at present. Exploitation of the land will bring changes, and the resulting ionic composition of this silent river will be a mute witness of the devastation then taking place. It will not be necessary to look at the gullies, to watch a land whose fertile topsoil is gradually diminishing: it will be a matter only of going to the river and measuring what it is taking away. For the time being the fazendas are thinly spaced, and their great changes are only to small patches of their vast domains. The Suiá Missú is still as it was beforehand, but this permanence from the past cannot last.

Apart from the gerente and his trim wife there are 120 other families living on the

Who will inherit this earth? ABOVE *Three men from Rio Grande do Sul who had come to see if an investment* ▷ *would pay.* BELOW *Xavante children being taught about agriculture at a mission.* OVERLEAF *The vaqueiros who lead hard, hot, dusty lives together with the cattle.*

Suiá Missú Fazenda. The axe men are impermanent and they come and go, in the main, without their families. A total of 120 full-time families is a small figure, bearing in mind the enormity of the place, those 19,000 head of cattle, the plans for the future, and the fact that the fazenda operates a hotel, an efficient electrical system and a fleet of lorries to bring in essentials such as rice, beans and fuel oil.

There is in consequence a variety of occupations. For the main part the inhabitants are cattlemen, the vaqueiros who are the cowboys of Brazil. They work almost entirely from the backs of their mules, and such partnerships can drive a herd of cattle through that difficult country with all the stop-start agility of a sheepdog on the hills. All day long it was a sudden burst of speed, a stopping, a furious pursuit of a single errant beast, and a steady whooping noise when everything was going smoothly. The men have to wear wide leather trousers to stop their legs being torn to shreds as they rasp through the undergrowth. They wear either tasselled, up-brimmed leather hats of north-eastern Brazil or the American style of ranch-hand stetson. Indeed they look remarkably like the fictionalized style of the celluloid cowboys, save that their shirts cling with sweat to their bodies. The dust clings to them, sweat seeps through the dust and everything is torn. Nothing has that clean simplicity of the movies. The men lasso the animals they want to catch, and they frequently miss, and when they succeed the animal comes down in a painful heap of flailing limbs. Naturally (and this must have happened in the United States as well, however much the films may steer clear of the point) a large number of the mule-men are Negroes. They, the sweat and the ragged clothes provide an essential authenticity to the Brazilian scene, and happily destroy all romanticized versions of this kind of labour. It is incredibly hot, wearisome and demanding. There is little occasion for all that carefree backchat drawl we know so well. Besides any word that is spoken comes out in Portuguese.

Wages on the Fazenda Suiá Missú are good by local standards. They sounded very good the way the gerente phrased them because he referred to all salaries as multiples of the minimum wage. This basis, he said, was 150 new cruzeiros a month ($36 or £15 a month at the prevailing rate of exchange). The basic manual labourer on his fazenda received one-and-a-half times this amount. The cowboys received more. The mechanics received three or four times the minimum wage. Even £60 a month, assuming any kind of validity for the rate of exchange between sterling and cruzeiro, was only £720 a year and it sounded like good money out there if only because it was such a substantial degree above the average. Grass planters, as with the axe men, received piece-work payment calculated on the assumption that a grass man could sow five acres in 11 days. That seems good going, bearing in mind the difficulty of the terrain over which the sower has to clamber when scattering his seed, but it makes the axe man's ability to chop down a similar area in only 47 days even more impressive.

◁   *Liana, symbol of the tropical forest.*

Although the fazenda is such a major enterprise the total wage bill is modest, mainly by virtue of the small numbers being employed. With 120 permanent families, and with 250 seasonal workers, there are as yet some 4,000 acres per worker at the best of times. The numbers will grow, and the density will increase, but the intention is to have the estate worked by the minimum possible number of people. The backlands may be developed but, Brasília and new roads notwithstanding, they will remain as backlands. The magnetism of the coast is unlikely to lose its virulent power.

Even if the average Brazilian were to experience a change of heart, and determinedly forget all about the east, the old lines of force affecting his money would still lead to and from the traditional seats of financial authority. The Mato Grosso's development in the west is being financed with money from the east. The fazendeiros—or their agents—fly in with the great bundles of cash, and all this money then percolates slowly eastwards to the big banks from which, counted and wrapped, it had emerged in the first place. The British expedition, with major food, petrol and wages bills to pay every month, had to collect its regular bundles of money all the way from Brasília. Once every couple of months the expedition lorry would make this journey, mainly to fetch equipment and deliver collections, but also to bring the money from east to west. Cheques, letters of credit and all the other securer means of transporting money were of little value in Aragarças and far less in Xavantina, and it was easiest to bring in the money in cash in suitable denominations. The British requirements were not unique in this regard, and many of the planes, jeeps and lorries heading west must have had similar bundles of money, probably wrapped in newspapers, as part of their baggage. Not only were our own employees scrupulously honest with this wealth but no hold-ups ever occurred along the long and frequently lonely road from bank to camp and there was no talk of any such avarice. The granite banks of the big cities were frequently raided; not so the up-country couriers so laden down with wealth beyond their own personal means.

In many ways the finances of a big fazenda like Suiá Missú were operated without any great need for mere cash. The workers lived largely on credit, and much if not most had to be deducted before each pay-day. The cattle were largely bought in the east and most of the produce would be sold in the east. It was possible to live on a fazenda for a long time and not see any actual money, let alone money changing hands. What, after all, was there to buy that could not be bought from the fazenda's own store and therefore be put on the slate?

Moreover, inflation had made the stuff so bulky and unwieldy, despite that trick of knocking off three zeros from the sum. Of this loaded problem I had personal experience. On my final visit to Brazil, having learnt the difficulty of exchanging such oddities as travellers cheques in a state like Mato Grosso, and knowing that even Brasília could be short of money in its vaults, I decided to take all I would need from Rio. Unfortunately it so happened that there had been a run on large denomination currency, and I could not be given notes larger than 5,000 old cruzeiros, now equal to five new cruzeiros, and therefore worth, at the existing rate of exchange, some fifty pence. It was to be an expensive trip, hiring air taxis to visit outlying fazendas, and making use of boats, vehicles and people, and it was therefore with a pile of money 15 inches high that I left the bank. A wallet could have bulkily absorbed not one per cent of that pile. A couple of money belts, purchased with forethought beforehand, were almost as inadequate, and the pile filled a major part of my suitcase. Although this valuable burden was to lie around in hotel rooms, wrapped for security inside some evil and ancient shirt, no one ever stole so much as an inch of it. Nevertheless, when an air taxi bill came to, say, $250 or £100 it was a pleasure to count out a couple of hundred 5,000 notes on the wing of the plane and thenceforth feel both lighter and more secure by that amount. Probably the pilot would fly that money and all his other earnings swiftly back to the East of its birth, but lesser sums took longer to return along the same inexorable path. Schoolboys often write essays about the life of a penny. The story of the return of Brazilian cash, whether wrapped in Arab garments or thumbed into near extinction from bar to bar, would also have much to say about that particular kind of economy.

Fazenda Suiá Missú is a scheme that would make most financial backers waver. Quite apart from the expense involved in tearing the place down and then in building it up again as cattle, roads and houses, there is the overriding problem that all its square miles are hundreds of miles from anywhere. A good head of beef is all very well, but less well if it is an unprofitable distance from the consumer. A large number of Mato Grosso consumers suddenly springing up, both numerous and wealthy enough to pay for herds of this nature, is extraordinarily unlikely. Beef is cheap enough on the fazendas—as indeed it should be, bearing in mind the numbers of animals trampling through the surrounding countryside—but it is still a luxury crop elsewhere. Within Mato Grosso state there are so few people, both relatively and absolutely, and so most of the beef will eventually head eastwards. Mato Grosso's population of about a million people is already eclipsed by a cattle population of about ten million, and Suiá Missú's few hundreds of people set against its many thousands of cattle only exacerbate this situation.

The backers of Suiá Missú are undaunted both by the amount already spent and the further problem of getting this money back again. Remarkably, despite the size of this place, the destruction, the creation, the establishment of a going concern, the perpetual ferrying of supplies, and the building up of a major quantity of cattle, the total bill for the first five years at this one fazenda was only $2.5m or £1,100,000. Certain initial expenses had been heavy, but future growth was to be even faster. These two factors, the early difficulties and the later scale of the operation, precisely matched each other because the estimated expenditure for the second five years was also expected to be £1,100,000. By then about 135,000 cattle would be grazing off 200,000 acres of cleared and seeded land, and would also be making use of a good few thousand acres of uncleared cerrado. That ten-year stage would be the limit, so far as investment was concerned. The fazenda would by no means be running at its maximum capacity by then, but it would start paying for itself. The killing of the cattle would start—10,000 a year to begin with—and income would therefore begin. The actual stock of cattle, despite this slaughter, would continue to rise and so would the annual culling. Within five years of that turning point, or so it was confidently hoped by the gerente and the powers behind him, all the investment would have been paid back. Thereafter Fazenda Suiá Missú would be on an exceptionally sound commercial footing.

It will be even sounder in the years to come because the eventual plan is to have a million head of cattle on the estate. The business will then be very big indeed with at least 500 head being slaughtered each and every day. The distance to Rio and São Paulo will then be no less, and the big markets no nearer, and it is assumed that all the beef manufactured on the fazenda will have to be flown from it in refrigerated aircraft. The first refrigeration plant will be installed to coincide with the turning point in five years' time, but its capabilities will be small compared with the final production. The current airstrip, for example, will have to be substantially larger, and surfaced, and far more capable if it is to deal with large transport aircraft taking out those frozen carcases of 500 animals every single day.

Moreover Suiá Missú is only one fazenda, although the most advanced in the area. There will be all the others, each with their 200 square miles or so of land, and each with their own batch of black vultures hanging over the slaughterhouses. The leap from the past to the future will take no more than a couple of decades, and everyone involved will wonder what has happened, whether they themselves actually laboured to make it happen or merely watched.

Dr. Erminio Ometto planned his Mato Grosso enterprise without either governmental involvement or assistance. He was rich enough to withstand a drain on his resources of £2,200,000 spread over a period of ten years, and had calculated the project with care. Even a final price was put on the total investment—12,305,826 new cruzeiros. However, five years after he had purchased the land, and three years after work had seriously begun at the fazenda, the government offered financial support.

Briefly, in any government-approved project, the private capital needs only to be 25 per cent of the whole and the state provides the remaining 75 per cent. The simplest way to produce this money is via tax relief, and the governmental contribution can be up to 55 per cent of the taxes owed by the firm (or man) setting up the project. To him that hath, therefore, shall be given once again, or at least not taken away. By not having to pay 55 per cent of his taxes a man can more easily provide the necessary capital for the next endeavour. Of the 12 million new cruzeiros which the Ometto project was expected to consume, over seven million would come in the form of tax rebate. As this figure cannot be more than 55 per cent of the total tax bill it means that Dr. Ometto must have been facing a tax bill of at least 14 million new cruzeiros over the same period of ten years.

The forest is going. There is no hope for such a luxury in a world always hungry for land. ▷

This means, bearing inflation and other difficulties loosely in mind, a tax demand of at least £100,000 every year. The rich men of Brazil can be extraordinarily rich and will undoubtedly be richer still when their Mato Grosso returns start coming in. The old Indian country is not only providing a quick return on investment but a convenient method of lessening tax demands, a concept about as alien to the communal Indian way of life as could ever have been devised.

To an outsider the most striking point about all the activity involving large quantities of capital is that the end product is considered only of marginal interest. When the squatter plants manioc or acquires a litter of spotted piglets he knows very well the reasons for their existence; not so the wielders of larger fortunes. Everyone in the praefecture of Barra do Garças is interested in building up large herds of beef, but the market is by no means certain, particularly its export side. This uncertainty is not considered of prime importance by the fazendeiros. Of more substantial interest is the fact that taxes have been used (instead of being kept by the government) and the land this money has been spent on has gone up in value not several hundred per cent but several hundred times. If there is to be a profit, if beef proves to be a saleable commodity, this remunerative reward will come along at a decently short interval like 10 years. If there is not to be a profit at least one's taxes will have been used to create a capital gains empire of mammoth proportions.

The governmental authority is also not noticeably concerned about the end product and whether it will sell in the chancy medium of world trade. Government aid is organized by development agencies, not trading organizations, and their primary aim is to develop the land, to see that it is both tamed and occupied. Production from that land, whether beef or something else, is secondary to them. As in building a bridge or a road the main objective is to create access. What is done with that access does not immediately concern those who provide it.

So far as the Xavantina/São Félix road is concerned it was both planned by the government, and was yet unplanned. It was built by government money and along a route thought by the engineers to be most satisfactory. Its present squatters and families are mainly living at the subsistence level, or very near it, and they are certainly quite unplanned. At the other end of the scale most of the major land exploiters are working with government assistance and yet without government control. The men in charge of the development agency are happy to see the forest come down and the land made ready, but do not concern themselves with produce. Obviously, if anything is to happen with this land, they argue, it cannot exist in its former capacity. Then it was fit only for Indians and for no one else. If it is to be made fit for the twentieth century it must first be cleared. And that, as the smoke rises thousands of feet into the air to black out the sun, is precisely what is happening. Fired by tax concessions and the thought of capital gains,

◁   *They had seventeen children and they had no rights, or every right, according to your point of view.*

and with the good chance of income as well if the beef market survives, the Mato Grosso is yielding its ancient authority. That streak of a road, fired like an arrow through the heart of the jungle, is being lethal to the old kingdom. One day they will wonder, as they already do in so many other parts of the world, where the forest used to stand. And whether it is true that there used to be trees as far as the eye could see.

To leave the Fazenda Suiá Missú is to drive along a road (*its* road) and to swerve from side to side in the puffy dust. It is to munch biscuits and tinned meat from the fazenda's store which, incidentally, sells no beer. It is to pass thousands of cattle still having to stumble over their pasture. It is also to worry about the destruction of the habitat. It had been disturbing to hear the gerente say that more rain would fall if the forest was cut down—if anything the converse is the truth—and to hear him confidently confirming this opinion with a few rain-gauge measurements taken over a short span of years. Central Brazil is lucky in having no strong winds to blow all that dust away.

The wholesale adjustment of the area is too enormous for anyone to predict precisely what will happen, save that the forest will never return. In the old days the border-line between forest and cerrado must have moved tremulously back and forth, as circumstances permitted or encouraged this to happen. The Suiá Missú area lies within this border-zone and must have alternated perpetually from forest to cerrado in uncertain fashion. What is certain is that, following the destruction of the forest and its razing to the ground, the forest will not reappear even if all the developers were to pack their bags and leave. The land would then be scrubland as far as the eye could see, much like certain wastelands of the United States. The Americans found the rich prairie grasslands and often made them poor. In Brazil, the story could so easily be repeated with the forests.

To drive south, having left the vast domain of the Fazenda Suiá Missú, and to drive as swiftly as the road will permit, is to receive a kaleidoscopic picture of various images passing by which make up the whole. There is, for example, a hut, walled in mud, poorly thatched and casual in its disrepair, but with one bright gleaming length of wire between two stout poles meaning that radio reception from Brasília and the south-east will be that much better. There is a steam engine, disregarded at present because its trailer has collapsed, but a prerequisite for some new fazenda further north. To the right of the road is an old squatter's home, but with the dried-out, spreadeagled shape of cow-hide across the door indicating that no one is at home. Can there be such an area anywhere else where so many people are in such need and where so little pilfering of possessions occurs? There will be valuables—of a kind—within that home or at least such pots, seats and cups as would be valuable to anyone without them, but they will be safe.

The people themselves, when at home in such desolate spots, will also be entirely safe. To arrive at a dwelling, perhaps with a consignment of many other men, or just by oneself, and to stroll up to a house plainly filled only with women and children, is to have thoughts oneself of the fear one's presence might be creating. After all it would be a long time indeed before the law, any law, either heard of or caught up with some misdemeanour in such a wilderness and policemen in the Mato Grosso are one of its greater rarities. I personally do not recollect seeing one but I, personally, never heard tell of any great need for one.

To the left of the road are a group of axe men, bees on their backs, and each with a file sticking high up from a pocket in his trousers. Further on a coatimundi scuttles across the road, and then climbs up a tree to look down at us past his bushy tail. Parrots hurtle past, confident in their proper element and make straight lines over the tree tops. They look marginally less perfect when a freshly cleared and deforested patch is beneath them, and their loud catcalling shrieks then seem more anguished than before. Up on a hill, dustily distant from the road, is a tin shack settlement, obviously with money behind it and with oranges, lemons, avocado trees and tangerines in its forecourt. At times there is nothing quite so luxurious, or so magical as a fruit hanging on its tree, and it can taste all the better when picked, hot outside and warm inside, for immediate eating. Such a fruit detour, however blatant its approach, is incredibly easy to make and the men in charge of the trees are immediately generous. 'Manager and his assistant both come from São Paulo', goes down in the notebook. 'They're convinced SP people are best people at doing anything. Also SP language best in Brazil (certainly it is easiest for English to understand). Perhaps three other states have same quality as SP, e.g. Rio Grande do Sul. For the rest they are *bom para nada*—good for nothing—or so they say to us.' Nevertheless the oranges taste delicious. There is no need for the diary to record that point as their excellence is entirely unforgettable.

The road itself is extraordinarily empty, bearing in mind its arterial importance to so many differing communities. After all it is the only way back to São Paulo or to anywhere else, save by air. Camp members trying to hitch-hike either north or south, and realizing the fatuity of trying to walk the distance, have stayed for six hours or so on the same spot before the first vehicle came along. The local tradition is to pick up anyone if possible but to carry on well past him before stopping, as if several miles of visibility was insufficient to stop in time. The very emptiness of the road is itself a danger because, every so often, there is a curve. After a few hours' driving any driver is likely to assume he is entirely alone in his pursuits, and he has lonely reason for his egocentricity. Consequently he has a tendency to drive round the few corners with as little presumption that he will meet another vehicle as that he will encounter tarmac, neon lights, roadsigns or any other unlikely incursion. To be wary of this danger, and to sound a horn while keeping righteously to the right-hand side, is of little value because few klaxons can invade the decibels surrounding any other vehicle on that battered road to reach the ear of its equally battered driver.

It was pleasant, when returning along the familiar road, to find changes, to discover that a tree had come into flower, that the dead dog had disappeared, that an empty house was now full of life. Occasionally the agent of some new fazendeiro had come to claim his all, and a motley collection of clearings and dwellings were evenly labelled with a regular series of signs saying all too clearly who now owned the place. Sometimes there were locusts *en route*, blundering along in their own interpretation of flight and being so easy to catch by hand when on their fluttering, crackly wing; but often they were entirely absent. The sugar cane by the roadside was either tall, green and white, like some gigantic bullrush army; or else it had been cropped and only dry stems lay here and there.

Such traffic as there was along this road, notably the fuel tankers going to and from the big fazendas, had caused a hotel to spring up out of the trees a hundred miles north of Xavantina. Known as the Pensão Gato it was of no great stature by normal standards, but it amply supplied all Mato Grosso needs. To arrive was to cause the assumption that a meal was required. To sit down was to imply that the time was right. The food then appeared, often without a word being spoken, save for the civilities of introduction. Plate upon plate of chunks of meat (a skilled carver would make a thin living in central Brazil), hard-boiled eggs, fried eggs in layers, dry manioc, pumpkin, paw-paw, banana, ladies fingers and, of course (otherwise the world would halt in its tracks), boiled rice and black beans. The rooms had beds in them, with clean blankets against the hard mud walls. There was a shower outside, provided a girl had filled the bucket, then raised it up to the pulley's height and placed a lamp nearby. A courtliness in this kind of welfare was wholly welcome. Pensão Gato also overcame that normal Achilles heel—or indeed Achilles leg—of most such establishments by having no lavatory whatsoever. Instead the great Mato Grosso beyond was more than adequate, provided all newcomers steered clear of the flocks of butterflies, unerring indicators of those who had gone before.

Even Xavantina, on the return journey, became a prince of cities. It had festivals when hundreds poured on to its straight streets. It lit fires to celebrate the day of St. John, or indeed any of the crucial Catholic occasions, and the neat, small stockades of wood burnt splendidly before every home. It had fireworks, and of the crudest kind, being uniformly content to do no more, and no less, than to make three loathsome, unrewarding bangs. By day, probably, it had fruit in its shops. It probably had torch batteries, and often had meat. It always had the *urubu* flying above, the vultures so infinitely more admirable the greater their distance. It had the ferry, if not always the ferryman, and the waters of the Rio das Mortes were always soothing to the scarred and scratched remains of insect bites of every calibre from tabanid to maruim. In its way Xavantina was an exciting stepping stone to all those fazendas to the north, to all those places it had helped to happen. In fact it had done so well that they were already overtaking it and were providing services even Xavantina could not muster, such as electrical supplies whose current did not alternate fitfully according to some generating whim. In time Xavantina may again catch up with its offspring, those burgeoning tax concessions along the road. In the meantime no right-thinking fazendeiro would dream of relying upon Xavantina for anything.

9 ATE LOGO

Before the British scientists had moved out of their forest camp they received an idea of what would happen to their precious and carefully-studied 20 kilometre square. A jeep arrived, and three stocky men climbed out of it. There had been all manner of visitors to that camp, but there was something immediately different about these three men. They strutted about as if they owned the place. Moreover, to support this illusion, they even said that they did. They said that they represented those who possessed not just the camp area but a huge territory on all sides of it.

Such a visit had always been anticipated in camp. After all the land certainly belonged to somebody, as every scrap of the praefecture of Barra do Garças had already been sold, and it was reasonable that someone should turn up one day to claim his own. However the anticipation of this event did nothing to lessen its seeming brutality when the moment did arrive. Like squatters the British knew that they had no rights to the land, and certainly did not pretend to any, but the passage of time had caused a kind of rightfulness to exist. After all who had put up the huts? Who had created all the picadas and had even given names to the prominent features of this place? Who had lived there for the past two years, because it was certainly not the three men who strode here and there across the compound, across our compound?

They came, they said, because they had heard of the British camp and had then heard that the place was being vacated. They thought it would be profitable to find out how much of it might be useful to them when they eventually started work upon their inheritance. So they pointed at this and that, at this row of huts, at that aluminium laboratory, at this water tower and at that piece of equipment, and suggested that these things should be left in their care. They had not objected to the British presence on their land and therefore something in the nature of a *quid pro quo* would not go amiss. They were neither demanding nor arrogant. They merely showed a practical approach.

Unfortunately, as Iain Bishop explained to them, there were plans to turn the whole area into a permanent study centre. This was the intention of the Royal Society and the Royal Geographical Society, and the Brazilian scientific authorities were currently examining the feasibility of such an idea. In any case, even if no such centre could be permanently maintained, Brazilian science would have to benefit from any equipment left behind. It could not go to the landowner, however useful his land might have been. The men accepted these points and then sat down for coffee.

They explained what they would do with the land. Of course they would burn the bulk of its forest, just as the other major fazendas were doing up and down the road. They would probably be planting rice in the areas of the gallery forest, and they would graze cattle on the scrubland of the cerrado. 'You will be amazed', they said, 'should you come back in a few years' time. You will not recognize it. There will be roads, and houses instead of these shacks, and the forest will have gone.' The British group listened, silently, and then yet more so, as they pondered the inevitable destruction. They had patiently measured, and counted, and examined, and soon the holocaust would roar through it all.

The three men then left, full of carefree shouts about the progress that was to come. At the top of the drive, where the turn-off joined the main road, they again emerged from their jeep and hammered two posts into the ground. Between these they nailed a board, firmly and blatantly, that gave the names of the syndicate of men who owned the area. It was not a very big board, and the names were illegible unless it was examined closely, but those red letters on that white background were as garish as a blot on a clean, white page. There were miles and miles of green on every side and then, suddenly, there was the effrontery of this notice-board. It had great power to it and that turn-off was never the same again. In the past it had been 'our' drive to 'our' camp; thereafter it was nothing of the sort. The claimants had claimed and the visitors were due to go.

Going was a sorry business. When the time came, and when the shuttling of scientists from London had dwindled and stopped, the Brazilian authorities had still not decided how they could make use of the place. They could not even offer a caretaker to look after the camp while negotiations were in progress, and therefore everything of value had to be stripped from the site in the hope that it would be useful when the research centre was opened up once more. It took time crating what had been created, packing up, pulling down, and sending away what had been such an effort to bring to the place. Local people, and even others from far away, came to watch, and to beseech, and to demand, in the hope that they would become richer than before. Of course the valuables all went back to Brasília, but one man's idea of a valuable commodity is not the same as another's. To see men lumbering out of camp with half a plank, or empty aerosols, or indeed with broken objects of any kind, was always sad, and these visits were perpetual until the final truck had driven away with the final crates. Thereafter they continued but more spasmodically. Even three and four weeks after that final lorry had gone there

The local people picked over the old base camp and removed everything of value to them. It could so easily have become a research station guiding future development in that area. ▷

were still the occasional pickers among the ruins, finding valuables with a yet smaller intrinsic worth than half a plank or an empty can.

With so much groundwork achieved in the area, with maps and collections made from every part of it, the 20 kilometre square could well have become a scientific reserve within the vastness of the Mato Grosso. It could have had much to say to the men invading the area. It could have recommended certain policies and, possibly even more helpfully, dissuaded the invaders from policies likely to destroy the very place they were invading. Perhaps the well-studied square was too much ahead of its time, for where on Earth are experts called in to assist with a certain problem until that problem is sorely advanced and help is crucial?

The disparity between the activities at camp and those on the nearby fazendas was blindingly conspicuous at every turn. One man, investigating the soil, might refer to the English journal in which his results would eventually be published while the fazendeiro, no less preoccupied with the self-same soil, plainly had no intention of reading a book of any scientific kind, let alone a publication from another land and in another tongue. There was the gerente, with 20,000 cattle already under his control, looking up anthrax in the book for the very first time. It is fervently to be hoped that he does not learn about it all too soon, as thousands of those animals succumb to the disease and teach him about it far more tellingly than a book could ever do.

There was also another gap between the visitors and the visited. In the main those coming to the area felt sorry that the forest was going, or even angry. Those cutting it down, whether wielding an axe or holding the money to pay for its destruction, seemed less concerned at such a critical change to the landscape. The British, although welcoming the thought of more productivity from all this empty land, were essentially conservationist, but they kept most of their resentment for the thought that the land's transformation might not be handled sensibly. If the forest had to go it should at least be replaced by something entirely beneficial to the community. If it were to be exploited, and then replaced by something akin to the devastation caused in so many other virgin lands, that would be a catastrophe greater still for it would mean that all those earlier examples had done nothing to blunt man's greed and unwillingness to learn.

There were occasions when the desire for conservation most definitely weakened. Perhaps it did so at the end of a long day's tramp through the dry forest, particularly if the ticks had been outrageously exploratory. Or if the sun had shone too brightly, and the sweat bees had been too demanding, quite suddenly a longing to have done with it all would pervade a flagging spirit. I remember once when a colleague, weary and hot, tripped on some trailing tendril of an epiphyte and fell headlong into a rotten

She too was a settler and lived near the Araguaia River. Any day she could wander into the surrounding wilderness, pick orchids OVERLEAF, *watch huge butterflies, admire oyster petals or even the odd shapes of a much burnt sedge. But what will the place be like when she too is old?* ▷

log, rich with ants of every calibre. A lot of noise came from that log, a lot of expressions of considerable dismay, but there were two words that were both unmistakably coherent. 'Stuff conservation', he had said, very loudly and fairly frequently.

It was at the end of such a day that a man, even if he had been a dedicated scientist all day long, would come nearest in his approach to the fazendeiro. He would wonder—in his despair—just how the Indian problem could be settled as no way seemed satisfactory. It was reactionary to attempt to keep primitive cultures alive in the twentieth century. It was wrong to keep them out of touch with the world in which they lived. It was virtually impossible to see that they got a fair deal, whichever course was adopted. There seemed to be so little hope for the Indian as an Indian, and the sooner he became a Brazilian, by whatever method, the better it would be for him and all his tribe. So much, in short, for the Indian.

What about the forest? Of course it could be beautiful, and there was a magic to it, and there was all the life dependent upon it, but surely it had to go. Enclaves could be kept, much like the reserves of every country, but they would be fragments of the whole. For the main part the axe would have to do its work, for of what use was a national resource unless resourceful men took advantage of it? It would be hard work, and expensive, and the circumstances would never be as congenial as those back in the east. Therefore it was right that a man should wish to make money out of his efforts, a lot of money, in fact as much as he possibly could.

The chances were that if an expert came along, someone perhaps from an international agency, he would make innumerable suggestions, all of which, apparently, would somehow be aimed at reducing the immediate profitability of the land. He would recommend maintaining or increasing the fertility of the soil. He would suggest moderation, and would propose that prevention is better than cure, even though it was not inevitable that a cure would always be necessary. There was every chance that he would be a pain in the neck, however wise he was, however honourable his motives. He would only be able to prevent, or limit, or stop, because every fazendeiro knew how to go about exploiting the country. If further advice proved necessary it could probably be acquired up and down the road from the other fazendeiros. There was more than enough work for everyone to do, without additional suggestions from well-meaning investigators.

Significantly, although the team at base camp tended to ask questions of anyone ready to answer them, those that they questioned very rarely returned the curiosity. A soil man might ask a fazendeiro—at length—about his land and his intentions, but the questioner would receive nothing in return about his own researches and thoughts on the very same subject. It was a one-way traffic of information, for the fazendeiros were welcoming, entirely hospitable, always gracious and never curious. Perhaps it

◁ *He had been rich, he said. Now he had nothing and they used him to help cut down the forest.*

was reticence, or good manners, or a style of life, but it could well have been a feeling of total self-sufficiency on their part. Besides, or so they might have argued, the British scientists in their camp had come to learn about Brazil, and therefore it was up to Brazil to tell them what they wished to know, to answer their questions and leave it at that.

The disparity was not just between the geographer and the man who was re-shaping the geography of the land. It was at all levels. The camp had medical doctors: the Xavantina hospital frequently had no staff whatsoever, not even a nurse or a doorman. The camp had wealth on every side, at least through the eyes of someone who could see no cash for himself or his family in any direction. Most scientists had flown in from another hemisphere, and many had scores of other countries within their experience. The caboclos had probably been to Goiás, possibly to another state, and had probably never even seen the sea. They knew the Mato Grosso, and that was their world, but it bore little relation to the rest of the planet. It was a frontier state, raw and uncompromising. It was presumably booming in its own somewhat lethargic manner, but it looked poor. It was changing overnight, and yet everywhere had an ancient look. Government policy was opening up the place, and yet the trappings of bureaucracy were not visible. Where were the officials in Barra do Garças? Did anyone meet an inspection officer? Did anyone ever see a policeman?

Few Brazilian scientists visited the area or even the base camp, and the excellence of those that came caused the British scientists to regret that there could not be more of them. Sadly those that did come were, in the main, only able to stay for a very short time. Too many had too many commitments elsewhere, and were possibly filling more than one vacancy in the establishment where they worked. Too few of them were able to take advantage of the colossal laboratory within the undeveloped recesses of their country. There was too much for them to do either within their place of work or the very moment they left it. There was no need for them to travel deeply into the interior to find subjects worthy of investigation. Consequently the new frontiers were left pretty much to themselves, to the developers from São Paulo, to the caboclos. The frontier did open up equally great chances for either success or failure. Time would tell which it would be.

Papers are now being prepared to take their place in the scientific literature. Copies or abstracts of these papers will find their way to Rio or Brasília, to the libraries of the universities, but none of them, probably, will cross the Araguaia or the Garças, or be made to travel past the 20 kilometre square, the place of their origin. That will subside and become indistinguishable from the rest of the land. That place will be a memory in the minds of those who worked there, but their work will not affect the axe men who will cut the trees down, and burn them, and thereby pave the way for the cattlemen who will drive in their herds past those empty picadas. The British scientists had arrived at this new road in order to be ahead of development, and so they were. They were ahead by an enormous margin, a gap which may widen yet further in the years to come between the developed and the undeveloped regions of the world. Somehow the two will have to come closer together, and both forms of expert will have to play their part jointly, the men who study the soil in every particular and the men who make it work for them.

The Mato Grosso is the last great area in the world that is immediately ripe for full-scale development. The Indians preserved it, and then yielded it as they either died or retreated from their former omnipotence. It took a little time before the pressures built up to make use of this new land, but it is now crumbling before them. The forest of the Mato Grosso is as mortal as the Indians who lived within its enormity, and many of the pictures in this book will become archival documents before many more years have passed. 'Was it really like that?' they will say. Let us hope that the area will flourish, and benefit mankind, and they will never say: 'Would that it were like that once again.'

'There were miles and miles of green on every side and then, suddenly, there was the effrontery of this notice board.' The claimants had come for their due, and that was that.

PARTICIPANTS IN THE XAVANTINA/CACHIMBO EXPEDITION

		Affiliation at the time of the Expedition	
Iain R Bishop OBE *Leader*	Mammals	School of Biology University of Leicester	April 1967 – October 1969
Angela Bishop	Secretary Catering Officer		April 1967 – October 1969

Geography

Professor Eric H Brown	Physical Geography	University College London	September – October 1968
Stuart G Daultrey	Hydrology	University College of Wales Aberystwyth	September 1968 – June 1969
Professor Alfredo J P Domingues	Geomorphology	Instituto Brasileiro de Geografia e Estatistica Rio de Janeiro	July 1968
Mary Mason	Rural Development	University College London	June 1969
Professor Lucio de C Soares	Geography	Deputy Director IBGE Rio de Janeiro	July 1968
Dr John B Thornes	Fluvial Geomorphology	London School of Economics	April – June 1969
John R G Townshend	Geomorphology	University College London	July – December 1968
Dr Anthony Young	Geomorphology	University of Sussex	February – April 1968

Soil Science

G Peter Askew	Soil Science	School of Agriculture University of Newcastle upon Tyne	November – December 1967 March – May 1968
David J Moffatt	Soil Science	School of Agriculture University of Newcastle upon Tyne	July 1967 – September 1968
Roy F Montgomery	Soil Science	School of Agriculture University of Newcastle upon Tyne	June – September 1967 September – December 1968
Dr Peter L Searl	Soil Science	School of Agriculture University of Newcastle upon Tyne	March 1968 – April 1969

Botany

George C G Argent	Plant Ecology and Bryophyte Taxonomy	School of Plant Biology University College of North Wales Bangor	August – November 1967 June – September 1968
Professor Graziella M Barroso	Plant Taxonomy	Jardim Botanico Rio de Janeiro and Instituto Central de Biologia University of Brasilia	October 1968

with   Dr Waldock D Maia
Dr Alcina M Lima
Ana Maria de Barros Lima
Maria José Chaves
Eunice Onishi (also January – February 1969)

Dr George Eiten	Plant Taxonomy	Instituto de Botanica São Paulo	August – October 1968
Dr Liene Eiten	Plant Taxonomy	Instituto de Botanica São Paulo	August – October 1968
Dr David R Gifford	Forestry	University of Edinburgh	June – September 1967 February – April 1968
Dr F Barrie Goldsmith	Plant Community Analysis	University College London	March – May 1969
Dr Gerhard Gottsburger	Pollination Mechanisms	Instituto de Botanico São Paulo	May – June 1968 August – September 1968
Dr Ray M Harley	Plant Taxonomy	Royal Botanic Gardens Kew	August 1968 – January 1969
Dr Rolf D Illig	Plant Genetics	Instituto Central de Biologia University of Brasília	November 1967
David Philcox	Plant Taxonomy	Royal Botanic Gardens Kew	November 1967 – April 1968
Professor João Murça Pires	Plant Taxonomy	Instituto Central de Biologia University of Brasília	May 1969
Dr Jim A Ratter	Plant Ecology and Taxonomy	Royal Botanic Gardens Edinburgh	June – September 1967 March – July 1968
Professor Paul W Richards	Plant Ecology	School of Plant Biology University College of North Wales Bangor	August – November 1967 June – September 1968
Dr Daniel Morreira Vital	Bryophyte Taxonomy	Instituto de Botanico São Paulo	May – June 1968

Zoology

Luiz Azevedo	Entomology (Bees)	Federal University of Paraná	July 1968
Dr Roger A Beaver	Ecology of Bark Beetles	University College of North Wales Bangor	September – December 1968

Claudionor Elias	Entomology (Bees)	Federal University of Paraná	July 1968
Dr Brian E Freeman	Entomology	Sir John Cass College London	August – November 1967 February – April 1968
Dr C Hilary Fry	Ornithology	University of Aberdeen	July – October 1968
Professor Jim Green	Freshwater Ecology	Westfield College London	September – December 1968
Dr Bill D Hamilton	Entomology (Wasps)	Imperial College London	May – September 1968
Christine A Hamilton	Entomology (Wasps)		May – September 1968
The Hon Ruth L Jackson	Mammals	University of Aberdeen	January 1968 – March 1969
Dr Bill J Knight	Entomology	British Museum (Nat Hist)	October 1968 – April 1969
Dr Margaret C Knight	Freshwater Ecology	Twickenham County School	October 1968 – April 1969
Dr Sebastião Laroca	Entomology (Bees)	Federal University of Paraná	July 1968
A G Anthony Mathews	Soil Fauna and Termites	University of Edinburgh	September 1967 – November 1968
Dr Rosemary H Lowe-McConnell	Fish Biology		April – May 1968
Dr Timothy R New	Entomology (Psocids and Neuroptera)	Imperial College London	September 1968 – May 1969
Dr Ron Pine	Bats	Smithsonian Institution Washington	June – July 1968
Professor Owain W Richards FRS	Entomology (especially Wasps)	Imperial College London	January – April 1968 September – November 1968
The late Dr Maud J Richards	Entomology (Grasshoppers and Locusts)	Anti-Locust Research Centre	January – April 1968
David H Thomas	Ornithology and Effects of Burning	University of Aberdeen	January – May 1968

Medicine

D Lynn Aston	Leishmania	University College Hospital London	June – September 1968
Dr Jorge Boshell-Manrique	Virus Research	Belém Virus Laboratory Rockefeller Foundation	June – July 1968
Kenneth S Brecher	Social Anthropology	Institute of Social Anthropology Oxford	July – October 1968
Dr Michael I D Cawley	Cardio-vascular Disease	United Bristol Hospitals	April – August 1969
Dr John Guillebaud	Cortico-steroids and 'Stress'	Anatomy School Cambridge	October 1967 – March 1968
Dr Philip Hugh-Jones	Medical Studies	King's College Hospital London	July – October 1968
Dr Hugh I Jones	Tropical Medicine and Spiders		January – April 1969
Dr Ralph Lainson	Leishmania	Wellcome Parasitology Unit Instituto Evandro Chagas Belém	June – August 1968
The late Dr Robert A Mills	Anthropology and Tropical Medicine	Cardiff Royal Infirmary	March – August 1968
Dr Philip H Rees	Tropical Medicine	Hospital for Tropical Diseases London	June – October 1967
Dr Jeffrey J Shaw	Leishmania	Wellcome Parasitology Unit Instituto Evandro Chagas Belém	June – August 1968
Dr Anthony P Thorley	Leishmania	University College Hospital London	June – September 1968
Dr Jack P Woodall	Virus Research	Belém Virus Laboratory Rockefeller Foundation	June – July 1968
Anthony Smith	Scientific Correspondent		November – December 1967 July – September 1968 May – July 1969
Douglas S Botting	Photographer		May – July 1969
Geoffrey Bridgett	*The Times* Photographer		July – September 1968

INDEX

Numbers printed in *italics* indicate illustrations

aerial exploration, 20, 21, 36, 39, 50
aerial photographs used as maps, 53, 77, 104, 228; in soil study, 139
African bees, *see* bees
agouti, 194
air travel, 54, 67, 68, 104, 108
Airi (Indian drug), 184
aldeias (Indian villages), 94, 95, 101, 127
Amado, Jorge, 18
Amazon basin: size of, 17; settlements of, 18, 40; fauna of, 141, 211
Amazon river: as a guide to relative location, 19, 21, 24, 32, 60, 93, 175; destination of road, 49, 67
Anaconda, *see* snakes
anaemia, 119
Andes mountains, 17, 19
Andrelinho, 105, *106*, 107, *107*, 108, *154*, 156–7
Andropogon bicornis, 206
anteaters, 194, 198, 199, *199*
anthrax, 256, 276
Antonio 1, *154*
Antonio 2, 157
ants: dominance in Mato Grosso, 29, 77, 132, 281; hills, 30; habits of, 71; prey of, 143 (*Eciton*), 148
Apewen, 34
Aragarças, 20, 65, 67, 86, 192; as a guide to distance, 41; bridges at, 42; expedition members at, 49, 155, 264; means of travelling to, 58–9
Araguaia river, 19, 34, 50, *52*, 59; meets Garças, 20, 40, 42, 59, *61*; cattle transported on, 255–6
Arawak (Indian language), 120
Areões river, 67, 69; Xavante community on, 94, 95, 101, 103, 125, 126
Argent, George, 209
Arjimeiro, 71
armadillos, 194, *199*
arrowroot, 211
Aston, Lynn, 174, 177
Astrocaryum, *see* palms

bamboo, 65, 78
bananas, 56, 65, 95, 221, 272; leaves for thatching, 239, *239*
Barra do Garças, 65, 125, 129, 156; sale of land, 60, 273; Praefecture of, 60, 108, 228, 269, 282
base camp, 55, *57*, 70, 77, 92; suitable location for, 69, 139, 197, 202; construction of, 71; life in, 76, 89, *160*, 281, *283*; aerial view of, *82*; activities at, 131–64 *passim*; medical studies at, 174, 282; departure of expedition from, 273–6
Bates, H. W., 131, 132
bats, study and collection of, 194, *196*, 197
bee-eaters, African, 200–2
bees: study and collection of, 144, *146*, 211; honey, 72, 144, 197; sweat, 72, 203, 235, 271; African, 144; stingless, 144; 'Europa', 203
beetles (coleoptera), 147, *159*, 176
Belém, 55, 155, 156, 174, 175

Bertolda, João, 86, 156
birds, collection and study of, 199–202; *see also* under individual common names
Bishop, Angela, 49, 53, 69, *159*, 161, *162*
Bishop, Iain, 47, 49, 53, 69, 150, 161, *162*, 174, 273
blood, analysis of, 167
Blue Dacnis (*Dacnis cayana*), *188*
Boa constrictor, *see* snakes
Bonifacio, José, 39
botany and botanists, 132, 150, 182, *206–7*, *208*, *209*; botanical collections, 211
Botting, Douglas, 111, 248, 250
Brasília, 20, 39, *40*, 41, 55, 56, 58, 161; Cathedral, *45*; expedition members at, 49, 54, 70, 274; University of, 55, 157; banking at, 157
Brasilieros: photographs of, *61*, *73*, *151*, *154*, *217*, *226*, *244*, *253*, *259*, *260–1*, *267*, *268*, *275*, *277*, *280*; employees of expedition, 69, 78, 80, 149–50, 155–8
Brazil nuts, 211
Brazilian Geographical Institute, 93
Brecher, Kenneth, 104, 107, 108, 113
Breder, Jezonais, 157
Bridgett, Geoffrey, 104, 107, 108, 113
Bromeliad, 7
Brown, Eric, 214
buffalo gnats, *see* gnats
Buriti palms, *see* palms
burning of vegetation, 140, 212, 214, *223*, *224–5*; at Fazenda Dr Paulo, 229–30; at Fazenda Suiá Missú, 255, 269; planned for study area, 274
butterflies, *15*, 147, *160*, 272, *278*

caboclos, 71, 83, 86, 229, 282
Cabral, Pedro Alvares, 17
Cachimbo, 41, 92, 93, 150, 156, 166, 191
Cachoeira das Pedras, 238
Cachoeira von Martius, 60, 68, 238, *239*
caciques, 105
Calliandra longipes, *207*
Callichthys, *see* fish
camp, English, *see* base camp
campo, 30, 199, 255
cancer, first case in Parque Naçional, 185
candiru, *see* fish
capim colonião, *see* grass
Capitão Vasconcelos, 36
capybaras, 105, 108, *159*, 194
Carib (Indian language), 120
Cascara sagrada, 211
Cascavel, *see* snakes
cashew nuts, 211
cassara, *see* manioc
Cassia, unidentified, *206*
Catasetum macrocarpum, *207*
cattle, Zebu, 228, 234, 237, 255–6, *257*, 263, 265–6, 269
Cawley, Mike, 121, *121*
cayman alligators, 22, 22–3, 31, 104, 106, *106*
centipede, *8*
Central Brazil Foundation, 20, 41–2, 59–60, 66–7, 68, 150

cerrado, 29–31, 42, 58, 66, *74*, 126, 141, 150, *214*, 228, 265; mammals in, 194; birds in, 199; burning of, 212; border between forest and, 69, 270
Chagas' disease, 113, 156, 191–2
characid genus (*Hoploerythrinus*), 204
cicadas, 71, 197
cichlid genus (*Aequidens*), 204
coati (*Nasua nasua*), *80*, 271
cocaine, 211
cocoa, 211
coffee, 211
coleoptera, *see* beetles
collections, illustrations from members', *205*
compass, direction finding by, 77–8
conservation policy, 53, 193, 257, 276, 281
Constancio, *154*, 157–8
coral snake, *see* snakes
cormorants, 105
Correia, Jader Figueiredo, 39
Cottango, 113
Cowell, Adrian, 166
cuckoo, black, 67
Cuiabá, 59, 125
Culiseu river, 67
Culuene river, 35, 67, 238
curare, 211
custard apple, 211

Darwin, Charles, 14, 191
de Castro, Raimundo Aselino, *see* Taituba
deer (*Capridae*), *81*, 194
Delonix regia, *208*
desalination in tropical climates, 92
de Santos, Raimundo Reiss, 155–6
Diauarum, 105, 108, *109*, 111, *112*, 113, 120, 121, 129, 168
diseases of Indians, *48*, 119, *167*, 173, 185; smallpox, 18, 39, 122, 165 (vaccination); malaria, 192; grippe, 111, 120, 122, 129; *see also* medicine and medical treatment
drugs used by Indians, 103–4, 183–4
dry season, 132, 139, 204
Dyott, Commander George M., 32, 34, 35

Eagle, Harpy, *11*
ecology and ecologists, 131
edentates, 194
electric eels, 204
ema, 31, 70
entomology and entomologists, 131–2, 144–5
erosion, 53, 59, 137, 258; prevention of, 129, 140
espundia, *see* leishmaniasis
'Europa' bees, *see* bees
exploitation of Brazilian interior, 18, 31, 58, 269, 276

Fawcett, Brian, 35
Fawcett, Jack, 34
Fawcett, Colonel Percy Harrison, 19, 32, 161, 220; death of, 34
Fazenda Cachoeira von Martius, 239–40, *241*, *244*, 245–50, *247*, 252

Fazenda Dr Paulo, 228, 233, 235, *236*, 240, 248, 255, 258; finance of, 237–8
Fazenda Suiá Missú, 251–2, *253*, 255–8, *260–1*, 263, 270; expenses of, 264–5; market for products of, 265–6
fazendas, 107, 176, 214, 227, 238, 274
fazendeiros, 120, 178, 227, 264; agents of, 228, 271, 273, *283*; beef trade of, 269; attitude to forest, 281
Fer de Lance, *see* snakes
Ferreira, Aurelio, *154*, 158
fertilizers, 256
Finch, Pileated (*Coryphospingus pileatus*), *188*
firing the land, *see* burning of vegetation
fish: study and collection of, 203–4, 209; *Sorubim*, 8; piranha, *88*, 104, *172*, 203, 204; *Callichthys* (catfish), 203, 204; candiru, 209
fishing techniques, *170–1*, 203–4
Flame-crowned Manakin (*Hecterocercus linteatus*), *189*
Fleming, Peter, 35
flies: tabanid, *63*, 72, 222, 250; fruit, 72; *pium*, 75, 89, 185, *241*, 246, 250; house, 197, 227–8; *see also* gnats, midges
Flycatcher, Rusty-margined (*Myiozetetes cayanensis*), *189*
Fonseca, Joaquim, 157
forests, 17, 21, 24, *28*; destruction of, 234–5, 281; *see also* cerrado, mata seca
fruit flies, *see* flies
Fry, Hilary, 199–202, *202*
Fundacão Naçional dos Indios, 101, *102*, 103

gaivota, 106
Garapú, 67, 68, 69
Garças river, 20, 40, 42, 59, *61*, 282
Gé (Indian language), 120
Geraldão, 70, *73*, 222
gerente of Fazenda Suiá Missú, 255, 256–7, 263, 270, 276
Gifford, David, 209, *214*
gnats, buffalo, 75
Goiânia, 36, 49, 55, 58, 121
Goiás, 19, 32, 59, 121, 216, 282
governmental policy in Central Brazil, 60, 68, 102, 282; lack of, 216, 222, 269; tax relief for developers, 266
grass: insects living in, 76; on burnt land, 234 (*capim colonião*), 255 (Colonial, Jaragua, Napier types), *279*; planters, 263
grasshoppers, 131; short-horned, study and collection of, 147; *see also* locusts
groundnuts, 211
guanaco, 193
Guillebaud, John, 94–6, *95*, 101, 177, 180
Guyana, 141, 203, 204
gymnotids, *see* electric eels

Hamilton, Bill, 140, 141–3, *143*, 145, 158
Hamilton, Christine, 143, *145*
Harley, Ray, 209, 211
Harpy Eagle, *see* Eagle
hawks, 71, 250
Helicteres macropetala, *208*
Hemming, John, 92, 93, *93*
herons, 23
hoatzin, *231*
honey bees, *see* bees
hookworm, 184, 191
Hugh-Jones, Philip, 104, 107, *107*, 108, *112*, 113, 114
humming birds, 2, 71
Hunt, David, 49
hypochondria, 179–80, 249

ibises, 105
Inát (fish poison), 184
Incas and Mayas, 178

Indian Protection Service, 36, 39, 94
Indians of the Mato Grosso, 17, 49, 68, 91–130 *passim*, 247, 283; photographs of, *16*, *37*, *43*, *48*, *90*, 95, 97–99, 102, 110, 112, 115–18, 121, 123, 124, 128, 130, 164, 167, 169–72, 181, 242–3; uncontacted tribes, 18, 122; defence of territory, 19, 24, 32, 93; forest skills of, 30–1, 71; legends, customs, culture of, 114; exploitation and demise of, 39, 53, 122, 281; physical appearance of, 83, 103; in Parque Naçional, 92, 103, 122–6, 130, 130, 185; medical information from, 94–6, 103–4, 174, 177; medical skills of, 183–4; *see also* diseases of Indians, names of specific tribes
ion content of ash, 140; of river water, 258
ipecacuanha, 211
Iriri headwaters, 93–4
Irwin, H. S., 49

Jacamar, *190*, 201–2; Rufous-tailed (*Galbula ruficauda*), *188*
Jackson, Ruth, 174, 197, *199*
jaguars, 31, 42, 193–4, 239
Jararaca snake, *see* snakes
Jararacuçu snake, *see* snakes
Jatobá tree, 184
Jonas, 128–9, 158
Jones, Philip Hugh-, *see* Hugh-Jones
Julio, *149*, *154*, 158, *214*

Kajabí Indians, 34, 108, 113, 125, *242–3*, 245
Kalalatiri (toxic beverage), 184
Kalapaló Indians, 34, 125, 185
Kamayurá Indians, 119, 125, 185
Katepũ-Eglũ (tattooing juice), 184
Kayapo Indians, 34
Kielmeyera, *208*
kingfishers, 23–4; *Martim pescador*, 67; *Chloroceryle aenea* (Pygmy Kingfisher), *189*; *Ceryle torquatus*, 200
Kolé, 185–6
Kran-Acorore Indians, 93, 125, 165–6, 173
Kuarup festival, 97, *98–9*, 100; wrestling at, *115*, *116–17*, *118*
Kubitschek, Juscelino, 40
Kuhítse (red resin), 183
Kuikuru Indians, 119, 125, 183, 185
Kumairuqú (ointment), 184

Lafoensia pacari, 206
Lainson, Ralph, 174
Lambert, Christopher, 92
laterite, 137
leishmaniasis (espundia), 156, 179, 235, 237, 249; research into, 173–6, *175*, 177, 192
Leo, 158
Lepidoptera, *see* butterflies
Lewis, David Maybury-, *see* Maybury-Lewis
Liana, 262
lip discs, *110*, 113
lizards, 105; *Tupinambis teguixon*, 200
locusts, 70, 272; *Schistocerca gregaria*, 147; *see also* grasshoppers
loofah, 111
Lycopodium eichleri, 206

macaws, 31, 42, 69, 113, 220, 240, 246
McConnell, Rosemary, 202–4, 209
Machu Picchu, 19
maize, 211
Makukawá-Inuhri (eyedrops), 184
malaria, 119, 179, 192, 249
mammals: study and collection of, 193–7; kept alive after capture, *190*, *198*, *199*
Manakin: Red-headed (*Pipra rubrocapilla*), *188*; Flame-crowned (*Hecterocerus lineatus*), *189*

Manaus, 20, 40, 41, *41*
manioc, 95, 180, 211, 221, 230, 269, 272
Manitsauá Missú river, 168
Mario (São Marcos missionary), 126
maruim, *see* midges
Mason, Mary, 220, 221
Mason, Richard, 92, 93, *93*, 94, 165
Mata collado (*Ryania mansoana*, the silent killer), *182*
Matampó, *37*
mata seca (dry forest), 24, 29, 150; mammals of, 194; birds of, 199; *see also* cerrado, forest
Mathews, Anthony, 147
Matipu, 185
Mato Grosso, state of, 19, 20, 32, 39, 50, 59, 69, 272, 282–3; town of, 32; opening and development of, 36, 40, 60, 212, 230, 283; research programme in, 47, 49, 131; insect life in, 72, 76, 144, 147–9; erosion in, 129, 137; medicine in, 174, 179, 192; fish collection in, 203–4, 209; statistics about, 215; government in, 216, 269, 271; status of women in, 221; wealth and finance in, 252, 264
Mauritia palms, *see* palms
Mayas and Incas, 178
Maybury-Lewis, David, 20
medicine and medical treatment, 103, 119, 163, 179, 180, 192
medicine men (pajés), 119, 180, 183, 184
Mehinakú Indians, 125
Mémat (beverage), 183
Merowé, 108
meteorological site, 76
midges (*maruim*), 75, 203, 246; *see also* flies, gnats
Mills, Bob, 183, 185, 191, 192
Minas Gerais, 32
Moffatt, David, *89*, 132
monkeys, 31, 108, 113, *196*; capuchin, 83, 194
moradores (caretakers), 222
mosquitoes, 76, 203; larvae, 91; nets against, 75, 113
moths, 75, 147, 197
Muscovy ducks, 24, 105
mutum, 31

Negroes, 18, 83, 86; as mule-men, 263
Nicolau, Padre, 126, 128, 129
nightjars, 7, 70, 203
Nilto, 158
Nõntutu (oral contraceptive), 183
Noto (diarrhoea remedy), 184

Ometto, Dr Erminio, 252, 266
orchids, 219, *278*; *Catasetum macrocarpum*, 207
ornithology and ornithologists, 132, 147, 199
otters, 31, 113; *Pteroneura brasiliensis*, 194
ox-bow lakes, 21–2, 24, *25*, 245

Pabru, 191
Paepalanthus speciosus, 206
pajés, *see* medicine men
palms: Mauritia, 29; Buriti, 71, 111, 127, 197; thatch from, 77, 239; Astrocaryum, *208*
pantanal, *52*
Paraná, 32
Pará State, 32, 47, 50, 150, 156
parceiro (share cropper), 222
Parque Naçional do Xingú, *90*, 92, 119, 121–2, *169–72*, 185; foundation and control of, 68, 114; area of, 102–3, 111; way-of-life in, 103, *130*; British doctors visit, 104, 108, 183; Indian languages spoken in, 120; tribes in, 125; *see also* Villas Boas brothers

287

parrots, 31, 69, 220, 271
Paulo, Dr, 229–30, 233, 235, *236*, 237
paw-paws, 113, 211, 272
Pensão Gato, 272
pharmacies, 65, *179*
Philcox, David, 180, 209, 212
Phimeria, 31
physiological deterioration in the tropics, 91–2
picadas, 36, 39, 68, 77–8, 93; cut through study area, *89*, 163, 282; to contact new tribe, 168; around new fazendas, 222
Pileated Finch, *see* Finch, Pileated
Pine, Ron, 197
pineapple, 211
piranha, *see* fish
pium, *see* flies
pollination, explosive, 211–12
pollution, 108
polypharmacy, 180
population, Brazilian, 56, 58, 83, 265
porceiros, 222, 227
Pororí (Txukuhamae) village, *242–3*
Porter, Duncan M., 212
Portuguese language, 86, 108, 120, 157, 263; spoken by Indians, 113
Portuguese nationality, 17, 83
Posto Leonardo, 36, 68, 108, 114, 119, 185–6, 191; ways of travel to, 104–8; integration of, 113; organization of, 120–1
potato, 211
praias (sandbanks), 106–7
prawns, 203
Psocoptera, 147
Puyalú (beverage), 184
Pygmy Kingfisher, *see* kingfishers

Qualea ingens, *218*
quinine, 211

racial barriers in Brazil, 86
radio communication, 108, 120, 248; reception, 270
Ramos, José, 156
Ratter, Jim, 150, 157, 209
Red-eyed Vireo, *202*
Red-headed Manakin (*Pipra rubrocapilla*), *188*
resin guaiacum, 211
Richards, Maud, 147, 161
Richards, Owain, 140–1, 147, 158
Richards, Paul, 150, 158, 161
Rimmell, Raleigh, 34
Rio Batovi, 178
Rio das Mortes, 19, 20, 34, 40, 41–2, 59, 94, 155, 157–8, 204; ferry across, 49, 66, 67, 272; bathing in, 66, 185, 209
Rio de Janeiro, 19, 20, 39, 105, 147; expedition members at, 49, 55; prosperity of, 216, 264, 266
Rio Sete de Setembro, 67, 238
Rio Suiázinho, 107
Rio Tapajós, 150
Rio Tuaturi, 113
road project, *see* Xavantina/Cachimbo road
roças, 221, 222
rodents, 194; carriers of leishmaniasis, 174; in captivity, 197
Rondon, General, 36, 39
Rondônia territory, 32, 36
Royal Geographical Society, 20, 47, 49, 53, 92, 273; Founder's Medal, 104
Royal Society, 20, 47, 49, 53, 91, 273
rubber, 211
rubber trees (*Hevea*), 18, 31; tappers of, 111

Salesian missionaries, 125, 126, 130
Salvador, 39
sand flies (*Psychodid*), 75, 174–5, *176*, 178
Santarém, 40, 41

Santos, 19
São Félix, 60, *193*, 252, 255, 256
São Marcos mission, *123*, *124*, 125–30, *128*, 252
São Paulo, 19, 32, 55, 185, 271, 282; home of Mato Grosso developers, 36, 126, 235, 237; bees escape from, 144; area measures determined at, 252; markets at, 266
seriema, 70
Serra do Roncador, 21, *35*, 40, 42, 50, 60, *64*, 92, 126
Shaw, Jeffrey, 174
sloths, three-toed (*Bradypus tridactylus*), 194, *195*, *213*
snakes, 71, *80*, 142; Fer de Lance, 132; *Bothrops*, *136*; coral, *152–3*, 198; Cascavel, 198; Jararaca, 198; Jararacuçu, 198; Boa constrictor, *201*, *210*; Anaconda, *210*
Snowy Egret (*Leucophoyx thula*), *187*
soil and soil scientists, 132, 137–9, 228, 258, 276, 281
soil pits, 86, 197
Sorubim, *see* fish
South American Plague locust, 147
Souza, Raimundo (Raimundinho), *154*, 156
Sparrow, Rufous-collared (*Zonotrichia capensis*), *188*
spiders, *62*, *63*, 148, 203
Spiranthera odoratissima, 208
squatters, 215, 216, *217*, 219–22, 228, 258
steam-engine, *226*, 229, 233, 238
Sterculia striata, 207
stingless bees, *see* bees
sting rays, 104
Stripe-necked Tody-tyrant (*Idoptilon striaticolle*), *189*
study area, aerial photograph, *84*; map, *85*; size of, 76–7; a scientific reserve, 274, 276
sub-camps, 132, 163
sugar cane, 221
Suiá Indians, 21, 108, 121
Suiá Missú river, 21–4, *26–7*, 29, 91, 166–7, 199, 204, 245, 258, 270; expedition along, 104–8, 111, 113
Suiázinho river, 91
sun-bitterns, 24
'Survival Handbook', 240
Swallow-Tanager (*Tersina viridis*), *188*
sweat bees, *see* bees

tabanids, *see* flies
Taituba, 95, 101, 143, 150, *151*, 155, 156, 157
tapirs (*Tapirus terrestris*), 31, 70, 105, *106*, 108, 194, *199*
tax relief for developers, 266, 269
tayra (*Eira Barbara*), 194
termites, 29, 30, *52*, 72, 86, 131, 197, 257; study and collection of, 147–9, *148* (*Syntermes grandis*); mounds of, *149* (*Cornitermes bequaeri*), 176
Thorley, Anthony, 174, 177
Thornes, John, 111, 258
Tibouchina aegopogon, 206
ticks, 29, 76, *79*, 132, 157, 192, 257
tobacco, 211
Tocantins river, 91
Tolotutu, *see* Nõntutu
tomatoes, 211
Tordesillas, Treaty of, 17
toucans, 69
trapping of animals, 174, 194–5; of sand flies, 175–6
tritoma bug, 113, 191
Tropical Diseases Institute, 156
Trumai Indians, 111, 125
tucunaré, 22–3, *25*
Tupi (Indian language), 120
turtles, 23, 105, *106*, *133*

twenty kilometre square, *see* study area
Txikão Indians, *16*, 37, 122, 125, 168, 183, 184; burial customs, 186, 191
Txukuhamae Indians, 108, *110*, 112; lip discs of, 113; on raiding parties, 166, 168

Upuyá (diarrhoea remedy), 184
urine, collection and analysis of, 94, *95*, 96
urubu, 272
urucu, 95, 184

vaccination, *164*, 166, 168
Vale dos Sonhos, 35, *35*, 65
vanilla, 211
vaqueiros, 227, 256, *260–1*, 263
Vargas, President Getulio, 41
venereal disease, 165
veterinary medicine, 256
Villas Boas brothers (jointly), 92–3, 104, 245; methods of aiding Indians, 103, 125, 166, 184, 185, 238; receive R.G.S. Founder's Medal, 104
Villas Boas, Claudio, 36, *38*, 113, 119, *121*, 168, 183, 186, 191; pacifies new tribes, 120, 122
Villas Boas, Leonardo, 36
Villas Boas, Orlando, 36, *38*, 103, 114, 119–20, 166, 177; at Posto Leonardo, 104, 108, 113
Vireo, Red-eyed, 202
von Martius rapids, 40, 68, 111, 245, 246
vultures, 132, 230, 257

Waiana Indians of Surinam, 96
wasps, 72, 131; nests, 83, *143*; study and collection of, 141–3; *Polybia liliacea*, 142; *apoica*, *145*; *Stelopolybia testacea*, 143, *145*
water hyacinth, 248
wattled jacana, *232*
Waurá Indians, 114, 122, 125, 178, 185
Weaver bird (nests), 105
Wellcome Parasitology Unit, 174, 175
White-eared puffbird (*Mystalus chacuru*), *189*
wolf, maned (*Chrysocyon brachyurus*), *190*, 194
Woodall, John, 174
Woodcreeper, Buff-throated (*Xiphorhynchus guttatus*), *188*
Woodnymph, Fork-tailed, nest of, *8*

Xavante Indians, 19, 20, 32, 34, 40, 41, *43*, 67, 94, 102, *102*; poverty of, 42, 66, 94; at São Marcos mission, 92, *123*, *124*, 125–30, *128*, 252, *259*; medical study of, 96, 101
Xavantina, 20, *41*, 41–2, 47, 65, 70, 86, 157, 204, 221, 222, 252, 255, 264, 282; ferry at, 42, 49, 67, *67*, 70; expedition members at, 49, 66, 69, 185, 272; road passes through, 50, 219, 238; Indians at, 94, 101, 102; Taituba at, 150, 155
Xavantina/Cachimbo expedition, 50, 54; doctors and medical research on, 103, 114, 165; employees of, 149–50, 155–8; members' reports, 282; list of participants, 284–5
Xavantina/Cachimbo road, 47, *51*, 66, 221, 237–8, 240, 251, 267; possible routes, 40–1, 228–9; building halted, 69; results of building, 215–9, 269, 272; effect on forest, 270, 282; traffic on, 271–2
Xingú National Park, *see* Parque Naçional do Xingú
Xingú river, 19, 21, 34–6, 40, 42, 50, 68, 92, 193, *232*; headwaters, *46*, 165; tributaries, 157; expedition along, 168
Xylopia aromatica, *207*

Yawalapiti Indians, 184, 185

Zebu cattle, *see* cattle, Zebu